W. J. FISHMAN

The Insurrectionists

METHUEN & CO LTD
11 New Fetter Lane · London EC4

First published 1970 by Methuen & Co Ltd
11 New Fetter Lane, London EC4
© *1970 by W. J. Fishman*
Printed in Great Britain by
Butler & Tanner Ltd, Frome and London
SBN 416 15550 2

To the memory of
my parents

Contents

Illustrations

(between pp 100–1)

Preface

I must acknowledge the great debt I owe to those major definitive works in items within my theme, on which I have drawn heavily. They include *Socialist Thought: The Forerunners 1789–1850* by G. D. H. Cole; *Robespierre* by J. M. Thompson; *The Socialist Tradition* by Sir Alexander Gray; *Origins of Totalitarian Democracy* and *High Tide of Messianism* by J. L. Talmon; on Buonarroti the authoritative texts of Elizabeth L. Eisenstein and Dr Arthur Lehning amongst others; on Blanquism the personal aid and voluminous writings of M. Maurice Dommanget and the scholarly thesis of Alan Spitzer *The Revolutionary Theories of Louis Auguste Blanqui*. On the Russian revolutionary tradition, I must single out from the many I have consulted the works of S. V. Utechin, Professor Leonard Schapiro, E. H. Carr and above all, the monumental survey in depth of the nineteenth-century Populist and Socialist movement contained by Professor Franco Venturi's *Roots of Revolution*. I also wish to record my gratitude to those staff librarians of the Archives Nationales and the Bibliothèque Nationale in Paris, the L.S.E. library, the British Museum and the Bodleian, for their patient guidance and assistance.

I must also express my warm thanks to those invidivuals who helped me on the way: to Professor W. N. Medlicott of the L.S.E. for his advice and practical aid which enabled me to embark on initial research projects; to my friend and mentor Professor Harry Hearder of the University of South Wales, whose constant vigilance and cajoling drove me to complete the task; to Dr Christopher Hill and Bridgit Hill for innumerable personal kindnesses and who, together with those tutors of Balliol College, generously gave of their time and hospitality to make my stay at Balliol such a fruitful and memorable one;

to my post-graduate students of Columbia University, New York, whose perceptive analyses in seminars forced me to amend many pre-conceived notions; to my College Secretary Mrs M. Barney, who undertook the initial task of typing the early chapters and reading the proofs, and my colleagues Mrs E. Whicher, Mrs M. Prescott and Mrs I. Chatfield for completing the scripts. Finally, my deep gratitude to my wife Doris, whose voluntary acceptance of a long grass widowhood and whose constant prodding also helped bring the venture to a finale.

It is self-evident that this is no attempt at an esoteric thesis on Jacobin-Communism within the specified period. One hopes that it will provide sufficient stimulation for the lay reader to read on in depth and the student to probe further into those areas which are still vague and untested. Above all it could, I suggest, focus the relevance of the nineteenth-century tradition to those major revolutionary ideas and movements which are emerging at this time.

WILLIAM J. FISHMAN

Acknowledgements

The author and publishers wish to thank the following for permission to reproduce the illustrations which appear in this book:

Bibliothèque Nationale, Paris, for fig. 4
The Hoover Institution on War, Revolution and Peace, for figs. 8 and 9
Paul Popper Ltd, for figs. 1 and 5
The Radio Times Hulton Picture Library, for figs. 2, 3, 6, and 7
Ullstein Bilderdienst, for fig. 10

PART I

Genesis in the West

Prologue

The notion of an egalitarian society goes back beyond the eighteenth century and can claim biblical authority. It was only in the eighteenth century, however, that it emerged as a realistic possibility. The age was one of paradox, of enlightened despots permitting, within certain limits, a degree of free enquiry. Philosophers were at liberty to engage in social criticism provided that this did not overtly threaten the *status quo*.

Although these *philosophes* held that society was mutable they showed some reservation as to whether their prescriptions for change could be applied in practice. Many were dissenting academics voicing their protests against political and social injustice. Most of them, whether from prudence or inclination, speculated on the possibility of a Utopia based on 'natural' law, but drawing on past myths rather than examining contemporary situations, to produce their models. They looked back to a golden age of classical allusion. In the same sense they advocated Spartan discipline and austerity as opposed to the artifice of the modern city and the new-fangled machine.

It is symptomatic of French domination in the realm of ideas in eighteenth-century Europe that the doctrines of a collective *communauté* were first sounded there. These drew their strength from social injustice. Yet by 1789 social injustice had been slightly mitigated, and did not itself set off the revolutionary fuse. This was unwittingly performed by the 'harmless' ideas of the philosophers. No one, including themselves, had taken their Utopias seriously. So they were treated with paternal laxity by authority. It was a fatal mistake. Their ideas were charged with dynamite. The French Revolution offered the opportunity to put ideas into practice, to translate ethical codes into activist programmes. The egalitarianism of the philosophers was the predominant force which drove the men of 1789 towards insurrection.

Rousseau's *Discourse on the Origin of Inequality* (1755) provided the revolutionary dynamic for the cause of equality. Here he proffered an analysis of society which foreshadowed Marx. He regarded the property motive as the factor which accelerated the degeneration of man. The acquisitive society was rejected and the communalization of land put forward as an alternative. The law had always supported domination by the possessors. History, therefore, was a record of continuous antagonism between rich and poor, master and slave, a class conflict which could only be resolved by force. In the unjust society the consequences of excessive corruption ensured the triumph of the personal despot who maintained himself as long as he remained the strongest. It was reasonable to suggest that 'as soon as he can be expelled, he has no right to complain of violence. The popular insurrection that ends in the death or deposition of a Sultan is as lawful an act as those by which he disposed, the day before, of the lives and fortunes of his subjects.' This was a rational justification for regicide.

In his *Social Contract* (1762) Rousseau offered a political means of implementing equality. Out of the web of complex dialogue emerged the concept of the Legislator who would direct the people towards the *communauté*. 'How can a blind multitude, which often does not know what it wills, because it rarely knows what is good for it, carry out for itself as great and difficult an enterprise as a system of legislature?' This could only be brought about by the Legislator 'the engineer who makes the machine'. He must have the gift of bringing to his task a disinterested high intelligence and absolute dedication. Only he could effect a transformation of the social order in favour of the majority. The élitist precept is defined. The practical working out of this will be seen in the thinking and activity of the radical insurrectionists during the nineteenth century. It pointed the way beyond revolutionary vanguardism to the totalitarian idea.

Contemporary philosophers underlined Rousseau's main

diagnosis. Gabriel de Mably, in three major treatises, rejected such geopolitical deductions which suggested that there are differences between men according to environment. It was the immoral activities of *frelons* (drones) and the practice of nepotism on the part of rulers that led to the unfair distribution of property, the root of universal discord. For the evils of private accumulation caused both civil and national wars. Mably contemplated the diseased society with pessimism. There was little chance of its cure but he had strengthened the attack on the rule of property. André Morelly not only joined in the attack, but also ventured a replacement by way of a blue print of the future *communauté*. Its ingredients were ominous. Every individual had to be *homme publique*, that is under state scrutiny and control from the cradle to the grave. Legislation was to be inviolate. Transgressors would be dealt with in two ways: a temporary separation from the social body for lighter offences; permanent separation or civil death for anti-state activity. The latter meant confinement in large caves sealed with iron bars and located in cemeteries, a ghoulish scheme which foreshadowed later totalitarian practice. It was Morelly then who first presented a crude definition of the totalitarian idea. It is not surprising that Babeuf should regard Morelly as the inspirer of his conspiracy.

Perhaps the most outspoken voice of social protest was that of the village priest Jean Meslier who focused his attack against the Church. He aroused the support of the established critics such as D'Holbach and Voltaire. The latter published and edited his polemical *Testament du Curé Meslier*. Meslier, alone of all his contemporaries, sounded the call for violence. 'I should like to see, and this will be the last and the most ardent of my desires, I should like to see the last king strangled with the guts of the last priest.' He exhorted the dispossessed to free themselves by revolution. 'Your salvation lies in your hands . . . keep for yourself with your own hands all the riches and goods you produce so abundantly with the sweat of your brow. Do not give anything to the proud and useless idlers, who do nothing useful in this world.'

As political and economic vicissitudes shook the old régime, these ideas took root amongst its sternest critics. But in its turn the Revolution redefined social antagonisms once the debris of feudalism had been swept away. An unexpected force had burst on to the streets of Paris, when in July 1789 the labouring poor, the militant *sans-culottes*, took temporary control of the Revolution. This movement from below was communicated to the provinces. The land-hungry peasants rose, fired the châteaux and burned the title deeds. The December (1789) decree on the transfer and sale of Church property extended their opportunities to own land. But not so in the city, where the poor men of the faubourgs had jostled the middle classes along the road to political power. Once there, the *bourgeoisie* found that they had conjured up a monster who was difficult to control. It was safe to argue, theoretically, for legal equality. But the prospect of its realization would be a threat to their existence as a class. When it came to the point, the rights of property would be ruthlessly defended. The fight to preserve those rights placed the *bourgeoisie* behind opposite sides of the barricades in 1848 and 1871.

At the same time the political liberty reluctantly doled out to the artisans was not balanced by an alleviation of their social and economic distress. Leaders of the *sans-culottes* voiced their protest with a repeated call to insurrection and posed a permanent threat to central authority. It was a popular appeal, for the labouring poor soon sensed that they would remain second-class citizens, helping with the harvest but permanently deprived of their share in the fruits of the Revolution. In the end even their political rights were forfeit. The Constitution of 1793 had only given them a short-term guarantee, and those who overthrew Robespierre annulled it. So the *malheureux*, the city 'multitude . . . united in one body and driven by one will', the cry for bread and the right of life, was a powerful ready-made weapon in the hands of a demagogue. But these, like Mirabeau, Danton and even Robespierre, found it impossible to fulfil their obligations to the dispossessed. Baffled ideologues, facing the insoluble problem of poverty, tried in the end to make a virtue of it. Poverty was elevated to the god head but suffering proved the relentless force which overwhelmed them one by one.

To the labouring poor the pursuit of freedom alone was meaningless. The Revolution, for them, would be a violent end to the indignities of deprivation. Those like Marat and Babeuf who understood, assumed the rôle of warring prophets of the dispossessed. The torch lit by these men was to be handed on, one to another, by the great insurrectionists until it reached its final destination at the Finland Station.

CHAPTER I

The Myth Makers

The great French Revolution established the tradition of the involvement of middle-class professionals in the proletarian cause. It is understandable that, in their sympathetic identification with the less fortunate, they were not only accepted but also assumed top leadership. For they provided the intelligence, the direction, and unlimited dedication. So-called working-class revolutions were hardly ever led by proletarians. From Robespierre to Lenin the caucus of revolutionary vanguardism was controlled by *bourgeois* or *déclassé* elements.

The ideas and significance in the revolutionary setting of Maximilien de Robespierre have endured a wide range of controversy. Robespierre was born in the small town of Arras in 1758, of a provincial lower bourgeois family. By 1789 he had had his full share of misfortune: orphaned young, his feckless father had deserted the family, leaving Maximilien not only to fend for himself but also to support a younger brother and sister. He was physically frail, but the incidence of poverty and early responsibility forged in him the qualities of toughness and ambition. These, combined with an unbending integrity, became for him a source of weakness as well as strength. At the age of seventeen, as a poor student maintained by a benefactor, he was selected, the best scholar of his year, to deliver a speech in Latin welcoming the new monarch, Louis XVI, when he visited the 'Collège de Louis-le-Grand' in Paris. They met again – seventeen years later at the bar of the Assembly, when Robespierre, as his chief accuser, demanded his head. In 1789 he was the small town deputy, with a local reputation as a radical holding questionable ideas on religion and the rights of the third estate. He had also gained a national reputation through his successful defence of the installation of a M. Vissery's lightning conductor against the opposition of the superstitious townsmen of St Omer, who had brought charges against the innovator of introducing an infernal machine. The year 1789 gave him his hour of opportunity, and he seized it. Increasingly, through the Jacobin Club, he was both to fulfil himself and his historical identity.

It is significant that Robespierre had to borrow his fare to get to Paris on May 5th. He soon entered the limelight (June 6th) with a vehement outburst against the wealthy Archbishop of Nîmes, who claimed to be concerned for the poor and who had suggested a conference between the three estates to seek a remedy in poor relief. Robespierre replied indignantly: 'The clergy should be reminded of the principles of the Early Church. The old canons provide for the selling of altar vessels to relieve the poor. But there is no need for such desperate remedies. All that is necessary is that the bishops and the dignitaries of the church should renounce that luxury which is an offence to Christian humility; that they should give up their coaches and give up their horses; if need be, that they should sell a quarter of the property of the church, and give it to the poor.' This had not been the first time that a rich dilettante had evoked such a violent polemic from him. Where is the traditional picture of the icy, rigid lawyer in the following sustained invective called forth the year previously? A prize had been offered on the death of the wealthy lawyer Dupray by the notables of his birthplace, La Rochelle, to the essayist who would submit the finest eulogy. They received an 'Eloge par M.R. . . avocat en Parlement'. All the evidence suggests that in style and content it was the work of Robespierre. It registers a fierce attack on the hypocrisy of Dupray's reputed compassion for the poor: 'You, who are for ever complaining about the crowd of unfortunates that wearies your eyes; learn to blush for your insensibility! Do you know why there are so many poor? It is because you grasp all the wealth in your greedy hands. . . . Why are they suffering the horrors of starvation? It is because you are living in luxurious mansions, where your gold pays for every art to minister to your comfort, or to occupy your idleness; it is because your luxuries devour in a day as much as would feed a thousand men.' There was fire in his belly when he spoke for the dispossessed. It was his speech of June 6th against the Archbishop which caught the attention of Etienne Dumont, biographer of Mirabeau, who commented, 'Everybody asked, "Who was the orator?" . . . it was only after some minutes of investigation that a name was repeated which, three years later, was destined to make France tremble. It was that of Robespierre!' Championship of the poor had projected him on to the stage; for this passionate sympathy for *les malheureux* occurs again and again in his utterances, and was perhaps the most attractive feature in his character. Here there are no lofty observations on cause and effect, but a deeply sustained emotion born of personal experience and near-identification. In July 1791 he published a defence of his actions in the Constituent Assembly, which is, in effect, not only a political testament in this idiom, but a personal revelation: 'I have always held that equality of rights belongs to all members of the state; that the nation includes the working class and everyone, without distinction of rich or poor. . . . I knew that I represented them [the poor] as fully as any other class. And I admit that I was bound to their cause by that imperious impulse which attracts us towards the underdog; for it was this impulse, more than any reasoned knowledge of my duty, which had always claimed my sympathy for those in trouble.' He explained further his advocacy of their cause by describing them as the most virtuous element of the people. 'And why so? Because it is precisely this class, which is neither corrupted by luxury, nor depraved by pride, nor carried away by ambition . . .' and so on. He reinforced this theme in his great speech (11th August 1791) concerning the rôle of 'Passive citizenship' given to the poor, which the Cordeliers Club printed in full and circulated in Paris as the 'charter of democracy'. In this he chides the rich and ambitious and balances them against their despised opposites. 'Do you honestly believe that a hard and laborious life engenders more vices than softness, luxury and ambition? Have you less confidence in the honesty of our workmen and artisans, who, by your standard, will hardly ever rank as active citizens, than in that of the courtier and the tax farmer, who on the same reckoning, will stand six hundred times as high? . . . among the poor, and under one exterior that we should call coarse, are found honest and upright souls, and a good sense and energy that one might seek long and in vain among a class that looks down upon them.'

Robespierre's ideas bloomed in the hot-house atmosphere of the Jacobin Club, housed in the old Dominican Friary in the Rue Saint Honoré. It was, paradoxically, a less inhibited debating area than the Assembly, although current problems were discussed in detail and conflicting views thrashed out in the open, under the watchful eye of a discerning public. Initially the Jacobins had stood for the breaking up of large estates, the abolition of feudal dues, and the removal of property rights invested in the church, all in tune with popular demand. 'They felt themselves not to be attacking property, but liberating peasant property in abolishing these dues, and, at the same time, to be liberating the property of all productive classes from exactions levied upon it by an unproductive nobility and a parasite court.'[1] In fact circumstances drove them to more and more radical projects. They moved in the forefront of national opinion; their legal enactments merely confirmed what was being actively forced on them by peasant and Parisian *sans-culotte*. In the revolutionary milieu greater pressure on the flanks was driving the Jacobins towards some modification of a society, whose socio-economic determinants they were only beginning vaguely to understand, and whose validity they began to question. Robespierre possessed both the skill and temperament to act as grand Legislator in the changing design. As the revolution increased in its dynamism so did Robespierre give increasing voice to his egalitarianism. It could be argued that it was an expedient to offset the threat of the *sans-culottes*, who had exercised their peculiar manner of dealing with

[1] G. D. H. Cole, *Socialist Thought*, p. 14.

'enemies' of the revolution on more than one occasion. The
September massacres (2–8th September 1792) may have been
a salutary warning to most of the future Conventionnel. But
Robespierre, who had assumed a diplomatic silence during the
terrible affair, soon showed where his sympathies lay. In a personal journal[1] issued that month he warns that the *bourgeoisie*
are unable to comprehend the intrinsic merits of the labouring
classes. 'The first thing a legislator must recollect is that the
people is good; the first thing he must feel is the need to avenge
the people's wrongs, and to restore its self-respect.' The legend
of the 'incorruptible' was taking shape. In him would be identified the personification of virtuous and democratic Paris against
the treacherous *bourgeois* and Girondins. On 25th February
1793 a proposal by Tallien in the Convention to send troops
to put down food riots in Lyons was opposed by Robespierre.
He openly asserted in the Jacobin Club that the riots were
due to the natural resentment of the poor who 'have not
yet reaped the reward of their labour. They are still persecuted
by the rich, and the rich are still what they have always been
– hard and pitiless.' By then the club was the true centre of
power. 'Here was the Capitol and here also was the Tarpeian
rock of the Revolution.'[2] Robespierre, as its most dominating
figure, was emerging as the all-powerful Legislator. Was it
expediency or emotion which carried him towards supreme
power by means of the reservoir of despair? The circumstances
certainly included both. On May 8th he pleaded at the
Jacobins for the formation of a revolutionary army, recruited
through the Sections and therefore based on the *sans-culottes*,
as a strike force to operate against internal enemies. The armed
worker would be state-paid, the cost of upkeep maintained by
taxes on the rich. Here, in effect, was a directive for the creation
of an army for permanent revolution. The plea was repeated
on May 13th. On the 31st of May, the outcome of Robespierre's
harangues against the Gironde was a popular uprising resulting
in the Jacobin take-over of the Paris Commune. The pressure

---

[1] 'Lettres de Maximilien Robespierre, membre de Convention, Nationel de
France, à ses commettants.'   [2] J. M. Thompson, *Robespierre*, p. 196.

from below was mounting, owing much to Robespierre's own propositions. A series of deputations demanded a tax on the rich to subsidize the price of bread; the removal of aristocrats from the armed and civil forces; a relief system out of public funds for the aged and infirm; and even a proposal to disenfranchise all except the working class. Was Robespierre playing with fire which was getting out of control? Or, as his words and activities appear to confirm, was he the most far-sighted of the Jacobins in realizing the need on all grounds – human, political and economic – of alleviating the suffering of *les malheureux*? So, 'whilst Roland denounced the Commune, Robespierre busied himself with drawing up a Labour programme'.[1] There is a logical culmination of ideas in this medium in his memorandum, 'Une volonte une', composed soon after the insurrection of May 31st. Here is the first unsophisticated élitist manifesto, evoking as a political weapon the permanent revolution. In Rousseauist terms he sees the ultimate will invested in the Convention, that is the Jacobin vanguard, which would sustain its power through a general assault by the armed *sans-culottes* on the *bourgeoisie*:

> What we need is a single will. It must be either Republican or Royalist. If it is to be Republican, we must have republican ministers, republican papers, etc. . . . The internal dangers come from the middle classes; in order to defeat them we must rally the people. Everthing had been so disposed as to place the people under the yoke of the bourgeoisie, and to send the defenders of the Republic to the scaffold. The middle classes have triumphed at Marseille, Bordeaux and Lyon. They would have triumphed in Paris too, but for the present insurrection. *The rising must continue until the measures necessary for saving the Republic have been taken.* The people must ally itself with the Convention, and the Convention must make use of the people. The insurrection must gradually spread from place to place, on a uniform plan: the *sans-culottes* must be paid and remain in the towns. They must be supplied with arms, roused to anger, and enlightened Republican enthusiasm must be inflamed by all possible means.

Yet one must be cautious and not read too much into this. Robespierre was fumbling with the dual problems of political

[1] J. M. Thompson, *Robespierre*, p. 339.

and economic discrimination against his Parisian supporters. Hence the apparent dichotomy of approach in his speech to the Convention (24th April 1793), when he was emphatic about the impossibility of an equal redistribution of wealth ('L'égalité des biens est un chimère!'). He hit on the compromise formula that the 'problem of the legislator is not to redistribute private property but to insist upon the moral duties of property owners'; from which he drew two corollaries – a state scheme for the unemployed, and a progressive income tax. This was certainly no economic reconstruction of society, but, simultaneously, he called for a system of radical reform which presaged the twentieth-century welfare state: 'Society ought to encourage with all its might the progress of public intelligence, and bring education within the reach of every citizen. . . . The people is sovereign; the government is its work and its property; public officials are its agents. . . . Every public position is open to all citizens. . . . All citizens have an equal right to share in the appointment of the people's deputies, and in legislation.' These clauses were written into the abortive Constitution of 1793. Over a century of political confrontation and social and economic struggle were to occur before their realization. Robespierre could not perceive that political and economic problems were interdependent, derived from common causes and, therefore, subject to a common solution. He tried to divorce the two and deal with each separately. He could not foresee the logical consequence of his political alignment; that if he were carried to power on the backs of the revolutionary masses he would be forced into a policy of social change, with some redistribution of wealth in their interests. He persisted in full measure in his championship of the poor, but achieved only *ad hoc* palliatives in ameliorating their social plight. He opposed the article in the Constitution of 1793, which gave the Primary Assemblies wider powers of meeting. He declared, 'The intrigues of the rich will spin out the meetings; the poor man will have to leave, to go to work, and they will proceed to carry out any measures they like.'

He moved towards dictatorship over the corpses of 'traitors'

and 'counter-revolutionaries', most of whom he equated with
the rich. His Republic of Virtue was threatened by enemies
within and without. The responsibilities of power, at a time
when France's energies and resources were being dissipated in
both civil and European wars, bore heavily on Robespierre.
He prevailed, and with his triumph the consciousness of his
personal rectitude grew. He attacked and destroyed both
Dantonists (who pleaded moderation) and Hébertists (who
preached a violent anarchism) on superficial grounds ('One of
the factions urges us to weakness and the other to excess. One
would turn Liberty into a Bacchante and the other into a
prostitute'); externally the battle for France's frontiers was
being won.[1] An overbearing strain of office, and a naturally
cautious and suspicious temperament, brought to him in
supreme power a fanatical belief in his own infallibility.

By 1794 Robespierrism, based initially on democratic expression and permanent debate, was thus transmuted through its
high priest to a form of Messianic redemption, conceived in the
surrender of the individual to the Legislator. Ultimately then
the philosophical realization of the General Will was given one
rational area of fulfilment, not in the group, but in the One.
He was the Messiah, the practical visionary, who alone could
lead his people into the promised land. Here, then, was the
first ingredient of Jacobin Communism. By 1794 the precedent
had been set. Secure in his own infallibility, Robespierre viewed
opposition as folly or treachery, either of which could only lead
to failure. Hence his merciless destruction of erstwhile friends
and collaborators. The compassionate young lawyer, who had
once voiced his detestation of capital punishment, had become
the Terror's pitiless inquisitor, another feature which was to be
inherent in the élitist creed. The execution of his old companion,
the poet Camille Desmoulins, even after an impassioned plea
for mercy from his close friends, exemplifies the dehumanization
of this convinced saviour of humanity; and when suspicion and
intimidation become the prime agencies of government, they
provide their own grave-diggers. Thermidor was inevitable;

[1] The victory of Fleurus, 26th June 1794, confirmed this.

and more so because Robespierre had little knowledge of political economy. His *raison d'être*, as far as the *sans-culottes* were concerned, was his ability to alleviate hardship by increasing real wages and curbing prices. However, the relaxation of the Law of Maximum,[1] in March 1794, favoured prices only and led to an inflationary process with a demand for higher wages from a growing number of trade groups. Deputations were dealt with harshly by Barère, and Robespierre soon became associated with the curbing of wages. His ousting, therefore, would spell finis to the hated 'maximum des salaires'. On the very day of Robespierre's fall, any attempt at his rescue was made impossible by the confusion at the Hôtel de Ville caused by workers protesting against the Maximum. He fell without a whimper, because he had failed, in the end, to recognize the primacy of the social question.[2]

In most other respects Robespierre was unsuited for the rôle of plebeian leader. He lacked the physical personality which would help sustain their uncritical acceptance. He was of slight build, almost undersized. His eyes, ice-like, staring, myopic behind the lenses, had a frightening effect on his audience. The overall image was one of a cold, delicate fop immaculately dressed in blue silk and lace fripperies. What a contrast to the wild men of the sections! Rough hewn and tattered from their long confinement in cellars and sewers – an experience which the fastidious Robespierre could never have shared – they were hatched out of the slum-ridden faubourgs. His basic religiosity, confirmed by his adoption of worship of the Supreme Being, proved repugnant to radical *sans-culottism* (although, like Lenin, he thought that too much energy could be uselessly expended on anti-religious activity – energy which could be far better directed towards more positive ends). So, in the last resort, he could never identify himself with the masses and lead them in a revolutionary transformation of society. One man could. He was Jean Paul Marat.

[1] See Professor George Rudé, *The Crowd in the French Revolution*, p. 135.
[2] When the Commune sounded the tocsin to free Robespierre only 13 out of 48 of the Parisian sections sent battalions – and then only to defend the Town Hall against the Convention.

In Marat was fused all the constituents for the popular insurrectionist. Contemporary sketches build up a terrifying portrait. He resembled a human gargoyle. He was short and sturdy, with a massive head. This was dominated by a large forehead, and a strong aquiline nose. The eyes, piercing in their intensity, would suddenly reflect the inner contemplation of the visionary. A filthy handkerchief was wound round his forehead. His skin was ridden with pullulating sores and swarthy with ingrained dirt from living in underground hide-outs. A brilliant demagogue, no one could challenge *his* revolutionary integrity. He spoke the language of the masses. His political roots were nurtured in the Cordeliers slums. He stood out in bold relief against worldly antagonists. He made his way to the tribune in an atmosphere of fearful anticipation. He harangued with demonic energy, his eyes rolling in frenzy. He fulminated against those enemies he had smelt out, demanding their destruction as a national catharsis. The actor predominated. His whole body moved in rhythm with his theme; his strong shoulders and artistic hands (those of a surgeon) were used to emphasize major points. His naturally weak voice rose to a crescendo in a high-pitched shriek. He was the personification of *la révolution à l'outrance*!

In the steps of the master Rousseau, his background and experience before 1789 were a preparation for the great day of *sans-culottism*. Marat was born in Boudry, Switzerland, of a heady mixture of Sardinian father and French Huguenot mother. From his own retrospections we discern that he was a wild undisciplined youth, a perpetual job-changer. In 1759 his mother died and he drifted away, ostensibly to study medicine with an inter-mixture of politics, literature and philosophy. But he was no professional lay-about. He worked, when he could, as a children's tutor or language teacher. His temporary pedagogic experiences were suffered in Toulouse and Bordeaux. He managed to survive for two years in the latter as tutor to the family of Paul Nairac, sugar refiner and later member of the National Assembly. It was here that he made his curious request direct to Louis XV for permission to accompany an expedition to Tobolsk aimed at observing the passage of Venus over the sun. It was, of course, refused. Marat never forgot that refusal.

For years he appeared to be a drifter, with ports of call ranging from Paris to Dublin. A short-term acquaintance with St Martin's Lane, London, and one year in Dublin were followed by a stay in Edinburgh. Soon after he appeared to have embarked for Holland, where he continued a vagabond existence between The Hague, Utrecht and Amsterdam. Yet these seemingly incoherent wanderings cannot have been purposeless. As an intellectual with a highly perceptive mind he must have spent much time as a student in the centres of learning which he visited. He settled for a time in Harley Street, where he profitably practised medicine. He established a worthwhile reputation as a doctor and appeared to be known to members of the Royal Society. In June 1775 he was granted a medical degree by the University of St Andrews on the recommendation of two fellow practitioners who vouched that he was 'a very distinguished master in arts, who has given all his attention to medicine for several years and has acquired a great skill in all branches of the science'. He was certainly fairly successful as a doctor, though not so to be considered, as in his own estimation, 'the physician of the incurables'. His consistent boasting of his medical prowess was later used as a weapon against him. The Girondin, Brissot, accused him of being a charlatan and a quack.

His residence in England gave rise to the curious tale, which circulated amongst the more respectable members of the Assembly, that under the name of Jean-Pierre le Maître he had been involved in a theft of medals from the Ashmolean Museum in 1768. He fled to Dublin with the loot, was caught and returned to Oxford to be tried. He was due to be hanged, but the privilege of scholarship proffered a remission to forced labour service on a Thames hulk, from which he was promptly saved by the intervention of an old pupil, who recognized his one-time master amongst the prisoners.

Medicine was not enough for this dynamic eccentric. In

July 1774 he had joined the Grand Lodge of Freemasons, then associated with the radical elements in London, in which he could actively participate in the fermentation of new ideas. Legend has it that some of his leisure hours were more romantically spent in the fashionable apartment of the then avantgarde painter, Angelica Kaufmann. It suggests the unlikely picture of Marat, on his knees, gazing passionately into the eyes of his mistress, as she sang to him to the accompaniment of a zither. Be that as it may, Marat had more serious interests, which even then he managed, *malgré soi*, to turn into farce. His first philosophical discourse, *Essay on the Soul* (1772), was sent to Lord Lyttleton, an old dodderer but would-be patron to young scribes. Marat was invited to discuss the theme at his home in Hill Street, Piccadilly, but the meeting ended in mutual incomprehension. His second essay, *Chains of Slavery* (1774), registers his first political involvement. Its inflated sub-title attacked the pseudo-liberty of British institutions: 'a work, wherein the clandestine and villainous attempts of princes to ruin liberty are pointed out and the dreadful scenes of despotism disclosed, to which is prefixed an address to the electors of Great Britain, in order to draw their timely attention to the choice of proper representatives in the next parliament'. His entry, as a foreigner, into political controversy provoked a sharp response from officialdom. He found the market for publication quickly restricted, then withdrawn; resulting, as Marat supposed, from payment or pressure by Lord North himself. Certainly distribution was curtailed, although sales were maintained in the quasi-radical societies in the north. His questionable danger as a radical was overborn by his reputation as a surgeon. In 1777 he returned to France as brevet-physician to the Comte d'Artois. In the storm of discontent gathering in those years, he found his *métier* in political criticism. In 1780 he produced a *Plan de Législation Criminelle* and took his stand as an egalitarian and a revolutionist. The plan embraced three themes. His basis for a legal system was an *a priori* acceptance of equality of rights and opportunities in contra-distinction to the prevailing extremes of privileged lord and propertyless serfs. He recognized the inability of the oppressed to elevate themselves other than by illegal means, given the injustices inherent in contemporary laws and institutions, and thereby questioned the need for citizens to observe them. Finally he openly advocated an equal division of property. In respect of the 'idle' needy, the establishment of National Workshops would sustain a dichotomy of economic support and the maintenance of self-respect.

Yet, up to the revolution his interests were still all-embracing. In the physical sciences he engaged in research into light and fire, and evidence (other than his own) suggests that he actually worked with Benjamin Franklin on the solar microscope. He published a number of treaties which brought him into conflict with the academic establishment, and in the process of continuous acrimony his delusions of persecution grew. He left the Comte d'Artois in 1786 and practised in Paris, where, as in London, his reputation as a diagnostician helped expand his connection. The future leader of the *sans-culottes* was making good from *haute-bourgeois* clientele at thirty-six francs a visit, with interesting sidelines. There is the story of the attractive Marquise de L'Aubespine suffering from T.B. and a licentious and neglectful husband, who came to Marat, in the last resort, after her previous doctor had given her only twenty-four hours to live. Marat offered a guaranteed cure, if she would put herself in his hands exclusively. He treated her ostensibly with a chalk and water concoction, but her health was not restored by purely medicinal means. Marat had long practised normal methods of curing frustrated women. The 'treatment' was continued to the Revolution.

1789 began his day of reckoning. The constant rejection of his extra-curricular scientific findings had turned him into a neurotic, with an all-consuming fire for ideas, which if either ignored or accepted, made him suspicious. He appeared early on the revolutionary scene as 'a Messianic enthusiast sustaining his vision by an orgy of anguished resentment'.[1] His frustrations, which he associated with the social establishment, could be

[1] Piers Compton, *Marat*, p. 65.

worked off in the raging storm of iconoclasm which prevailed. In August he was already formulating a 'Projet de Déclaration des Droits de l'Homme et du Citoyen, suivi d'un Plan de Constitution juste, sage et libre'. He repeated a now recurring theme: the social contract to be based on the people's sanction; the nullification of inequality by division of property and the more equitable distribution of wealth. The peasant had quickly learned the lesson by taking affairs into his own hands. This was not lost on Marat, who, as possibilities of alleviation in favour of his urban *sans-culottes* proved chimerical, stepped up his call for revolutionary violence. On 12th September 1789 appeared the first edition of his *L'Ami du Peuple*. He struck the note immediately – a note he would never cease to repeat. The workers of Paris were exhorted to become their own vehicle of justice. In assuming the rôle of self-sacrifical devotee of 'les *malheureux* he urged them on with his own frenzied revolutionism. He had deliberately rid himself of his lucrative practice to take up the life of the impoverished oracle. His energies would be utilized in the making and directing of violent demonstrations against authority. On October 5th, as the Court held feasts whilst the poor faced famine, angry Parisian women, roused by the harangues of Marat amongst others, marched to Versailles. Marat was immediately marked out as a dangerous agitator by an Assembly conscious of its own insecurity. On September 30th, Marat had been brought before the members of the Commune to be interrogated by Bailly, who reported that the residents of Filles St Thomas had accused Marat of incendiarism. His prompt reply was that as that district was inhabited by bankers and financiers, parasites who thrived on inegalitarianism, it was expected that such an accusation would be made against him. As self-appointed 'ami du peuple' it was his duty to expose anti-patriotic elements in word and deed, even though he had to live on bread and water to maintain publication. He probed everywhere. A scurrilous attack on a municipal secretary, de Joly, brought a warrant for his arrest, and he went underground. As revolutionary enthusiasm grew, he broke surface. His presses were released and he

c

settled in the heart of the Cordeliers district. But he could never operate in the open for long. Constant threats of arrest followed short intervals of liberty, but, be it in cellar or attic, *L'Ami du Peuple* continued its thunder. His vituperations increased with the pain and discomfort brought on by an incurable skin disease which racked him (pruritis, caught in the unhygienic hovels underground, from which he could only find relief by immersion in a warm medicated bath!). Marat smelt out treason in high places. In May 1790, he declared Mirabeau, then at the height of his popularity, a paid hireling of the King. It was proved true soon after Mirabeau's death. He attacked a Civil List grant of twenty-five million to Louis, at a time when the *sans-culottes* suffered hunger. The publication of *The Damnable Scheme of the Enemies of the Revolution* (14th July 1790) once more meant confiscation of his presses and forced hibernation for nearly two years. Continually on the run from the police, he was consequently the darling of the poor, whilst his journal still pursued its clandestine exhortations to the *sans-culottes* to continue their public castigations and blood letting.

Marat was the first of the 'insurgés' to advocate terror as a means of disposing of the class enemy. He demanded the destruction of *émigrés* and aristocrats. 'When I find that, in order to spare a few drops of blood, one risks shedding floods of it, I am indignant, in spite of myself, at our false maxims of humanity.' He focused his diatribes on the monarchy, and opened full blast after the flight to Varennes. 10th August 1792 was the day of his deliverance, when the invasion of the Tuileries confirmed the power of the *sans-culottes*. But although Marat stood as their mouthpiece he surmised that an uninformed mob was unfit to rule; that terror must be organized and directed by an authoritarian intelligence. Again he was the first to demand a dictator, one chosen for his revolutionary integrity, who could detect counter-revolution and deal with it ruthlessly. And why not himself? He asserted his suitability for the rôle – as Robespierre, who actually filled it, was never to do. It was Marat therefore who eased the passage for Robespierre. For him, terror and dictatorship were both essential to enforcing the egalitarian principle.

He brought his own peculiar measures to terrorization, which never lacked popularity with the masses. They saw him working all hours, composing speeches, writing articles, his door always open to any citizen for suggestions or complaints. They knew that his journal was printed out of his own meagre funds, so that he lived in constant penury. When he sounded the tocsin for action his ragged followers poured into the streets. The September massacres (2–8th September 1792), the classic Maratist exercise, had their positive results in relieving fear and tension as the foreign invaders drew near. They also procured his election to the Convention (September 9th) supported by Robespierre and the Jacobins. (They dared not do otherwise.)[1] Yet even in triumph he stood alone on the crest of the Mountain. In the Convention he was friendless, for no one dared befriend him. On September 25th he issued his *Journal de la République Française*, with the ominous sub-title: 'That misery should be relieved, let the fortune of the wealthiest be reduced.' It stimulated a violent attack on him for his excesses. Danton defended him with the plea that his rashness was due to cellar life, which had ulcerated his soul. But the outcast of the Convention remained the hero of the *malheureux*. He, alone, of all his contemporaries, completely identified himself with them, and zealously guarded their interests. He was the first of the great line of professionals, who lived and breathed revolution almost twenty-four hours a day. The inarticulate saw him writing his speeches for *them* and the socially maimed viewed their physically tormented spokesman as a human wreck submerged in a shoe-shaped bath in the centre of a bare room; a flat board traversed the bath, on which was deposited his parchments and a thick cube of bare wood holding his ink and medicines. His sympathetic identification with the mass is confirmed by his attitude during wage pressures, which contrasted with that of Robespierre. By 1791 artisans' pay had hardly risen since the Revolution, although

[1] 450 out of a possible 758 had registered the vote in his favour.

there was a labour shortage. This meant constant demand for higher wages. The first to exert pressure were the journeymen carpenters, who, supported by the Cordeliers Club (in which Marat was a leading member), met in their premises. Marat opened his *L'Ami du Peuple* to the workers, and in June 1791 a letter appeared purporting to have come from 560 building workers engaged in the construction of the Panthéon, accusing their master builders of being 'ignorant, rapacious and insatiable oppressors'. The Assembly reacted to higher wage demands from the carpenters and farriers by passing its 'Loi Le Chapelier'. Marat alone protested. (Robespierre and the Jacobins did nothing to erase it and it persisted for another century!) When he suspected corrupt officials behind the grain hoarding during a bread shortage, he wrote that this could be easily dealt with by a show of violence on the part of the *sans-culottes*. On the day the article appeared there were attacks in the sections against provision stores. Was it coincidence or was Marat, as usual, in tune with the feelings of the people? Certainly a more perceptive view than Robespierre, who, in later bread disturbances (September 1793) expressed surprise at rioting over 'paltry grocers' goods'!

It was the call for the sacking of a few bread stores that soon led to Marat's impeachment (24th April 1793). His trial was followed throughout France, and his vindication was the culminating point of his power. On May 31st his call to arms in Paris brought an end to the Gironde. It was the sounding of the tocsin which set off the tragi-comedy of June 2nd: a terrified Convention, fleeing in all directions from the *sans-culottes*, who had surrounded the building, rounded up like sheep by the frenzied Marat who cried: 'I call upon you to return to the posts you have abandoned like cowards!' They returned to acquiesce in the proscription of the thirty-one Girondins. Thus Marat's last act paved the way for Robespierre. On July 13th Marat was stabbed to death. He had twenty-five sous in his possession.

The advent of Marat proclaimed a turning point in the direction of revolutionary élitism. He had assumed absolute social identification with the Paris *canaille*. He beat in rhythm to their moods, transformed their desperation into action, and elevated violence to a creed, which could, momentarily, alleviate their sufferings. Unlike Robespierre, he could act out the rôle of prophet with conviction. It is not surprising that in the great myth he is the revolutionary's revolutionary. He underlined the message to Robespierre who was driven to assume the one aspect of chiliasm to which he was temperamentally unsuited: that violence controlled through centralized terror could work for longer duration. Elitism, as a concomitant to violence, had emerged with a margin of success. But equality, the final objective of the grand design, was as elusive as ever. It needed the supreme prophet to bring this, the most subtle of illusions, to reality. The Thermidorian reaction set the stage. The Messiah was already waiting in the wings.

CHAPTER 2

Prophet and Apostle:
Babeuf and Buonarroti

'The lot of the poor, always downtrodden, always subjugated and always oppressed can never be improved by peaceful means. This is doubtless one of the striking proofs of the influence of wealth in the legal code. . . . The great point is to enlighten them [the poor] and make them aware of their rights, and the revolution will function infallibly without any human power being able to oppose it.'[1] Thus presaged Marat in 1789. Jacques Roux, the red priest of the Gravilliers section, was to pose the corollary that 'freedom was an empty phantom when the rich man can, through his monopoly, exercise the right of life and death over his fellow men'. The elimination of Robespierre provoked the conditions which appeared to validate both these assumptions.

The plebiscitary democracy of 1793 was replaced by a limited franchise of the propertied classes. (The poor were significantly declared unfit to rule and deprived of the vote.) The abortive constitution of 1793 had, in effect, proclaimed the right to work, and the Committee of Public Safety, through the *livre de bienfaisance*, that is social assistance, had pegged prices and controlled production and distribution centrally for the benefit of the poor. War was conducted with resources provided from taxation which bore heavily on the rich. Under pressure from the *sans-culottes*, the Law of Maximum was passed (September 1793). Prices and wages were maximized to a limit of one-third and one-half respectively above those prevalent in June 1790. In the period of peak war effort the demand for labour forced

---

[1] Marat: cited by Max Leroy, *Histoire des idées sociales en France*, Vol. 1, p. 282.

up wages dramatically. In certain instances these rose to over three times the 1790 rates. In March 1794, with Hébert out of the way, the Commune relaxed prices. The inevitable response for higher wages followed from a multi-variety of groups. The *bourgeois* interests of the Commune hardened against this. Warning signals came when, on 21st April 1794, a deputation of tobacco workers to the Hôtel de Ville were met by official hostility and five were arrested. Barère now brought labour agitation within the definition of counter-revolution and ordered the arrest of agitators by the public prosecutor. The hated 'maximum des salaires', which the wage earner believed would go with Robespierre, persisted. In fact his fall eased off all restraints on entrepreneurs. Prices were freed, inflation ensued to the enrichment of speculators. The overall result was soon evident. Unemployment soared, free distribution of bread to the poor of Paris ceased. Again the *sans-culottes* faced starvation. Again, in hatred and despair, they sought the fulfilment of the Messianic prophecy – the One who would finally usher in the egalitarian millennium.

Noël François Babeuf was born in 1760, the eldest son of a salt tax collector in Picardy, traditional home of rebels and revolutionary thinkers such as the Jacquerie, Calvin and Saint-Just. His father combined pride and self-elevation as becomes an old soldier relegated to civilian status; and he transmitted these characteristics to his son. Noël's education, like that of his great successor Proudhon, was informal, but he read assiduously the works of Rousseau, Morelly and Mably. He grew up against a background of rural oppression based on land shortage, where land was farmed in increasingly large units. Hatred between peasant and landowner prevailed. Born among the dispossessed, Babeuf would always associate his background with his own personal humiliation and this led him to early political involvement. At sixteen he was employed as 'archiviste feudiste', a research clerk in feudal claims. Whilst studying the yellowed parchments of old charters, he discerned the swindling and deceit involved in land property deals. The ill-treatment he received at the hands of landlords and their agents inculcated in him a violent class hatred of the aristocracy. The very existence of his work convinced him of the need to erase a society that sanctioned legal robbery.

At seventeen he gained employment near Roye at the house of the Count de Bracquemont, Seigneur de Damery. His domestic responsibilities grew burdensome with his father's death in 1781 when he became breadwinner for the whole family. The next year he married the Countess's housemaid and, although by 1783 he was a successful *commissaire à terrier*, his personal problems became overwhelming as he then had to maintain two families. Yet a restless daemon for instruction drove him towards a philosophical speculation on society, which would soon bring him directly into the maelstrom of contemporary politics.

For three years (1785–8) he engaged in a lengthy correspondence with Dubois de Fosseux, secretary of the Académie Royale des Belles Lettres d'Arras. The institution awarded prizes to the best essayist offering solutions to current local and national problems. Babeuf submitted a discourse involving a rationalized road-building scheme in the rural area of Artois. It arrived too late, but stimulated a personal correspondence between Fosseux and Babeuf that was to prove invaluable to the latter in his education as a social revolutionary. In 1787 he was suggesting to Fosseux a theme for discussion that revealed him as an advocate for a social transformation of society. Here, in vague terms, he was already asserting the egalitarian principle:

> What would be the state of the people whose social institutions should be such that the most perfect equality would reign among the individual members and that the land on which they lived belonged to no one – if, in short, everything was in common, including the products of all kinds of industry?

He was yet unable to define the social order he was seeking. In his writings we detect both a feel for a centralized *communauté* and for a universal distribution of land. From his agitation amongst the local peasants to a later correspondence with a member of the Assembly (1791) he appeared to be overbalanced in favour of what Jaurès would call 'un communisme parcellaire'.

In the tense days before 1789 he threw himself wholeheartedly into revolutionary activity. He assumed the editor-
ship of the *Correspondant Picard* in which he thundered against
the régime. The outbreak of revolution sparked off his chiliastic
fervour and led him to the forefront of the *insurgés*. The demand
for *feudistes* ceased, and unemployment provided him with the
opportunity for full-time action. He ranged everywhere, organizing strikes and boycotts; he led attacks on châteaux and
burnt government offices. In the working-class sector of the
provincial town of Roye, he fomented popular agitation and
learned the art of political demagogy. His self-delusion grew
as the Revolution manifested its destructive potentialities. He
appointed himself prime defender of the oppressed and Messiah
of the Revolution. In his autobiographical notes (1794) he
declared himself '*avant la Révolution archiviste et géomètre. Depuis
la Révolution, propagandaire et défenseur des opprimés.*' He was convinced that he was one of the elect, 'better than many of their
brethren'; one of the esoteric few who were joined in the 'terrible
mystery' that would enable them to change the world 'to its
greatest advantage'. To him was granted the supreme rôle for
the deliverance of the French people. The prophet had found
the philosopher's stone with which he could transmute mass
oppression into mass liberation.

He agitated fiercely for the introduction of his own version of
land division. To effect a rational equality in distribution
Babeuf advocated plots to be allocated for life only and which
were not to be sold. Allotments were to be given to people of
all trades. This maintained current practice which recognized
that the agricultural worker could not support his family on
one job alone but was forced to seek additional income elsewhere. Above all he early formulated the proposition that
property was the basic evil in society which inevitably led to his
re-appraisal based on a centralized *communauté*; and he first trum-
peted the call to revolutionary violence in the battle for expropriation, which would reverberate across the nineteenth century:

> Private property is the principal source of the ills which burden
> society. . . . Go then my friends, batter, upset, overturn this

society. . . . Take what suits you everywhere. What is superfluous belongs by right to him who has nothing.

He exorted the landless and propertyless artisans. 'Cut without pity the throats of the tyrants and patricians, the gilded millions, all the immoral beings, who might oppose our common happiness.'

It is no wonder that this self-styled defender of the oppressed *'un des hommes, moroses, extravagants propres à troubler l'ordre et la tranquillité publique'* was constantly imprisoned between 1789 and 1791 for ultra-revolutionary activities. As with Marat the emergence of a more radical element into positions of authority in 1792 registered a change in his fortune. He was elected to the post of administrator and archivist of the Department of the Somme. His turbulent nature soon brought him into conflict with the local representative Dumonge, and he was coerced into leaving but managed to gain a similar assignment in the Montdidier district. Once more he quarrelled, not unnaturally, with the pro-Royalist President of the district. A charge was brought against him of forging a signature on an act of sale of national property, which could neither be proved nor disproved. He refused to face trial and escaped to Paris where he suffered a long period of hunger and despair. He subsisted mainly on friends' charity until early 1794, when he gained a minor post as secretary on the Bureau des Subsistances under the Paris commune. Like Marat, he too had short-lived respite from perpetual misfortune owing to his persistence in the self-appointed task of watchdog of the Revolution. He discovered evidence of faked accounts and speculation and was quick to expose his departmental chiefs, accusing them of plotting an artificial famine. He was now a marked man by eminent counter-revolutionaries, who managed to manipulate his arrest by the Montdidier authorities on the old charge of forgery. In July 1794 the accusation was quashed in court. His hour of vindication almost coincided with the downfall of his hero, Robespierre (July 27th). For a brief period, in articles written as editor of the popular *Journal de la Liberté de la Presse*, he turned on the deposed leader whose authoritarian rule had demonstrated the rejection of the democratic constitution of 1793. But his inherent acceptance of the egalitarian principle soon brought him to redirect his fulminations against the commercial parasites, *les honnêtes gens*, who were systematically undermining the short-lived gains of the *sans-culottes*. Forced into hiding, he published a clandestine political sheet *Le Tribun du Peuple*, in which he violently attacked the Thermidorian clique. Henceforth there would be no compromise with the parvenus and speculators, who, in his view, were destroying the Revolution. At Tallien's orders he was quickly seized, removed from the danger point, Paris, and cast into prison at Arras. It was there, in the birthplace of the 'Incorruptible' that he infused Robespierrist dogma with the Maratist dynamism. The resultant crystallization of ideas was momentous. Babeuf, in the cells of Arras, had analysed and reassessed the radical experience of the Revolution to the point where he could logically conclude that a collective egalitarian society could only be brought about by violence and through the leadership of a highly motivated *élite*; that is, that communist élitism was the only force that could effect a social transformation of society. Here then was the point of take-off of modern Jacobin Communism.

This was confirmed in Babeuf's mind by the failure of the spontaneous insurrection at the rising of Prairial (20th May 1795) when the *sans-culottes* made an unco-ordinated assault on the Convention. Defeat and repression paralysed action in the revolutionary sections. Babeuf was then convinced that the time was ripe for a centrally organized conspiracy by his élitist group, who, under cover of the revolutionary masses and soldiers brought in on their side, could seize power by a lightning coup. His opportunity came when, as a result of abortive Royalist uprisings, he was released by government amnesty. In September 1795 he returned to Paris prepared to play out his final act. In October the 'Society of the Panthéon' was formed from residual dissidents of the Left. Their maxim was a return to the conditions of 'Bread and the Constitution of 1793'; their goal – ostensibly, political and economic equality for the dispossessed. They met in the crypt of the Convent of Ste Geneviève. Filippo

Buonarroti, future apostle of Babouvism, paints a dramatic picture of the early meetings of the conspirators:

> The dim paleness of the torchlight, the hollow echo of voices, and the constrained positions of members standing or sitting on the ground or leaning against pillars, impressed everyone with the grandeur and the peril of the whole enterprise, as well as the courage and prudence it required.

The police spies moved in. In January 1796 the Directory ordered the re-arrest of the editor of the *Tribun*, which Babeuf managed to avoid by running faster than the police agent sent to detain him. He disappeared in the labyrinthine alleyways of the *arrondissement*, where he was joined by his fellow conspirators. In February, General Buonaparte made his second entry into the counter-revolution as the officer detailed to seize the keys to the Society, disperse its members and close down permanently this 'cave of brigands'. Clubs and public gatherings were prohibited throughout Paris. Repression and a flood of debased currency, the assignats, stimulated revolutionary fervour among those who had known power through the *sans-culottes*. In March, Babeuf, whilst in hiding, was called upon to unite and lead the Parisian militants towards the final seizure of power.

He responded and the secret directory (*comité-insurrecteur*) of the Conspiracy of the Equals was born. It consisted of six ultra-revolutionaries at the head, of whom two, other than Babeuf, were to be of significant importance in Communist tradition. One was Filippo Buonarroti, who emerges as the next great link in the chain of revolutionism. Fortunately for posterity he was also a scribbler. His chronicle of the Conspiracy of the Equals was to be read with serious application by the great insurrectionists of the nineteenth century. The second was Sylvain Maréchal, poet and atheist (he had been imprisoned prior to 1789 for his blasphemous writing and had subsequently produced an atheist's dictionary) who composed a *Manifesto of the Equals*, which he submitted to the Babouvist Director.

Flamboyant and extravagant in language though it was, it contained, in less sophisticated terms, the basic precepts of

Communist ideology that presage Blanqui and Marx. The following extracts reveal crudely the early recognition of a class struggle as an historic process. Here was a clarion call to social revolution as the pre-requisite for a classless society.

People of France!
    For fifteen centuries you have lived as slaves and therefore in misery. For six years you have stood breathless, waiting for independence, happiness and equality.
    EQUALITY!! the first desire of nature, the first need of man, chief bond of all legitimate society! . . . Ever since there have been civil societies man's finest birthright has been recognized . . . but so far has not once been achieved; equality was nothing more than a legal fiction, beautiful but sterile. . . . We aspire to something more sublime and more just, the Common Good or the Community of Goods! No more individual ownership of land, the land belongs to nobody. We lay claim to, we demand common enjoyment of the fruits of the earth; these fruits exist for all.
    We declare that we can no longer suffer the great majority of men to toil and sweat in the service of the few and for the pleasure of the small minority.
    People of France!
    The highest of all glories is yours! Yes, it is you who must be the first to offer the world this moving sight. . . .
    On the morrow of this true revolution, men will say to each other in amazement: What! Was the common good to be had for so little? We had only to will it. . .?

Yet there is one declamation surpassing all these that brought strength to the great myth of the Revolution. Destined to pervade the theses of the important socialist activists of the future, it is written, as though by accident, into the general preamble of the Manifesto: '*The French Revolution is only the forerunner of a much bigger, much more solemn revolution, which will be the final one.*' The revolutionary dynamic implicit in this is unmistakable. What clearer holy writ for action could be given to the men of 1848, 1871, and to those beyond France in 1917? The message would be received and adapted by both Blanqui and Marx. It was Lenin who would guarantee its fulfilment.

The conspiracy itself took a month to hatch out (April–May 1796). Its construction gives weight to the argument that it is the progenitor of modern revolutionary techniques. Planning and direction was in the hands of the secret committee. Agents, selected for their revolutionary integrity, were sent to undermine the state forces – that is, the police and army in the immediate area. The *Manifesto* and *An analysis of the doctrine of Babeuf* were widely distributed and read avidly by dissentient workmen and soldiers. A coterie of a dozen agents controlled dissemination of propaganda and organized the formation of Babouvist cells amongst the Paris police legions and in the large barracks at Grenelle. (In the latter, prostitutes were used to deliver the 'great' message with their normal services!) One of the most effective agents (and chief *agent provocateur*) was the army captain Georges Grisel. An unscrupulous realist, he urged that material gain should be the crux of their appeal, that is to loot, an end to tyrannical discipline, and the prospect of the easy life outside the service. He played on the baser needs of the soldier, without whose support, he was shrewd enough to realize, no revolution could succeed.

Babouf's propaganda bore fruit. The removal from Paris of two battalions of police suspected of Babouvist infection was ordered by the government. It aroused an outbreak of local hostility which panicked the government into dissolving these units. They were promptly seized on by the secret committee and inveigled into joining the advance guard in the planned take-over. A meeting of the 'General staff' took eight days to complete arrangements. Secret ammunition dumps had been set up and government weapon stores pin-pointed for looting. A secret call to former Montagnard supporters to converge on Paris was sent. They would strengthen the insurrectionary army. An *Acte insurrecteur* was printed for distribution to the Paris workers at the moment of uprising. It was a remarkable document – a blue-print for later would-be revolutionaries.

It warned that the call to action would be heralded by tocsin and trumpets. The citizens would then seize arms at all points of 'disorder' and march to the centres of assembly. Six revolutionary generals, recognized by special tricolour cockades in their hats, were to head the three forward divisions. The treasury, ministerial houses, and other listed headquarters of civil power, were to be attacked and occupied. Government officials were to be despatched without mercy if they offered resistance. Bakers and wine merchants, under threat of immediate execution, were to distribute their wares gratis. The Directors were to be destroyed, buried beneath the ruins of their mansions. Government troops were enjoined to support the insurgents. If they refused, barricades were to be erected and the troops attacked. Women and children were then exhorted to hurl stones and pour boiling water on the military. All existing institutions would be declared null and void, and a reign of terror was to be imposed until all opposition was eliminated. The people must act without thinking. 'It is essential that they should first commit acts, which would prevent any retreat.' Only then could they be tied irrevocably to the revolutionary leadership.

The democratic constitution of 1793 was still to remain a pipe dream. Babeuf had already renounced democratic sovereignty. Dictatorship was the long-term guarantee for success. The past had already demonstrated that people, who had been so long in a state of inequality, would remain corrupted until re-educated to a *nouvelle vertu*. This would come with the implementation of the community of equals. Only then would the people be capable of determining their own destiny. Meanwhile 'the social reformer must take a large view of things, he must mow down all that hinders him, all that stands in his way'. A form of war communism would ensue. All private stores of food, clothes and other necessities were to be expropriated and redistributed through government depots. The property of émigrés and 'enemies of the people' was to be handed over to poor patriots. Pawned goods were to be recovered without payment. The climate would thus be prepared for the implementation of an egalitarian society. Sovereignty would rest in the Insurrectionary Committee until success was confirmed by 'regenerating laws . . . drawn up in such a manner as not to leave a single, poverty-stricken citizen in the state'. A commissariat of chosen leaders would be attached to districts for the purpose of imposing the will of the central authority. A school for training future leaders was to be introduced as an insurance for the perpetuation of the new order. These would be drawn initially from pre-Thermidorian patriots. Opponents who refused to submit would be detained in hard-labour camps, which were rendered 'inaccessible . . . having administration directly subject to the government'. Instead of remaining idle, they would partake in the task of national reconstruction 'forced, however reluctant, to seek in it their only means of safety'. The Grand National Assembly, controlled by a Supreme Administration, would be directed towards the pursuit of happiness through the right to work. Money, as a means of exchange, would be abolished. Each would work for the good of all and receive, in kind, according to his needs. Personal luxury and profit seeking was to be avoided in order to sustain an 'honourable mediocrity'. Government would consist of three types of assemblies, within which a system of checks and balances could be maintained. Representatives, however, would be elected on the ultimate basis of political reliability. The whole would work on the assumption that *all* were servants of the state. It was, therefore, naïvely presumed that, in such a system, government could be so simplified that any individual could undertake any of its specialized tasks (Lenin, alas, was to repeat this theme almost verbatim in *State and Revolution*). The Babouvist millennium had been defined. But Babeuf would never see it fulfilled.

For the master plan was doomed before it began. The government was kept aware of every stage of the conspiracy through its spies and informers led by Grisel. On May 10th, when final preparations were being made, loyal soldiers raided the headquarters and rounded up the main body. Babeuf and Buonarroti, absent at the time, were seized later. Babeuf's end was traditionally dramatic. After a prolonged trial (February–May 1797) in which he offered a brilliant defence, both he and a co-conspirator were sentenced to death. As the verdict was announced, both drew out concealed daggers and stabbed themselves. The wounds were terrible but not fatal. The next morning both were dragged, in agony, to the guillotine, where with dignity and courage, they faced their executioner.

The end was but the beginning. The legend of Babeuf could not be stilled. The image that he projected would not fail to arouse both the sympathy and emulation of his successors. Babeuf was unique in that he was the only élitist revolutionary whose roots were undoubtedly plebeian. He had shared the wants and privations of *les malheureux* as no other had. He was the prisoner of a humiliating past, the subject of contempt and derision of those Picardian landlords and metropolitan parvenus, who had fashioned themselves for the easy life. He was the most attractive of all; handsome and unruly, wild and generous, single minded in his passion for the cause, which he saw as ultimately the elimination of human want. His fanatical sense of mission grew stronger as hunger and desperation bit deeper. The will to power is implicit in all self-styled prophets. Yet all the fulminations, torchlight conspiracies, fiery manifestos, add up, in the final account, to strong moral protest against socio-economic injustice. Can only the generous acknowledge courage and nobility in this protest?

The consequences of Babouvism place its originator firmly at the start line of modern Communist tradition. They demonstrate the principles which would influence his successors, and the problems, which, in the more sophisticated context of nineteenth-century growth and change, would become more formidable. To sum up, Babeuf utilized many of the Utopian ideas of the philosophers, which were yet vague and untested, to postulate a means of effecting a political and economic reconstruction of society, which was practicable. Although a countryman himself, he preached urban centralism, that is society based on dictatorship of town over country. He recognized that a politically emancipated peasantry was still under the spiritual tutelage of landlord and curé. He anticipated the dangers arising from peasant opposition to direction from the centre on the sales and distribution of their products.[1] Finally he set the seal of his authority on the view that the *only* means of ushering

---

[1] See Blanqui's views on this theme in Chapter 3.

in the egalitarian *communauté* was through a revolutionary working class led by an élitist vanguard.

Babouvism, in its own time and setting, could never have succeeded. Only the nucleus of an urban proletariat existed then. In the later, more potent environment of industrial exploitation combined with political reaction, it was to gain additional strength. An almost insignificant conspiracy was rescued from obscurity by the imagination of its sole leading survivor and chronicler. The apostolic succession was assumed by Filippo Buonarroti. In the new milieu he preached the old gospel, and extended his preachings over the frontiers of Europe.

Filippo Buonarroti (1761–1837)

Buonarroti, 'the first professional revolutionist'[1] was born in the opposite end of the social spectrum to Babeuf. Both his parents were aristocrats – his father was a direct descendant of Michelangelo's brother Buonarroto. He was nurtured on privilege. He attended an exclusive Jesuit school and showed an early flair for music[2] and mathematics. In 1773 he was appointed a page at the court of the enlightened Archduke Peter Leopold of Tuscany, who was the first ruler to abolish capital punishment, the infliction of torture, and to question the Inquisition as 'the harshest despotism'. Such progressive ideas must have rubbed off early on the young Buonarroti.

In 1778 he was admitted to the University of Pisa as a law student. Pisa was a centre of liberal ideas and experimentation. He was taught and guided by Professors Christoforo Sarti, a disciple of Locke, and Giovanni Lampredi, a Rousseauist tutor in French political thought. The latter, as Buonarroti later records, 'accustomed me to the rigours of reasoning, drew my attention to an awareness of my position and to the fundamental principles of the social order'. He embraced Rousseau amongst the 'philosophes' and joined the band of the faithful. 'From then on, I had the deep conviction that it was the duty

---

[1] The appropriate sub-title of an excellent study of Buonarroti by Elizabeth L. Eisenstein.

[2] See p. 42. He used his talent as a music teacher to convert his students to his 'cause'.

of a man of means to work towards the overthrow of the social system which oppresses civilized Europe.' This was not quite true. For at twenty-one he married the beautiful noblewoman Elisabetta de Conti, and accepted the title of Chevalier of the Order of Saint Stephen from the Duke. Nevertheless, it was not long before this young man, the most gifted of his caste, deliberately turned his back on privilege and embraced social revolution for the purpose of destroying it. He had found the Rousseauist creed irresistible. In one sense this amalgam of intellectual grace and humanitarian protest places Buonarroti in the forefront of the Romantic insurrectionists.

Being the subject of constant government scrutiny soon forced him into an almost pathological commitment to conspiracy. In about 1786 he appeared to have joined the Masonic Lodge of Weishaupt's 'Illuminati', a radical society engaged in disseminating anti-clerical and egalitarian propaganda. The Florentine authorities caught on to his activities, raided his home, and discovered a hoard of subversive literature. His father's influence saved him from gaol, but he continued to propagate his radical views as editor of the *Gazette Universale*. In the local setting he employed his pen on the side of the *petit-bourgeois* progressives against the combined old guard of *haut-bourgeois* and aristocrat. 1789 found him in a state of jubilant excitement. He hailed the Revolution: 'I had been waiting a long time for the signal; it was given. Some of the articles of the first Declaration of the Rights of Man . . . confirmed my hopes and succeeded in inflaming me!' He had to be involved. The clandestine period – the fiery words and secret conclaves – was temporarily over. He left Italy for Corsica. The French authority quickly assessed the talents of the young firebrand and offered him the post dealing with clerical affairs and government land. His precipitate anti-clericalism succeeded in mobilizing the 'unenlightened' peasants around their priests to oppose him. In 1791 the locals rose in rebellion at Bastia, seized Buonarroti and dumped him on a ship going to Leghorn, where he was promptly gaoled by the Tuscan police. It would take him some time to learn the Babouvist dictum that *'l'infâme'* was the most difficult to uproot in the countryside, where the peasant is bound to his priest. Conversely he came to see that the town workers would provide the shock troops for the destruction of the old order; and in the process the town proletarian would have to face the antagonism of his rural opposite. The Great Revolution would clarify this through the attacks of the Girondins and Vendéeans against 'red' Paris.

A firm request to the Grand Duke from French Corsica brought about his release. He returned to pursue what was to become a life-long activity. He formed local political clubs on the French model, this time under government sponsorship, and organized conspiratorial committees throughout northern Italy. He became a prime suspect in Italian police files. With Corsica as his base he travelled to and from the mainland, with an almost contemptuous disregard for the police who pursued him relentlessly. He added spice to his escapades by editing, under the Jewish pseudonym of Abraham Levi Salomon, a clandestine journal, which he distributed *en route*. Besides these romantic interludes it is suggested that his Corsican experience finally cemented his ideas on revolutionary egalitarianism. Did not Rousseau himself, in the *Social Contract*, advise that Corsica, under the 'good' Legislator, could be converted into a model society? And had not the master preceded this with his *Project of A Constitution for Corsica*, wherein he had first given practical application to basic Rousseauist tenets? Buonarroti's revolutionary *élan* was awarded recognition when he was directed to join an expedition to St Pierre and Sardinia (January 1793) as an exporter of the new message – with a sword in one hand and the Declaration of Rights in the other. In return he was appointed Legislator of St Pierre (renamed Ile de l'Egalité) which he ruled with considerable success. He came to Paris to plead the union of his island with the mainland. In voicing his attacks there on Paoli (leader of the movement for Corsican independence against France) he established a friendly relationship, which was later to be to his advantage, with the young Corsican officer, Napoleon Buonaparte. Meanwhile his voluntary involvement in France's affairs gained him the reward of French citizenship by the Convention (27th May 1793).

It was then that he met Robespierre. It was the first great turning point in his career. He was fascinated by this disciple of Rousseau. He attended the meetings of the Jacobin Club and was even invited to the sanctuary of the holy one himself – Robespierre's lodgings at the Duplays. But there is no convincing evidence that a personal friendship grew up between them. However, Buonarroti did get to know him at close quarters, and what he saw he admired unreservedly. Henceforth he became a passionate devotee, a remarkable conversion considering that the two personalities were completely antithetical. Although a non-factionist in political attitude, he would back his hero against any opposition; and his hero in return must have judged him of some value. In April 1794 Buonarroti was posted as National Commissioner for occupied territories east of Menton. In Oneglia, in northern Italy, he found himself responsible for the administration of 35,000 people. Here he could use his opportunity for making this small area the focal point for revolutionary ideas and experimentation, from which would stem the new movement into Italy. He carried out his assignment to the letter: exports were prohibited, assignats made currency, the Maximum imposed with forced requisitions and all. He was baffled by the unfavourable reaction to this so he offered the locals the benefits of additional enlightenment, which might win their co-operation. He set up a system of primary and secondary education for the young, in order to indoctrinate them with the uplifting principles of the French 'philosophes'. Still there came no response. Then it registered. He was up against the old obscurantism of priest and landlord. The setting up of surveillance committees and revolutionary tribunals were of no avail. The ungrateful recipients of the new order would agree to a union with France, on condition that their church, then used as a hospital, be restored to its spiritual function. Added to these frustrations was, what he thought, an inadequate economic policy laid down by the Committee of Public Safety. He sent in his resignation, pleading that he wished to undertake 'other means of contributing to the solution of the problems of the world'. It was refused and he continued to do battle with his recalcitrant folk. Robespierre was overthrown and Buonarroti was almost forgotten until complaints reached the Thermidorian government that this neglected Robespierrist was attempting an illegal confiscation of Genoese nobles' land. He was recalled to Paris and thrown into prison at Plessis (March 1795). This was the second turning point.

In prison he met Babeuf and completed his education as a professional revolutionary. In the circumstances of incarceration with its own disciplines he was then able to finalize his own *raison d'être*. He also presents an emotional scene of prison life and conveys a pattern of experience, which would be shared by his successors:

> The victims, whom the aristocracy had plunged into them, lived frugally in the most intimate fraternity, honoured one another for their chains and poverty, devoted themselves to work and study, and conversed only on the calamities of their common country and on the means of bringing them to an end.

His release from prison with Babeuf found him also penniless and homeless. He managed to scrape a bare subsistence by teaching music or Italian to individual pupils, some of whom he converted to his brand of Jacobinism as a by-product. As became a true follower of Rousseau, he left his wife for long periods, although he did manage to find time to give her a son whilst in Bastia (1790). In 1794 he replaced her with a Genoese mistress, Teresa Poggi (in whose divorce he was named as corespondent) who lived with him for twenty years. Political activity absorbed most of his time and energy and he moved back into the circles of anti-government conspiracy. His generous nature responded to the call of Babeuf. He was admitted into the highest ranks of the conspiracy. What is generally unknown is that, as chief adviser and co-ordinator between the Dutch Jacobins and French Babouvists, using Jacques Blauw the Dutch ambassador as intermediary, he helped synchronize an uprising in Amsterdam (8th May 1796). When Babeuf's plot blew up, he was arrested and condemned to deportation by a Vendôme court. He was transported in an iron cage (an experience shared later by his successor Blanqui in 1850!) to Fort National in Cherbourg. His aristocratic charm, however, appeared to have captivated both the court at his trial and his subsequent captors. His prison conditions were, to say the least, curious. His mistress Teresa was allowed to stay with her lover for all purposes. She not only kept up his morale with her 'wifely' ministrations but also acted as a courier for illicit correspondence with underground Jacobins in the capital. Through them Buonarroti issued inflammatory propaganda to build up the pressure of popular discontent. His constant plotting from within roused the prison authorities to rid themselves of this nuisance. In March 1800 he was transferred to the island of Oléron but was still granted a subsidy of three francs a day. Why was he such a favoured prisoner? Napoleon was now master of France. He had probably remembered the dedicated Italian Francophile who had strongly backed his anti-Paoli policy. Both, on sound evidence, had been tainted with Robespierrism. The first consul could afford to be magnanimous towards refractory old comrades, and the bizarre Italian would always inspire respect and affection even from adversaries. In December 1802 he was moved to Sospello in Alpine France. His plottings continued, but notwithstanding this he was given ticket of leave for Geneva in 1806. It became his headquarters for almost fifteen years of unremitting hatching of conspiracies. It also established his reputation as the first of the full-time professional revolutionaries. Equally important at this juncture was his association with, and infiltration into, alien organizations in order to forward the interests of his own élitist cabal. This tactical principle was exemplified in all his future relationships with, what were really to him, auxiliary bodies. It was another precedent that would lend itself to copy by political ideologues obsessed with their own rectitude. After all élitist consciousness gives such activity its own *mores*, since the end subscribed to was the morality of universal equality. Nothing could be immoral, which contributed to the making of the *communauté*. Such was the new(?)

vertu. It is easy to see how the exponents of irrational or illiberal radicalism would make a necessity of this *vertu* for ends other than 'justice' or 'equality'.

Buonarroti's foundation of the society the 'Sublimes Maîtres Parfaits' in 1809 exemplifies this process of infiltration by a self-styled élite. It also confirmed Buonarroti's permanent adherence to the principles of Babeuf's conspiracy. In operation the society registers the point of injection of Babouvist theory into the broader mainstream of European socialism. Where Babeuf saw France, Buonarroti saw Europe; although Buonarroti never ceased to regard France (and for France read Paris) as the mainspring without which no revolutionary movement outside its frontiers could operate.

The ultimate aims of the society were clearly defined. They were to republicanize Europe, to 'break down the marks of private property', and to 'create with the ruins of the private land a social patrimony'. An insight into its construction and influence is given by the closest of Buonarroti's young comrades – Joachim de Prati. He was one of many young European intellectuals attracted as much to the magnetic personality of the leader as to the romanticism of conspiracies. (His devotion to the man lasted longer than his belief in the cause.) After an adventurous career as an international agent, organizer in the Greek Liberation Army, and finally, contact man between the London Italian Carbonari lodge (La Vendetta Italiana) and lodges in Brussels, he settled down to a middle-aged respectability in London. Here in 1838, after the death of Buonarroti, de Prati contributed, anonymously, his autobiography to the *Penny Saritist*. It recounts as much of Buonarroti's revolutionary activities as his own. It is invaluable as a text on conspiracies between the years 1810 and 1831.

De Prati was initiated into the sections of the 'directing committee', into the Great Firmament itself, in 1810. He gave an all-embracing description of the 'Sublimes Maîtres Parfaits'. It operated through various secret societies with differing structures in other countries. It was, therefore, international in scope, working in and through Masonic organizations to further its own political aims. Top leadership was absolutely secret, presiding over a three-tiered hierarchy and led by the supreme directors – the Great Firmament. The lower strata were deliberately sealed off from above and below to offset penetration by the secret police. Organization was based on the principle conceived in 1795, that 'the principal agents . . . institute, organize, or direct the clubs we look for without appearing to institute, organize, or direct anything'. The primacy of a secret caucus was an axiom which persisted throughout Buonarroti's career:

> With respect to doctrines, which one assumes are held in a pure form by the leaders, they would be better preserved and transmitted by them, than by the crowd of initiated whose opinions, whatever one does, will never be altogether fixed nor uniform. With respect to action, whether preparatory or definitive, it is absolutely necessary that the impulse come from above and that all the rest obey. This society is nothing else but a secret army, destined to fight a powerful enemy.

There is no mistaking the implication. The Great Firmament was the esoteric *élite*, and the ordinary members were the vanguard to be employed as thought fit by the elect who were imbued with pure doctrine. Buonarroti conceived himself in the Messianic rôle. 'Midst the collapse of free institutions, midst the general corruption of sentiments one cannot find . . . future regeneration save in a secret corps guided by a pure and dictatorial authority.'

On the broader map of Europe he extended his attack from Geneva on all governments, attacks which reached a crescendo during the era of post-war reaction. He engaged in his Machiavellian policies of undermining institutions on two fronts. First against contemporary society; second against similar groups, which were to be controlled through infiltration by 'fellow travellers'. He expressed a cynical contempt for the masons as 'nothing more than entertainment centres or schools of superstition and slavery'. The extension of his empire of conspiracy brought its own weaknesses. There were the dangers in the centre of being cut off from the political realities on the periphery; and thus of over or underestimating a revolutionary

situation. This could lead to misjudgements, when the leadership would direct action into a vacuum. The abortive coups of
Blanqui mainly resulted from this.

Was Buonarroti's society the spectre that haunted Chancellor
Metternich, that urged Stendhal's Prince of Parma to look
nightly under his bed for hidden Jacobins? Metternich was
convinced that the *Männerbund*, a German secret society pledged
to unite and republicanize Germany, was associated with 'that
secret centre, which has . . . directed the greater part of the
secret societies of Europe for years'. Prati's reminiscences reveal
a network of conspiracies emanating from Geneva, with
Buonarroti at the centre spinning his web. Police records in
France, Austria and Italy appear to confirm it. Recent evidence
gathered by such eminent historians as Armanda Saitta in Italy,
and Arthur Lehning in Amsterdam, suggests that in European
conspiracy 'Buonarroti was a true divinity; if not omnipotent –
at least omnipresent!' Prati's account of his own rôle in the
scheme ties up with all other evidence. He explains, in detail, the intricate organization built up across national frontiers.

As early as 1810 Prati had met deputies from committees in
Paris and Geneva, who were preparing for General Malet's
conspiracy against Napoleon. With the restoration of the Bourbons in 1815, extreme radical opposition was centred round a
'*Comité directeur*', which included the republicans Voyer d'Argenson, Charles Teste, and Pierre Leroux (coiner of the term
'Socialism'). All of them were in contact with the Great Firmament, that is Prati and Buonarroti, who were the '*diacre mobile*' –
the top initiates. During the years of monarchical reaction a
pyramidical organization was built up on an ever-widening base.
In April 1820 Prati met Wilhelm Snell and Carl Follen, the
latter a teacher in the University of Giessen. They formed a
directory of three. Their task was to recruit twelve men from
different countries to undertake the formation of secret societies.
They were to seek recruits from all classes – nobles, soldiers,
students and workers. Ultimate political aims remained a
secret invested in the original triumvirate. The *Männerbund* was

an offshoot of this and a parent body to the *Jünglingsbund* its
student auxiliary. Links were to be established with parallel
societies in Italy and France. Snell was to be chief organizer
in Germany, Prati in Italy, and Follen in Paris. Metternich's
suspicions appeared to be justified.

In France Follen met d'Argenson and Joseph Rey who had
founded the secret 'Union' in 1816. In August 1820 they were
involved in the military conspiracy of the Bazar Français,[1]
which failed. Rey escaped to Switzerland where he joined up
with Prati and Snell. They agreed to the internationalization
of secret societies and to their control from a central base. In
1821 Prati was in contact with refugee insurgents from Piedmont and Lombardy in his new post of general agent in charge
of the expansion of organizations in Switzerland, the Tyrol and
Germany. Other 'Union' escapees from the August plot, Jou-
bert and Dugred, returned to France from Italy to arrange the
formation of the 'Haute Vente' of French Carbonarism. An
underground assault on Metternich's Europe was being prepared ostensibly in breadth and depth. Behind all was the
ubiquitous presence of the arch-conspirator Buonarroti.

But all the central directives, secret rendezvous, nocturnal
to-ings and fro-ings across borders came to nothing. It was an
'International' that might have been. By 1823 the conspirators
were either imprisoned or dispersed. The insurrections in Naples,
Piedmont, and Spain were crushed. Early that year a student
agent, Andryane,[2] was caught with incriminating documents
referring to the 'Sublimes Maîtres Parfaits' and its clandestine
activities. The great diaspora began. The French agent Ange-
loni was expelled from Paris (14th March 1823) and fled to
London, where he died a pauper. Prati, on the way back from
assisting the Greek Liberation Army, was ordered out of France.
He entered Switzerland, where he was in turn expelled
(7th May 1823), and likewise came to London. Six days later

---

[1] Some old disgruntled ex-army officers and N.C.O.s opened a shop in Paris
to collect money. The funds were to be employed for buying arms in order to
effect a military coup in favour of the restoration of Napoleon or his son. The
conspiracy was poorly planned and proved abortive.

[2] See his 'Memoires d'un Prisonnier d'Etat au Spielberg'.

Buonarroti received his marching orders in Geneva, with a passport to London. He never arrived. He stopped off incognito in the Vaud canton, where the police only discovered him eleven months later. He was finally expelled from Swiss territory in April 1824.

Buonarroti arrived in Belgium with a new mistress, Sarah Disbains. Before leaving Geneva, he had suggested to Teresa the idea of a *ménage à trois*. Teresa, a Latin and highly jealous, utterly refused to share him with a 'Swiss snake' (yet she persisted in writing to him until his death). Brussels, where he lived for the next six years, was an immigrant centre for the old fugitive leaders of '93 and '94, who wrote memoirs and debated the pros and cons of the activities of the great ones during the Revolution. They met at the *Café des Milles Colonnes*. Here Buonarroti joined them. In their never-ending dissertations he was the consistent defender of Robespierre, and in spite of this, he was accepted by all. His extravagant views they regarded with indulgence – perhaps a mental blockage in an otherwise sane and affable eccentric. Yet his unrelenting Robespierrism was to prove his greatest strength. For a new generation of Frenchmen had grown up after Thermidor under the stultifying restrictions of Bourbon rule. The young turned back, beyond the years of Napoleonic 'gloire', to the classical age, when the Mountain had saved France by heroic utterances and ruthless deeds, and Buonarroti's sustained apologia for the Terror and his eulogy of Robespierre added strength to the legend. It was resuscitated on two fronts: by three published works each influenced directly or indirectly by Buonarroti, and by his persistence in operating through or controlling the secret societies reborn in the 1820's.

These works were required reading for the extreme oppositionists in France. The first was the *Réfutation de l'Histoire de France de l'Abbé de Montgaillard* (1828) by Paul Mathieu Laurent, a follower of Saint-Simon, who, aligned with the attacks on the obscurantism of Charles X, re-evaluated the Jacobin dictatorship in its favour. The publisher, Charles Antoine Teste, became first assistant to Buonarroti when he resumed his conspiratorial activities. Teste was also connected with the publication of the second apologia, the *Mémoires de René Levasseur (de la Sarthe)*, in four volumes, edited by Achille Roche (1803–34) who drew on the notes of an ex-Conventionnel to defend the régime of 1793–4. Roche was placed on trial. It was Karl Marx's early reading of his works that directed his interest towards the Great Revolution. It also shows conclusively the influence of Buonarroti, who contributed the third and most important work on this theme. In 1828, there first appeared in Brussels his two-volumed chronicle of *Conspiration pour l'Egalité, dite de Babeuf*. It more than strengthened contemporary political trends. It struck at the roots of the gradualist schools, such as those of the Utopians Saint-Simon and Fourier. Moreover, it not only rehabilitated Robespierre, but also transmitted the Babouvist theme in the revolutionary tradition to a developing industrial proletariat. An English translation was made by Bronterre O'Brien in 1836. In 1844 it was read by Karl Marx, who with Engels toyed with the idea of producing a German edition. Marx always kept a copy in a prominent place on his shelves.

The *Conspiration pour l'Egalité* is Buonarroti's political testament. He indulges in polemical and denunciatory thrusts (which anticipate the methods of his twentieth-century successors) to bring out in relief, by laudatory invocation, the rectitude of the Left. The Committee of Public Safety becomes the model for 'illustrious legislators' who brought about

> the astonishing metamorphosis by which so vast a population . . . but a season before, the sport of voluptuousness, cupidity, levity and presumption cheerfully renounced a thousand factitious enjoyments, rivalled one another in zeal to offer up their superfluities on their country's altar, thundered in mass on the armies of the coalesced sovereigns and contended themselves with demanding for their *all*, bread, steel and equality.

The Robespierrist dictatorship represents the archetypal rule by devoted élitists. The old system had rendered the masses 'poorly qualified to make a useful choice', so the *élite* must lead them, with coercion implicit in the process. Here was the 'despotism of liberty against tyranny', in which the new order will ensure that 'the country takes possession of every individual at birth and never releases him till death'. Defence of the social patrimony was to be maintained by compulsory military service for young men 'constantly encamped on the borders of the Republic'. It would serve as propaganda by example to 'the servile soldiery of the despots of Europe'. Internally would be enacted the consummation of the Revolutionary experience. The worship of the Supreme Being and the immortality of the soul was to be recognized. Censorship of writers would be rigidly enforced on the basis of 'publication [being] useful to the Republic'. Judgement would be given by a board of censors – 'conservators of the National Will'. Academic concentration on the arts and sciences was to be avoided since the arts 'led to the taste for superfluities . . . and frivolities', and the sciences to affectation of an undeserved and dangerous superiority. Sartorial design would be simple and patterned to identify individuals. Clothes were to consist of uniforms varying according to the age and occupational group.

Magistrates were to be placed in charge of overseas trade so as to dispense with merchant entrepreneurs and profiteers, 'a race of vampires that would be unknown to the country'. The state economy would be based on agriculture (understandably so, since Buonarroti had no personal experience of a highly industrialized society, such as in England). Industrial centres were not to be retained for purely commercial enterprises, which were associated with vice. They were to be transformed functionally, for use as bases of virtue, where government quarters, libraries, bridges and amphitheatres would vie with each other as purveyors of the new enlightenment. Pre-Thermidorian legislation would be extended to embrace the total nationalization of wealth and production based on 'a grand national community which maintains all its members in an equal and honourable mediocrity'. Heavy taxation would deprive the wealthy of their privileges. The possessors could either voluntarily surrender their property or leave the country. (Buonarroti deflates the 'Constitution of 1793' since 'one regrets to find in it the old deplorable ideas on the rights of property'.)

The drones and work-shy faced the threat of internment in hard labour camps. The new society would achieve perfection when every being, every activity was state controlled. For even the 'human heart' was to be part of the 'body politic', in which family kinship was sacrificed to love of State. This, to Buonarroti, was the ultimate triumph – when 'the Legislator would have been able to render all affections of family and kindred subordinate to this sentiment'.

For the last fourteen years of his life (1823–37) Buonarroti remained the focal point around which Republican secret societies revolved. Hardly had he been defeated, as in 1823, than he was up again re-mustering his invisible army between Paris and Brussels. He was behind the activities of the French *Charbonnerie* where the old and new Republicans joined to undermine the Legitimist régime. Evidence testifying to his involvement in a multi-variety of groups is found in the correspondence between Charles Teste and himself. The July Revolution provided no respite from his plottings. In August 1830, after a written request to the new government, the old man, now the Grand Nestor of the old Revolution, was allowed to return to his beloved Paris after thirty years of exile. But not to enjoy the quiet and repose earned by an old campaigner who is approaching his end. He quickly discerned that the Orleanist monarchy was the old in borrowed robes, that its class function was as anti-egalitarian as the régime it had usurped. Refreshed in his spiritual home he stepped up the process of sapping and mining, using as his tools the radical youth disillusioned after July. In August 1830, we find Prati joining the 'Amis du Peuple', 'Having obtained . . . permission from the invisible church, I offered myself as a member . . . in order to train this society in our political creed.' He had the usual task of infiltrating the society in order to influence it in the interests of the 'invisible church' (*Penny Satirist*, 2nd February 1839). It was this society which included in its front rank the young Auguste Blanqui already committed to an implacable hostility against rule by *bourgeois* functionaries. They met openly once a week in a circus in the Rue Montmartre. Blanqui led the left wing, which was centred round the old triumvirate, Buonarroti, Argenson and Teste. The latter worked silently in the background. Yet the dynamic impact of the old revolutionist on Blanqui was irrevocable.

Why could Buonarroti attract to himself so many men and women of high calibre and win their endless devotion? Physically he was of middle height, about five feet five inches, but tallness was suggested by a handsome patrician elegance set off by a powerful leonine head. First impressions were those of aloofness and a cold exterior, but these were quickly dispelled. The warmth and kindliness of this humane and generous man soon broke through. He would wax deadly serious on political issues only; the gay and lively conversationalist inevitably took over. The image of an urbane wit was reinforced by his gadabout existence: his insouciance over ownership of things, places to live, a change of mistress.

He was a superb teacher of music and revolution. Essentially his was a perennial appeal to youth. He could not suffer old bores gladly. To the young, he offered a passionate devotion to a cause, a self-sacrifical pursuit of the *bonheur commun*, an end to the degradation of *les malheureux*. Had he not renounced both social station and a secure future for the miseries of imprisonment and the perils of the hunted? He drew on the idealism of youth by his contempt for the 'smug' *bourgeoisie*, who lives were circumscribed by the unedifying limits of material self-interest. Legend decreed that, politically, his own moral stature was impeccable. He could, therefore, demand and obtain absolute obedience. His selfless, unrelenting pursuit of an egalitarian *communauté* won him his greatest disciple in old age.

Yet it was this very inflexibility that bred its own paradoxes. In voicing his own decisions he would brook no opposition. He was firmly secure in his own egocentricity, but distrusted selfishness in others. Like Robespierre his political vision could embrace all humanity, but the lonely sufferer could go unheeded. Both imposed justice without mercy; both could deal out retribution to those who denied the revealed word. The oracle, to the very end, persisted in his conspiracies and pontifications.

Only when alone did he meditate in 'august melancholy' on man's inability to inaugurate the 'incorruptible's' dream – the *regnum* of pure virtue and the fulfilment of Babouvism.

He died on 16th September 1837. Blanqui, under police surveillance at Jancy, was forbidden to return to Paris where his mentor was to be buried. The *National* pertinently reported the death of 'the former general commissioner of the Convention . . . after an existence consecrated by seventy-seven years of virtue'. The day of the funeral over a thousand French and Italian artisans followed the bier to the Montmartre cemetery. His old comrade, d'Argenson, provided the vault, Charles Teste conducted the service. A bronze figure of Buonarroti by the radical artist David d'Angers broods over the vault. Buried with the old conspirator was a bound volume of his *Conspiration pour l'Egalité*. A huge wreath provided by the workmen bore the inscription, 'Buonarroti, great citizen, friend of equality, the people bestow this wreath, history and posterity will consecrate this ovation.' The last memento of the elect was provided by the doyen himself. It is inscribed on the tomb:

> My life story, troubled, full of sacrifices and sorrows, marked by an ardent longing for the happiness of others, that is what you are called upon to judge.
>
> (Defence, High Court of Vendôme,
> 21 Floréal, Year V of the Republic.)

History provides its own judgement. Buonarroti pursued the theme of conspiratorial techniques, which he believed could bring exclusive power to an *élite*, that would act in the name of the masses. He, therefore, rejected spontaneous insurrection *per se* and the possibility of its aftermath of democratic rule. Blanqui accepted these principles and adapted them to a changed milieu, which appeared to provide more scope for their fulfilment.

CHAPTER 3

Blanqui

The France of Blanqui contrasted sharply with that of Babeuf. Economic changes had been profound and these, in turn, produced a like reaction in the political sector. Industrialization had taken root, an urban proletariat was expanding, although both developments were not as rapid as those which had taken place across the Channel. The best general test of a nation's industrial life under modern conditions is the rate and character of the growth of its towns.[1]

In 1801 Paris had the largest town population in Europe (548,000) after London. Lyons registered 109,000; Marseilles 111,000, and no British town other than London existed with these numbers. By 1851 the population of Lyons had doubled; Paris almost so. Marseilles had grown by seventy-five per cent. Only two other towns showed a dramatic growth: St Etienne (16,000–56,000), a coal mining centre where the first rail link with Lyons was completed in 1832; and Roubaix (8,000–34,000), developing primarily through worsted weaving and mixed fabrics of cotton and mohair for clothing and furniture coverings. Paris was involved in almost all aspects of industry, both as a capitalizing agency and in the finishing processes. Entrepreneurs, who provided materials and patterns, were centred here. Also the capital was the control centre of finance, since the Bank of France, except for some provincial competition, virtually maintained its monopoly. Economically, in relation to current expansion, Paris was still the focal point of French investment and overall development.

Considerable advancement had taken place in the textile,

[1] See J. H. Clapham, *Economic Development of France and Germany 1815–1914*, Chapter III.

metal, railway and coal industries, although not at a pace comparable to England. On analysis certain causes emerge. From 1789 to 1815 France had experienced a disorganizing revolution and a destructive war. Her resources had been strained to the limit, her losses in man-power immense, and, in the end, her own territory invaded and ravaged. Hence official reports after 1815 on individual industries show that few were ripe for reorganization and in fact most had retrogressed to the position they had held in 1789. Everywhere there was a shortage of capital and skilled labour, with limited access to raw materials previously cut off in the blockade. A fundamental defect was France's limited resources of cheap quality fuel, which Britain had in abundance. Nevertheless there was vital and energetic application to economic tasks. The most acceptable statistics record that only fifteen establishments in 1815 used steam engines, mainly for pumping in the mines. By 1820, sixty-five engines were already employed in the mines. In 1830 the figures show 625, with a total horsepower of 10,000. By 1848 there were 5,200, with a corresponding horsepower of 65,000. This suggests an overall decline in the average (16 H.P. in 1830 to 12½ H.P. in 1848), but this may be accounted for by the spread of engine power to the smaller textile mills. Cotton development in Alsace exemplified the process. Around Mulhouse there was rapid industrial acceleration between 1815 and 1850. Here experiments with a power loom began after 1823; by 1830 there were already 2,000 in operation and by 1846, 10,000: and here spindles rose from half a million in 1828 to 1,150,000 by 1847 – that is one-third of the total in France. Figures for railway line development showed the construction of 38 kilometres by 1831, rising to 1,831 kilometres by 1847 with a parallel increase in output of metals and coal. Annual coal production, which in 1815 had barely touched 900,000 tons, rose to 1,774,000 in 1828 and reached 5,153,000 tons in 1847. Consequently the output of pig iron rose as follows: approximately 100,000 tons in 1815; 221,000 tons in 1821; 591,000 tons in 1847.

An industrial proletariat was in the making, certainly in

organic development from the bare nucleus of 1796. Metal-workers rose from 25,000 in 1830 to 38,000 in 1847; miners from 15,000 to 35,000 within the same period, and textile workers doubled their numbers. But by 1848 no overall clear-cut division between the small handicraftsman and wage earner had emerged. The former had still a fair chance of acquiring master's status. Yet in 1848, both their interests and social attitudes appeared almost identical. Paris, as usual, polarized their relationship. Here, on the eve of revolution, 7,117 work-shops employed more than ten workmen; 32,583 worked alone or employed up to two workmen. In the seventh district there were 57,988 wage earners against 10,324 employers. Certainly no large-scale proletariat in the classic idiom, but nevertheless undergoing the common tribulations in those areas associated with a maturing capitalist economy.

Labour codes bore heavily on the workmen. The revolutionary legislators had swept away the guilds. In 1791 both masters' and men's associations were declared illegal, but this only proved effective against workers combining to protect their standard of living. Napoleon's Civil Code confirmed the rights of employers in wage disputes. Under article 1781, the master's opinion was to be decisive in law over wage fixing, and this right was sustained until 1868. Additions to the penal code consolidated this decision: articles 291–4 prohibited the association of more than twenty people, and articles 414–16 declared striking or picketing a criminal offence. In 1803 the 'livret' was introduced – the workman's employment book, which recorded the names of his employers, and their reports on his work. No man with a previous unsatisfactory labour record could hope to be re-employed. After 1815 workers' rights got worse, not better.

Living conditions in towns were deplorable, with little hope of respite. Families shared one room and for outworkers this meant living and working under conditions of extreme congestion. Rooms were let weekly, and rent paid in advance. In times of recession evictions were common. Rent was assessed as an average of ten per cent, and food seventy-five per cent, of a worker's wage. Saving was, therefore, impossible. For example, in 1831 the Lyons weaver worked sixteen to eighteen hours a day with one hour recess for meals, and a 'good' weekly wage on piece rates was 1 franc 50 sous. This was well below subsistence level, and unless more income could accrue from children's earnings families constantly faced starvation. The factories were the new Bastilles, long hours and unhygienic conditions undermined the health of the worker and led to a corresponding increase in tuberculosis. A survey of the national physique between 1835 and 1845 revealed a degeneration in the health and stature of army recruits, particularly those from the highly industrialized Lyons area (Lyons focused the issue). Industrial pockets in Paris and elsewhere were modified repetitions of the same theme. It is in this setting that we must study the making of a social revolutionary.

Louis Auguste Blanqui was born in 1805, at Puget Theniers near Nice, the second son of Jean-Dominique Blanqui, ex-Girondist Conventionnel, who had survived the Terror to become a *sous-préfet* under Napoleon. The Restoration meant the loss of home and office, but thanks to a timely inheritance settled on Madame Blanqui, the family was saved from destitution. In 1818, the eldest son Adolphe was offered a post as a junior master at Bourg-la-Reine near Paris and suggested that Auguste should accompany him to be educated at the Lycée Charlemagne in Paris. There Auguste became a brilliant student of the classics, excelled at mathematics, history and geography, and at the annual Lycée presentations was held up as a paragon of scholarship.

He left the lycée a promising academic, but was also politically committed to a vague radical republicanism by joining the Charbonnerie. He had already taken part in student demonstrations, and discoursed endlessly on political issues in student cafés in the Latin quarter. In 1822 he was an onlooker at the execution of the four sergeants of La Rochelle, who had conspired against the monarchy, and the manner in which they faced death, recalling the mythical heroism of Babeuf and Darthé, left its mark on an impressionable youth. Meanwhile,

Adolphe brought his gifted young brother into journalism, as a reporter on the *Courtier Français* and the *Journal du Commerce*. But not for long: Auguste, looking for more secure employment, applied for, and was chosen, as tutor to the son of the ex-Bonapartist, General Compans. For two years he pursued the rôle of an anchorite in the lonely Château de Blagnac on the banks of the Garonne. It was here that he must have finalized his creed. He assumed a Spartan mode of living – no intoxicants, a frugal diet of bread, fruit and vegetables. His window was open in all weathers, and in winter he would often wake to find frost on his bedclothes. Perhaps he was already preparing for the grim life of *l'enfermé*, of self-sacrifice and incarceration, which was to be his lot for nearly forty years.

He returned to Paris in 1826, during the peak period of monarchist reaction, to complete a university course in law and medicine. As a student he was already strengthening the threads of his revolutionary background. Involvement with the Charbonnerie was to have a permanent influence on his revolutionary technique; but it was amidst the student discourses and demonstrations in the Latin quarter, and among the artisans of the faubourgs, that he received his education in the art of revolution. Soon the paths of the two brothers were to diverge: the elder achieving honour as a state economist and the coiner of the phrase 'industrial revolution', the younger becoming in turn both persecutor and persecuted under a succession of French governments.

Auguste's first taste of action came in 1827 as a leader of the Paris students demonstrating against the Bourbons. Thrice engaged in riots and thrice wounded he barely escaped with his life; and, what is more relevant, he became a marked man by the police. During an innocent visit to his birthplace, he was seized by the local police and taken into custody. It was a short-term introduction to what was to be a recurrent life-long experience. Returning to Paris in August 1829, he worked as a reporter on the *Globe*, the organ of the 'Doctrinaire' parliamentary opposition led by Guizot. Contemptuous of the academic and legalistic gyrations of the constitutionalists who controlled the paper, he sought the company of the workers and students, who, in the side-streets and cafés, plotted the violent overthrow of the régime. Here was the repository of the myth of Babeuf and his still-living apostle Buonarroti.

The hour of opportunity came on 28th July 1830 and found him ready. Seizing a musket and tricolour, he appeared on the barricades in the 'three glorious days' that ended the Bourbon monarchy. The story is told by Mlle de Montgolfier, a writer who had befriended Blanqui, that on the night of the 29th, as the last shots rang out, the door burst open and Blanqui appeared, his face blackened with powder, his eyes bloodshot, his clothes torn. Flinging his musket on the floor, he cried out triumphantly against the lawyers and poets who had vacillated in the hour of decision – *'Enfoncés, les Romantiques!'*[1]

The régime which followed provided a more rational basis for the economic change which was developing, and brought its authority to bear on the process of acceleration. It emerged as a government controlled by a *bourgeois* king that worked for, and in the interests of, a financial coterie. The banker Lafitte declared: 'From now on the bankers will rule.' The political arm of the state was once more directed against the workers and artisans, the very groups who had fought and won on the barricades only to have their victory snatched from their hands. The perceptive Blanqui quickly recognized the changeover in terms of replacement of one exploiting group by another. It brought the young intellectual to a more sophisticated analysis of social change as he prepared to join combat against the *bourgeois* parvenus. An economic crisis in the autumn revealed the deep schism in society. In Paris printers and bakers broke the new mechanical presses and baking equipment, and artisans rioted. Blanqui headed the formation of a republican student federation. He was expelled from the University. In January 1831, a student assault on the Procurer General and Minister of Education led to his arrest and imprisonment for three weeks. In letters to Mlle Montgolfier, Blanqui already referred scathingly to the *bourgeoisie* who had reaped the fruits of the

[1] 'They've had it, the Romantics!'

July revolution and now wished to hang those true fighters who
had wrought victory by arms in 'the three glorious days'. The
'republicans' had committed the cardinal error of discarding
these arms in the hour of triumph, leaving them at the mercy
of the bayonets of the 'government of the *bourgeois* classes'. Was
not this a more positive reiteration of the 'permanent revolution'
anticipated by Robespierre? According to Blanqui, the *bourgeoisie* were determined to use their power to cast the masses
back into servitude, the logical consequence of which would
be a second revolution – one, with equally matched protagonists, that would produce a holocaust greater than 1789!
Contemporary socio-economic conditions were propitious for
an ideology which openly proclaimed class warfare, for labour
was being alienated more and more from the means of production. Blanqui was first to identify this process.

Out of a cocoon of specific generalities, there emerged the
chrysalis of a political theory, which suggests itself as the precursor of Marxism. In January 1832 Blanqui was brought to
trial on the charge of conspiracy. In this dramatic dialogue,
during cross-examination, Blanqui openly proclaimed the class
struggle as an omnipotent historical phenomenon:

> 'What is your profession?' asked the Judge.
> 'Proletarian,' replied Blanqui.
> 'That is not a profession.'
> 'Not a profession?' retorted Blanqui. 'It is the profession of thirty
> million Frenchmen who live by working and are deprived of all
> political rights.'

The tone was set for a declamation which has certainly been
construed as 'the first socialist manifesto of this epoch'.

> 'There is a war between the rich and poor. The rich have made it
> so, for they are the aggressors. . . .'

He proceeded to assert that all previous conflict between the
feudal nobility and the rising merchant classes had now been
transposed by a final struggle between the dominant *bourgeoisie* and the proletariat – the last form of slavery.

'It appears that here, under new forms and between other adversaries is the war of the feudal barons against the merchants, who they plundered on the high road.'

The jury, if not convinced, were sympathetic. They urged his acquittal, but the magistrates saw the danger. He was sentenced to one year's imprisonment for 'disturbing the public peace by arousing the contempt and hatred of the citizenry against several classes of people, which he had variously described as the privileged rich or *bourgeoisie*'.

At this stage, had Blanqui already arrived at a mature stage of Socialist theory through a perceptive appreciation of current social and industrial trends? Marxists deny this and dismiss his views as 'primitive'. Lenin declared: 'Blanquism is a theory that denies the class struggle!'[1] Criticism is directed against Blanqui for not defining his terms absolutely in his categorization of classes. But who could at any juncture? Are clear-cut definitions of class strata with overlapping areas ever really possible? Blanqui's conception of the 'people' is written down. They were the sector deprived of their 'instruments of labour', whose benefits accrued to a tyrannical minority who had brought about this alienation. Evidence is confirmed in an early article 'Qui fait la soupe doit la manger' (1834). Here he asserts that exploitation must exist as long as economic and political power is controlled by this minority. 'It is this monopoly and not some political constitution or other which enslaves the masses.' The same year, in the one and only issue of *Le Libérateur*, he confirms his dedication to the 'exploited worker' and declares his belief in 'a social transformation from the Republic'. In a handbill *Propagande Démocratique* (1835), he reiterates the theme: 'the end for us is the equal distribution of the burdens and benefits of society – it is the complete establishment of the reign of equality . . . without this radical reorganization all modifications in the forms of government would only be illusions, all revolutions merely comedies played for the profit of a few ambitious people'. In all this, where is Blanqui's denial of the class struggle?

[1] Lenin, *The Congress Summed Up* (1906).

Henceforth Blanqui and his party were committed to the violent overthrow of society in order to attain equality through a socialism based on 'the illegitimacy of capital'. How would this be achieved? What kind of leadership could profitably direct the great uprising? He had the historical precedent conveyed to him by Buonarroti. Now steeped in the Babouvist tradition of conspiracy, Blanqui conceived of a revolutionary *corps d'élite* – a body of dedicated men, well-trained, well-armed and sworn to secrecy, who, at the right strategic moment would seize the main centres of power. Revolutionary execution would be effected by the spontaneous insurrectionism of the armed workers. The miseries of capitalism would now provide the raw materials and opportunities for insurrection. After the coup, under the umbrella of a revolutionary reign of terror, capitalism would be abolished and a communist state imposed from above. No definition of the new society is given. Its structure would work itself out by trial and error, provided the direction was in the hands of the Blanquist guardians. Here he parts company with Proudhon ('Communism and Proudhonism argue vigorously on the bank of a stream, whether there is a field of corn or wheat on the other side. Let us cross first, we will see when we get there'): but not with Marx. For neither Blanqui nor Marx believed that one could draw up a blue-print of the archetypal communist society. It was this blending of conspiratorial élitism with communism in a developing capitalistic *milieu* which was to set Blanqui apart from his contemporaries. His first practical attempt to hasten the millennium came with the remarkable rising of 12th May 1839.

Released from prison by a general amnesty on the occasion of the marriage of the Duc d'Orléans in May 1837, Blanqui again entered into conspiracy in the clandestine 'Society of the Seasons', with two picturesque co-revolutionaries, Armand Barbès and Martin Bernard. Classic techniques were designed to effect a closely knit organization based on a hierarchical caucus. Supreme command was invested in the *élite*, who were to constitute the leaders of the new government. The rank and file, sworn to a strict code of secrecy and obedience, were kept unaware of the names of their leaders to prevent infiltration by the Orléanist police. Each cell was called to assemble immediately at fixed points in Paris, by an order from its group leader. No one, except the triumvirate, knew which order was the call for action. Each turnout was a dress rehearsal.

In April 1839, a parliamentary crisis accompanied an economic one. Mass unemployment aroused discontent and tension among workers and peasants. Blanqui, sensing an opportunity, decided to strike after careful preparation. Training periods were instituted and the sections assembled at various centres, where Blanqui, unknown to his followers, inspected them and memorized the face of each individual. A thorough military appreciation of the situation was carried out. Secret ammunition dumps were set up, gunsmith shops were pin-pointed for looting, and maps were prepared, with detailed outlines of barricades strategically sited for defence and attack. It was a masterpiece of planning, the significance of which was not lost on later revolutionaries. Blanqui selected the day – 12th May, a Sunday. He learned that new provincial regiments had just replaced the old, and were therefore unconversant with the mazes and alleyways of the faubourgs. Sunday would also see high officers and senior government members and officials away at the races at the Champ de Mars, which would mean the withdrawal of many police from the central district. The vital question was, 'How would the Paris workers react?' ‘ Blanqui expected them to rise and rally to him when the *coup* was struck. After seizure of the capital, the revolutionary tide would overflow into the provinces to bring about the national uprising. He was wrong. And it was a lesson he would never learn.

On the afternoon of the fine spring day, the sections were assembled at their start line – groups of seemingly ordinary citizens lounging or seated at cafés along the Rue St Martin and St Denis. Suddenly Blanqui appeared among them, issued orders to the leaders, and led the forward contingent on the first looting expedition to the gunsmiths in the Rue Bourg l'Abbé. After the distribution of weapons and ammunition the mass, divided into three groups, moved off to attack set points. As the columns diverged, they shouted slogans for the populace to rise. There was no response. At the first sight of arms, the astonished crowds fled, leaving the deserted streets to the marching insurgents.

The first clash came with the military at the Palais de Justice. Barbès called upon them to surrender. A shot was fired, killing the lieutenant in charge, and general firing broke out. The soldiers, out-numbered, fell back, and the building with its arsenal was soon captured. The first power centre was won. The next objective was the Préfecture of Police, whose occupants, now alerted, barricaded themselves against the coming attackers. Seeing that the breakthrough would require a long siege, Barbès left a section there, and pushed on to meet the other columns, which were converging on the Hôtel de Ville, and capturing vital police stations on the way. After a small scuffle, the great prize, the focal point of Parisian government, was in their hands. Plans had succeeded beyond the leader's expectations. On the steps of the Hôtel de Ville, Barbès proclaimed the Republic – to the open air. Amongst the bombast appeared the traditional theme: 'Let exploitation perish that equality may stand triumphant upon the ruins of royalty and aristocracy.' Blanqui was named Commander-in-Chief of the Republican armies and leader of the provisional government. But this was no 1830. The farce could not endure for long. The Government ordered out the National Guard; military garrisons were alerted, and the Municipal Guards detailed to attack the captured buildings. Within an hour, the Palais de Justice, the Hôtel de Ville and the police stations were retaken. The Blanquists retreated behind the prepared line of barricades, where troops and insurgents joined battle. At Ménilmontant and Montmartre, in the rues Richelieu and Feydeau, the fighting raged. By nightfall, with Paris swollen with troops, the end came. Barbès, wounded, was taken prisoner; Blanqui and Bernard were in flight. The insurrection had one immediate success – it solved the ministerial crisis. A right-wing cabinet was formed under the veteran Marshal Soult, whose first job was to bring the Blanquists to trial.

Why had the *coup* failed? Engels, in retrospect, viewed such a launching in prescribed terms: 'Insurrection is an art, quite as much as war or any other, and subject to certain rules and proceedings, which, when neglected, will produce the ruin of the party neglecting them.' Blanqui had studied the art but neglected to define the priorities making for victory. He was the prisoner of an inflexibility of method, unmoved by error. After careful pre-planning, he utilized the element of surprise, always to achieve nothing. One of his weaknesses lay in his old-fashioned belief in the 'spontaneous insurrection' of the masses, which he naïvely presumed would be automatically harnessed to a *coup* of his own timing. Therefore he ignored as irrelevant, and continued to ignore, widespread propaganda among the workers. The participation of the masses in the uprisings of 1848 and 1871 came in spite of him. He was a prisoner during both. Yet one can see why he eschewed a closer relationship. Safeguards had to be met against an efficient secret police, whose agents achieved a high record of penetration into underground organizations.[1] The larger the organization, the wider the contacts, the easier it was to undermine. Faced with this dilemma, Blanqui could hardly tackle the problem of 'mobilizing' the masses. The other weakness lay in his commitment to the barricades as the centre of a *tour de force*. Trotsky suggests: 'The insurrectionary tactic of Blanquism corresponded to the character of the old Paris, the narrow streets and the military system of Louis Philippe. Blanqui's mistake in principle was to identify revolution with insurrection. His technical mistake was to identify insurrection with the barricades.' A technical mistake also on the part of Trotsky. Could not the 1917 *coup* be classified as Lenin's (and Trotsky's) identification of Bolshevik insurrectionism with mass revolution?

In Maratist fashion, the hunted Blanqui went underground; a troglodytic existence in cellars and sewers, sustained by his

[1] See L. de la Hodde, *Histoire des Sociétés Secrètes et le Parti Républicain de 1830 à 1848*.

wife[1] and worker friends, meeting them in obscure and deserted by-ways, always expecting arrest. The inevitable happened as he was about to escape to Switzerland on October 13th. Through the treachery of an informer, he was caught boarding a stage coach. In January 1840 he was tried by a Chamber of Peers and sentenced to death – a sentence which, with that of Barbès, was commuted by the king to imprisonment.

For eight years, at the prisons of Mont Michel and Tours, he assumed the rôle with which he was always associated: *l'enfermé* – the unbending prisoner of five régimes, in self-sacrifical dedication to the cause of the revolutionary overthrow of *bourgeois* society. The brooding figure in the narrow cell, prematurely aged by ill-use and suffering, became a myth that fired the imagination of young radicals and roused them against the ineptitude and corruption prevalent in the last years of the Orléanist monarchy. In December 1844, apparently dying in hospital through years of physical neglect, he was offered a pardon by the Minister of Justice, who feared responsibility for the death of his, now, widely-reputed charge. Blanqui indignantly refused in characteristic terms:

Tell the gentleman that I proclaim solidarity with my comrades. Does he believe, by any chance, that the tortures of our imprisonment have broken that solidarity? It was that which upheld us in our terrible struggle; it was that which has been our strength. Let the Minister send me back into the nearest prison. This prospect would be a pleasure to me, compared with that of an odious pardon.

He made a miraculous recovery; and by the spring of 1846, on Sunday afternoons, his bed became the centre of a tutorial group composed of workmen, who came to study revolution from the lips of the master. Time for action was again approaching. The potato blight, together with the worst wheat harvest for years, led to severe shortages and rising prices which sparked off discontent. In neighbouring villages peasants had broken into wheat stores to prevent distribution of grain. Nearby Tours witnessed combined peasant and artisan riots, ruthlessly

[1] He married Suzanne Amélie Serre, daughter of an architect in 1834. She died in 1841.

suppressed by the military. Blanqui was denounced by a police spy as the chief instigator and, with twenty-eight workmen, was charged at Blois with incitement to rebellion through the dissemination of communist propaganda. Acquitted for lack of evidence, he was forced to live under police supervision until his day of deliverance – the February Revolution of 1848.

That year confirmed the legend. Blanqui dominated the turbulent scenes on the narrow stage of Paris. To the respectable – conservative or moderate – he was the sinister incarnation of bloody anarchy. De Tocqueville, the aristocratic liberal, records:[1]

> It was then I saw appear in his turn on the tribune a man whom I have never seen since, but the recollection of whom has always filled me with horror and disgust. He had wan, emaciated cheeks, white lips, a sickly, wicked and repulsive expression, a dirty pallor, the appearance of a mouldy corpse; he wore no visible linen; an old black frock coat covered his lean, withered limbs; he seemed to have passed his life in a sewer and to have just left it.

The historian, Alfred Delvau, presents a more balanced picture:[2]

> Auguste Blanqui is small and thin; his head, shaved like a monk's, is worthy of the brush of Holbein or Ribera. His eyes, deep sunken in his head, are dark and flashing. His face is pale with sickness, his body bent under the weight of physical and mental suffering. There is nothing in Blanqui of the professional conspirator, the street corner orator.
>
> At first sight, Blanqui does not appear very sympathetic; but that is because suffering is not always very agreeable to watch. One is disposed to obey him, but not to love him. He does not attract; he dominates. Blanqui replaces the physical strength that he lacks by a virility of the soul, which, on certain occasions, is all-powerful.

This was nearer the image prevailing among a small band of devotees who haunted the faubourgs of the Left: that of the selfless martyr whose actions constituted an unremitting struggle

---

[1] De Tocqueville, *Récollections.*   [2] *Histoire de la Révolution Février.*

against the injustices perpetrated by the privileged, and whose reward was the prison cell. Arriving in Paris on February 25th, he soon made his impact. Within twenty-four hours he had created the Central Republican Society; and 500 of his friends, new and old, flocked to hear him. The red flag, which had flown on the barricades, had been ousted by the tricolour. His followers pleaded that the revolution should be taken a stage further towards final rule by the Paris workers. He challenged the Provisional Government on the flag issue, but urged caution on the second:

> If we attempt to place in power those men whose names are compromised in the eyes of the *bourgeoisie* by the sentences they have received for their political activities, the provinces would take fright, would remember the Terror and the Convention, and would perhaps recall the King. The National Guard itself has only been our involuntary accomplice, for it is composed of frightened shopkeepers who are quite capable of undoing to-morrow what they have done today.

A shrewdly prophetic analysis. He did not intend to repeat the mistake of May 12th. On the rostrum, in his dry sharp tones, he continued to harangue his audience, urging vigilance and readiness for further action. He became the watchdog of the Provisional Government, which in return focused on his person all its hatred and suspicion.

Again and again he returned to the attack. He opposed elections for the Constituent National Assembly by national suffrage on the grounds that an ill-educated peasantry, still under the influence of landlord and *curé*, would vote for reaction. (A conclusion reached by his forebears Babeuf and Buonarroti!) His petition was rejected. On March 16th, a procession of right-wing companies of the National Guard protested against a decree abolishing property qualification for membership. Blanqui, at the head of the club leaders and 200,000 workmen, followed with a counter-demonstration and placed a resolution before the Government demanding postponement of elections fixed for April 23rd. It lay on the table. The Government of moderates soon revealed that they were

more afraid of Blanqui than of counter-revolution from the
Right. By the end of March he was the fountain-head of its
most cohesive opposition.

The blow fell on March 31st. Taschereau, a moderate
Republican, produced on the front page of his new *Revue
Rétrospective* the headline: 'Affair of May 12th, 1839.' Under it
was a printed document, the copy of an alleged confession by
Blanqui to the Orléanist police, betraying the secrets of the
conspiracy after his arrest. The evidence was such that it could
neither be proved nor disproved. (An historical parallel can be
recognized in the 'smear' campaign against Babeuf.[1]) But the
timing of the revelation – with obvious Government sanction –
and Blanqui's own vehement justification at his trial in January
1840 render it suspect. His printed reply on April 14th, a brilliant and poignant *cri de cœur*, pin-points the source and reason
for the accusation:

> 'You have sold your brothers for gold,' they cry. Gold, to go
> to slow death in a tomb on black bread and water. And what have
> I done with this gold? I live in a garret on fifty centimes a day.
> My entire fortune at this moment is sixty francs. It is I, with
> broken body and frayed clothes, who am blasted with the name
> of traitor, while the lackeys of Louis-Philippe, metamorphosed
> into brilliant republican butterflies, dance on the carpets of the
> Hôtel de Ville and peer in disdain over their well-filled stomachs
> at the poor Job escaped from the prisons of their master.

He ended his defence with the counter-accusation:

> You needed the Taschereau and behold it was discovered.
> *Is fecit cui prodest*. The infamy of its origin is betrayed by the
> shameful detour of its publication. Reactionaries, you are cowards!

Even if the 'Taschereau' attack was not Government sponsored,
it certainly worked to the Government's advantage. Both a
commission of enquiry and an action for libel by Taschereau
supported by Barbès (now Blanqui's jealous rival), faced
Blanqui. It spread confusion amongst the ranks of the militants,
and gave the Government its opportunity; with the forces of
order now ranged behind them, the rulers struck back. On

---

[1] See Chapter 2, p. 30 above.

E

April 16th the regular army was recalled to Paris and an attempt was made to arrest Blanqui. Elections held on the 23rd registered an overwhelming victory for the Right, as he had predicted; the peasantry were reacting in form against 'red' Paris, and respectable citizens voted, to a man, for the *bourgeois* republicans. The opposing forces were mobilizing for a second, more bloody, fray in class terms. The first clash came on May 15th, when a demonstration of the Left in favour of Poland ended in an invasion of the newly elected Assembly. Blanqui, reluctant to precipitate action without preparation, favoured caution, but was swept along by his followers, lifted bodily by workmen, and set on the tribune. In an impassioned speech, he spoke of the Tsarist atrocities in Poland, but, more relevant to the fears of the Government, also called for wider social rights, including permanent creative employment for the Paris workers. Not to be outdone by his rival, Barbès, after a frenzied declamation, led a procession to the Hôtel de Ville, which, as anticipated by Blanqui who had withdrawn, ended in a fiasco. The National Guard and regular army units concentrated within the hour; Barbès and the would-be insurrectionists were rounded up. Blanqui, after the usual betrayal by a police spy (the price was 6,000 francs), was seized in hiding and transferred to Vincennes prison. The Central Republican Society was shut down – the Government was resolved to crush the socialists once and for all. Decrees were issued prohibiting the right of assembly. Tension mounted during the warm June days, reaching a climax on the 21st with a decree virtually abolishing the National Workshops – relief labour centres for the unemployed. The challenge was taken up. At the Panthéon, where Babeuf had hatched his Communist conspiracy over half a century before, the 'red' faubourgs mobilized. The first great class battle was fought out with the workers deprived of their natural head, Blanqui, who, impotent in his prison cell at Vincennes, heard the distant thunder of the great insurrection he had striven so hard to bring about.

The next two decades confirmed him in his legendary rôle as the eternal prisoner, as unrelenting and uncompromising towards the régime of Napoleon III as he had been towards its predecessors. He read widely, taught his fellow prisoners political economy and was always a thorn in the flesh of the prison authorities. An attempted escape from the penitentiary of Belle Île reads like a chapter from the *Count of Monte Cristo*, but with a less happy ending. Once more Judas money caused his speedy recapture. His influence extended beyond the prison. He attacked not only Buonapartists but also the exiled moderates, Ledru-Rollin and Louis Blanc. In response to a request from a Blanquist refugee in London, Barthélémy, he wrote a toast 'Avis du Peuple', to be read on the third anniversary dinner of the February Revolution. He pilloried the *bourgeois* democrats and socialist reformists as the traitors of 1848:

> What menaces the revolution of tomorrow?
> The danger which broke the revolution of yesterday; the de-plorable popularity of the bourgeois disguised as tribunes of the people.
> Ledru-Rollin, Louis Blanc, Cremieux, Lamartine, Garnier-Pagès, Dupont de l'Eurc, Flocon, Albert, Arago, Marrast. A sad list! Sinister names written in letters of blood on the paving stones of democratic Europe. . . .
> It was natural for reaction to cut the throat of democracy. The crime is that of the traitors whom the people had accepted as guides, and who delivered them up to reaction.

It ended by demanding that a revolutionary government should arm the people and 'disarm the *bourgeoisie*. . . . He who has arms has bread.'[1] Marx was one of the minority who greeted it enthusiastically, had it reprinted and smuggled into Germany. Most radicals in exile received his diatribe with a storm of resentment, to which Blanqui replied, giving further warning against those who were 'lulling the masses to sleep with this sad monotone of conciliatory moderatism'. These were the days when 'le vieux' – the old one – became his title as the venerable oracle of proletarian socialism. While the Proudhonists and Trade Unionists compromised with the régime, Blanqui almost alone kept alive the concept of its destruction by revolution. His disciples amongst the workers

---

[1] M. Dommanget, *Auguste Blanqui à Belle Île*, p. 66.

and students perpetuated his name, anxiously awaiting his return. 'When HE comes' became the watchword of a new generation of Blanquists,[1] many of whom had received their political education in state gaols.

Released in 1859, he was soon back again for conspiracy. Here he found a new band of devotees who did not, however, accept his leadership uncritically. Such Blanquists 'of the second rank' included Georges Clemenceau (the war leader of 1917–18), Paul Lafargue (Marx's future son-in-law) and Gustave Tridon (later Communard leader). In prison hospital in 1865 he edited a journal *Candide*, which was quickly suppressed for sedition. That year, aided by friends, he escaped to Belgium, where, with constant incursions across the border into Paris, he prepared for the overthrow of the Second Empire. His second hour of opportunity came in 1870. Napoleon III's last gamble – war – ended in the disaster of Sedan on September 2nd. It was the Blanquists, Martin and Granger, under orders from 'le vieux', who led the Parisians into the Assembly and forced the proclamation of the Republic. A Government of National Defence was set up, dominated by middle-class liberals. Blanqui, who had thrown himself wholeheartedly into the struggle against the German invaders, for the first and only time called for co-operation on the grounds that 'in the face of the enemy there are no more parties, no more differences of opinion'. Soon perceiving that the administration feared the armed Parisians more than the Prussians, he fulminated against them in his patriotic journal *La Patrie en Danger*. The news of Bazaine's surrender at Metz, and confirmation of the report that Thiers was seeking an armistice brought the angry Parisians, in traditional manner, to the Hôtel de Ville on October 31st. Blanqui, following in their wake, installed himself as Commander-in-Chief and issued orders to the Blanquists to seize the main centres of power in Paris and, to commanders of forward units, to hold fast and continue the fight. Lack of aim and communications among the

[1] Paul Lafargue, 'Auguste Blanqui – Souvenirs Personnels', in *La Révolution Française* (20th April 1879).

insurgents helped the Government to rally its supporting units of the National Guard. A truce was called and a compromise reached, on the basis of a Government pledge to hold early elections – a pledge immediately broken by the issue of warrants for the arrest of the insurgent leaders. Blanqui, forced into hiding during the remainder of the siege, left the capital the following February, sickened at its surrender to Bismarck. At Loulié he was seized on March 17th, one day before the *raison de souffrance* of his whole life – the declaration of the Paris Commune. Both sides understood that without him the Commune lacked a head. While the members of the Central Committee, predominantly Blanquist, offered to exchange all its hostages for Blanqui, Thiers refused, declaring that 'he was worth an army corps'. Once more what should have been his greatest hour found 'le vieux' behind prison bars, as his leaderless disciples met their doom in the blood and fire of the barricades.

The next eight years saw the old man, personification of fifty years of revolutionary struggle, languishing in the prisons of his Republican gaolers. Together with the Commune, his legend grew beyond the borders of France. In March 1879, though still a prisoner, he was adopted election candidate for a constituency of Bordeaux. Garibaldi himself, hero of the *Risorgimento*, sent a message urging the electors to support 'the heroic martyr of liberty'. Blanqui's subsequent election aroused international interest. In April 1879 *The Times* in London published an account of 'A Visit to Blanqui' by its Paris correspondent. Although his election was declared invalid, it helped to bring about his final release. The remaining months of his life were spent, as always, campaigning – though less conspiratorially – for the socialist republic and receiving tremendous ovations all over France. On 27th December 1880, after speaking at a mass meeting in Paris, he suffered a stroke and died on New Year's Day without regaining consciousness. Two hundred thousand workmen followed his cortège to the Père Lachaise cemetery, where the old fighter was interred, symbolically facing the *Mûr des Fédérés*, at which his beloved Communards had made their final stand.

Given knowledge of this background, it is still fashionable for historians, Marxist and non-Marxist alike, who, tied to the cult of success, dismiss Blanqui as a naïve activist, obsessed with 'La Révolution', but devoid of constructive theory. It is a presumption which can easily be challenged. The acceptance of a sense of continuity between present-day politics and its historical antecedents must lead to reappraisals on both sides. In this way Blanqui's rôle may fall into clearer perspective.

Benoît Malon[1] places him firmly in the tradition outlined above, that is, in the Jacobin communist growth whose roots lie in the élitist and egalitarian manifestations of the Great Revolution. 'Blanqui's work gives us a sort of synthesis of Babouvist revolutionism and scientific socialism.' Maurice Dommanget, the unrivalled authority on Blanqui, goes further and assesses Blanquist theory as both the precursor and essence of Marxism: 'The liaison between Babouvism and Bolshevism by way of revolutionary Marxism is realized, so to speak, through Blanquism. . . . Blanqui formulated, in nearly the same terms as Marx, the law of accumulation.'[2] The first is acceptable, the last is strongly questioned. It was against the parochial background of small shopkeepers, artisan masters and skilled labourers of Paris that Blanqui reasoned out his economic theories. Capitalist accumulation was derived by equating individual saving and abstinence to selfish hoarding, which he exemplifies in 'Gobseck' – Balzac's rapacious usurer. Hence he postulates the theory of underconsumption on the part of the masses, whose spending is reduced by capitalist extraction of interest from the worker's product. His approach to capital, interest and exchange is incompatible with Marxist theory. But not so on the political level. Here Marx isolates Blanqui's rôle in the contemporary setting with sympathetic regard (a rare sentiment on Marx's part). Analysing the events of 1848, Marx declares: 'the proletariat rallies more and more around revolutionary socialism, for which the *bourgeoisie* has itself found the name of Blanqui. This socialism is the declara-

---

[1] 'Blanqui Socialiste', *Révue Socialiste* 11 (July 1885), p. 597.
[2] M. Dommanget, *Auguste Blanqui à Belle Île*, pp. 7–11.

tion of the permanence of the revolution, the class dictatorship
of the proletariat as the inevitable transit point to the abolition
of class differences generally.' In *The Eighteenth Brumaire of
Louis Bonaparte*, he views Blanqui and his comrades as 'the real
leaders of the proletarian party, the revolutionary communists'.
We have already seen how Marx greeted his *Avis du Peuple*
in 1851, and we shall consider later how much Marx must
have drawn on Blanqui's experience for his own political
theorizing.

Before venturing the claim that Blanquism is the progenitor
of Bolshevik practice, we must look back to the one tenet of the
revolutionary fathers which obsessed him, that is, a violent
anti-clericalism. To the end he was convinced that an organized
church and the acceptance of God were the source of all social
evils. It was the task, therefore, of the revolutionist to combat
spiritualisme, wherever it may be. He vented his acid wit against
all things *spirituelle*. Whilst in hospital in Tours he wrote
scathingly: 'On the day of the Holy Communion the Sisters of
the Hospital of Tours are ferociously unapproachable. They
have eaten God. The pride of that divine digestion gives them
convulsions. These vessels of sanctity become vials of vitriol.'
Blanqui's almost pathological hatred of religion makes sense,
when we recognize that he identified this question with the
political *status quo*. The priests kept the masses ignorant and,
therefore, prolonged their slavery, which in itself was as much
a state of mind as a social condition imposed from without. To
The Times correspondent[1] he insisted that, of all the necessary
reforms, 'first and foremost France must be unchristianized.
She must be rid, not only of Catholicism but of Christianity.
The Catholics are now the masters. We have still the Inquisition.
It no longer burns, but it imprisons. The magistrates sentence
according to its orders. Journalists are condemned because
they turn religion into derision in the name of reason. . . .
The real conspirators are the Catholics and the Clericals. From
the Bishop to the beadle they are all astir.' Renunciation of
God and the Church was to him the prerequisite for revolu-

[1] 'A Visit to Blanqui' (28th April 1879).

tionary integrity. The history of human endeavour was marked by two great hindrances – personalized religion and its cowled advocates. These, triumphant during the dark ages of Mediaevalism, had destroyed at the roots the flowering genius of the Classical world. No one could be neutral (such as the Positivists) since it left the way open to Christianity. Neutrality or submission meant the betrayal of the Revolution. The most heinous crime he attributed to Robespierre for his resuscitation of the dying monster on the altar of the Supreme Being. This had confused the People and deadened the spirit of the *révolutionnaire*.

It ill becomes dogmatic Marxists to denigrate Blanqui for his so-called *petit-bourgeois* anti-clericalism; to classify those who attack religion violently as mere *petit-bourgeoisie* expressing an outlet for their own sense of inferiority. Marx was not backward in voicing his own hatred and contempt. Lenin was to pursue a policy of more subtle duplicity: verbal execration of the 'opium of the people' but for expediency, at the hour of decision, minimal pressure so as not to alienate those still tied to the chains of faith. In his view: "The unity of that genuine revolutionary struggle of the oppressed class to set up a heaven on earth is more important to us than a unity in proletarian opinion about the imaginary paradise in the sky.' Blanqui would not have it. The enlightened could not serve two such incompatible masters. It was God *or* the Revolution.

But 'le vieux' is further discredited by the 'orthodox' for the patriotic chauvinism in his anti-Prussian tirades in 1870. Lenin in his *Lessons of the Commune* (1908) observed that 'Blanqui . . . a true revolutionary and an ardent advocate of Socialism could not find a more suitable title for his newspaper than the *bourgeois* cry *Our Country is in Danger!*' This view is re-echoed by future historians in the U.S.S.R. It ill becomes criticism too from that quarter. There is certainly a parochialism in Blanqui's approach to both national and international affairs. France, to him, was an idealized Paris writ large. His political ethos was conceived among 'this Parisian folk, the precursors of the future, the leaders of humanity, this prophetic and martyred people'. Here, amidst the *déclassés* and artisans, was the reposi-

tory of French genius – the standard-bearers of the revolutionary
mission they must bring from the centre to the whole patrimony.
For the first stage to ensure France's rôle was the Parisification
of France. Only then would there be justification for 'the
voluntary abdication of Paris in favour of her children come
to their majority'. The next stage embodied Blanqui's unique
form of patriotism: his view of the Messianic rôle of France –
the vanguard of world revolution – in whom was crystallized
the revolutionary potential for the liberation of the oppressed
proletariat *everywhere*. It may be argued that there is no narrow
nationalism here. To the end he adhered to his ultimate objective. In an unpublished letter to the French army he reasserts
the common interests of *all* workers, with special reference to
those of Germany and England, who have 'but one enemy –
the oppressor, who forces them to kill each other on the field
of battle'. Yet in 1870, it was only realistic that France, as
bearer of an historic rôle, must first be defended against Bismarck's 'troop of slaves'. His invectives against the barbaric
hordes strike a chord in recent memory. Was not the Soviet
Union to be defended by *all* workers, everywhere, since she
alone sustained their hope in the millennium? And what of the
Russian Communist Party's stand in the great Patriotic War of
1941–5 against the Nazi 'savages'?

Blanqui brought to maturity the views manifested with less
sophistication by Babeuf and Buonarotti. By 1848 he had already
rejected an alliance with *bourgeois* and reformist elements.[1] The
problem posed was to convert an inchoate uprising into an
élitist victory, ostensibly in the interest of their worker protagonists. He was convinced that the vanguard must control the
revolution from its inception so as to ensure its own victory at
the end. Blanqui gave final directives to Socialist participants,
which Marx accepted eagerly. The French political scientist
Andler noted that 'the circular of the Central Committee of
the Communist League in 1850 presented a new tactic, the
tactic of Blanqui, adopted by Marx – the permanent revolution'.[2] In Blanqui's clipped terms the message was clear. 'If

[1] See also p. 60 above.   [2] See also p. 83 below.

socialism is not its [the Revolution's] author it will not be its master. It must make it, not allow it to be made. The morrow belongs only to the victor.'[1] It was the acceptance of this 'revolution in permanence', first by Trotsky and Helphand (Parvus) and later at the crucial stage by Lenin, which made inevitable the October revolution.

What of victory? How would it be consolidated? Early days would expose the class enemy defeated but still strong enough (with the aid of a reactionary peasantry) to launch a counter-attack. Blanqui rejected National Suffrage as a swindle by which 'a majority acquired by terror and gang rule is not a majority of citizens but a herd of slaves. It is a blind tribunal which for seventy years has heard only one of the two parties. It owes it to itself to listen more to the opposite party for seventy years. As they were unable to plead together, they will plead one after another.' It would take twenty years for the demolition of 'the formidable bastion of ignorance'. The answer was the dictatorship of the *élite* until the body politic was cleansed. The crediting of the term 'dictatorship of the proletariat' to Blanqui must be treated with reserve. In line with Jacobin dictum the dictatorship would be drawn from the intellectual *déclassés* and enlightened artisans of Paris. The lessons of 1848 and 1871 were not lost on 'le vieux'. To the end he grouped the peasantry in the ranks of the counter-revolution. We are left in no doubt of the fate prescribed for the *bourgeoisie*. 'The day the gag comes out of the mouth of labour, so will it enter the mouth of Capital!'

Although we have stated that Blanqui had never pre-planned post-revolutionary organization, he did essay some minimum provisions for making the new régime work.[2] Priorities were the neutralization of the army to parallel the arming of the workers, and a special police whose first task was the elimination of religious organizations. Priests and the enemies of the workers since 1848 were to be driven into exile. The nation in arms was to replace the regular army, the lower civil service

[1] Blanqui MSS 9583, p. 387, Bibliothèque Nationale.
[2] His ideas on this are scattered throughout his collected essays, *Critique Sociale*.

scrapped and the magistrature ended. Justice would be enforced through a national system of trial by jury. There seems no immediate urgency for an economic transformation of society. Any attempt at a withholding or flight of capital would bring harsh retribution. Initial reforms would be surprisingly cautious – progressive taxation; credit, import and export control; a few selected national monopolies and the setting up of 'workers' associations'. This reluctance to expropriate capital immediately after the seizure of power is symptomatic of the many contradictions in Blanqui's credo. It may be explained through his concern that the revolutionary *élite* should set up training institutions to enforce universal enlightenment. Only then could their implacable enemies, the peasantry, be won over to Communism. One discerns in his constant repetition of this theme that Blanqui regarded education as the prime requisite for socio-economic change. 'Ignorance is at the same time the instrument and the victim of violence.'[1] Education was the 'only real agent'.[2] Eventually, 'thanks to universal enlightenment, no one man can be the dupe of the other'.[3] This could be taken as a gradualist plea, which evoked its own dangers. Blanqui, himself, recognized that this might be employed in rational argument to postpone social change until *all* had been re-educated. He attempted to overcome the dilemma by attacking 'ignorance' and capitalist 'vampirism' together:[4]

> Of these two harpies which is the mother? Which is the daughter? Study of the past and observation seem to prove that ignorance is the mother. A dangerous conclusion, nevertheless, which will furnish pretexts for the adjournment of the social question, pretexts which have long been used in order to postpone indefinitely the emancipation of the Negroes. The attack ought to be opened and carried out simultaneously against these two bastions of iniquity.

Was Lenin as deluded in 1917, as he was in 1906, when he vigorously rejected the accusation that Bolshevik theory

---

[1] *Critique Sociale* I, p. 212.
[2] Blanqui MSS 9581, p. 23 (1848), Bibliothèque Nationale.
[3] *Critique Sociale*, I, p. 185.   [4] *Critique Sociale*, II, p. 41.

suffered from 'Blanquist error'? Certainly Lenin remedied the Blanquist weakness of overstressing organization and tactics to the detriment of strategic and objective conditions. In a ponderous explanation he distinguishes his own brand of Marxist emancipatory theories in three ways. A successful insurrection is ultimately dependent on 'the revolutionary upsurge of the people' led by the advanced class. The latter is no conspiratorial group divorced from the people but one in constant touch with, and deriving its strength from, the masses. Finally one takes strict account of tactical possibilities in terms of the historical dialectic. Only when the vanguard is at its strongest and its class enemy at its weakest can a successful insurrection be launched. Was this the actual situation in 1917?

There was more in common between the two than Lenin was prepared to accept. Both were dedicated professionals to the very ounce of their being. Axelrod complained of Lenin that he lived and breathed revolution twenty-four hours a day. Blanqui, to the end, persisted in his unbending commitment, which had sustained him through his long martyrdom. 'Le devoir d'un révolutionnaire, c'est la lutte toujours, la lutte quand même, la lutte jusqu'à extinction!' The irony is that Lenin would achieve victory through Blanquism. This was deemed outdated by Engels back in 1874. In a letter to *Der Volkstaat* the old master had already dismissed Blanqui as a revolutionary of the past in his analysis of the essence of Blanquism:

> In his political activity he was mainly a man of action believing that a small and well-organized minority, who would attempt a political stroke of force at an opportune moment, could carry the mass of the people with them by a few successes at the start and thus make a glorious revolution.

Yet eleven years later he was to revise his estimation, when he applied it to the contemporary Russian situation. He prophetically asserted:[1]

> This [the Russian] is one of the exceptional cases where it is possible for a handful of people to make a revolution i.e. with one

[1] Letter to the Russian revolutionary, Vera Zasulich, 23rd April 1885.

small push to cause a whole system, which (to use a metaphor of Plekhanov's) is in more than labile equilibrium, to come crashing down, and thus by one action, in itself insignificant, to release uncontrollable forces. Well now, if ever Blanquism – the fantasy of overturning an entire society through the action of a small conspiracy – had a certain justification for its existence, that is certainly in Petersburg.

Lenin had read his Engels. He would not have overlooked this in the making of his own revolution!

Blanqui, still the impractical revolutionary? The evidence is sufficient to discount this. He was a generator of ideas about men and society, unco-ordinated though they were. Ideas alone do not make revolutions. His comments on socio-political developments and his theory of revolutionary action certainly presage Marx. Ideas become ideologies when they are sufficiently convincing to boost revolutionary armies and provide them with holy writ to justify action. Therein lies the weakness of Blanquism. His brilliant polemics did not add up to an exclusive ideology, which could, effectively, challenge revealed 'truths'. By 1881 Jacobin Communism in the West had been put to the test and found wanting. The Commune had represented both its consummation and its defeat. Henceforth the dry bones of Blanquism would be given new flesh by being transplanted into the Marxist faith. Marxism would prove the more persuasive as a motivating force. Yet twentieth-century communist insurrections would still be undertaken by the voluntarism of a resolute few, determined, through violent change, to establish an undetermined society. Blanquism would be more than vindicated.

CHAPTER 4

The Marxist Intervention

That Marxism covered Blanquism with a convincing theory is only one facet of the case. It was, indeed, a gifted synthesis, in which many of the ideas of Marx's great precursors were fused and coagulated. Hegel, Saint-Simon, and Feuerbach had all contributed to the formulation of Marxist theory. Few, however, have evaluated the debt which Marx owed to Blanqui. Marx, himself, was committed to high praise of 'le vieux' but reveals little else. Lenin's observations have already been commented upon. Stalin placed him amongst those 'leaders in time of storm, practical leaders, self-sacrificing and courageous, but who are weak in theory'. Research in depth has recently modified these propositions. The outcome is the possibility of viewing Blanquism as the vital artery through which Babouvism was injected into the main flow of Marxist–Leninism.

In the field of philosophy, Blanqui's attacks on the Positivists accord with Marx. Blanqui decries their scepticism as a system of doubt, which at its culminating point resembles a religion itself, in that the characteristics of negativism and nihilism then transpose positivism. In other areas Blanqui and Marx part company. Blanqui's subscription to the view that 'the material causes of poverty, such as capitalism and all other forms of exploitation, exist because of ignorance',[1] is in antithesis to Marx's dictum. 'It is not the consciousness of men that determines their being but, on the contrary, their social existence that determines their consciousness.'[2] Despite the divergences in their economic theorizing, Blanqui comes close to Marx in his analysis of monopolist polarization. 'On the ruins of small scale

---

[1] Blanqui MSS 9592, Pt 3, p. 159, Bibliothèque Nationale.
[2] Karl Marx, *Critique of Political Economy*.

enterprise has arisen the terrible financial, industrial and commercial feudality, which is cleverer and more oppressive than
the old aristocracy, and holds our society in fee.' Blanqui decreed
that this tendency would sow the seeds of capitalism's own destruction, since intensified 'association' would accrue to Labour
too, and thereby facilitate the transformation to communism.

There is abundant evidence elsewhere of common ground.
The controversy over their individual interpretation of the term
'proletarian' is meaningless. Both were right, but Blanqui more
so. Blanqui's thirty-two million in 1852 still consisted of 'those
without property, or with very little property and living only
by their hands'. Their class opponents were 'all those living on
their revenue and the exploitation of the workers'. It was the
former – a small proportion of workers and a majority of *petit-
bourgeois* in the *sans-culottes* tradition – who manned the barricades in 1830, 1848 and 1871. By 1871 their adversaries moved
into sharper focus. Both Marx and Blanqui designated class
according to its relationship to the means of production. Both
viewed current legal systems as institutions for strengthening
control by the ruling class through their defence of 'the rights
of property'. Both rejected limited economic reforms as a means
of extirpating *bourgeois* privilege, and preached revolutionary
action. We have already cited Marx's recognition of the rôle
of Blanqui in 1848 and his prognosis, derived from the latter,
in his famous address to the Central Committee (1850). Marx
here gave practical meaning to the tactic of 'permanent revolution' – the tactic of Blanqui. Marx warned the workers to arm
themselves separately during the early stages 'to dictate such
conditions . . . that the rule of the *bourgeois* democrats will, from
the outset, carry the seeds of its own downfall, and their subsequent extrusion be considered facilitated'. In detail he
advanced the proposition that 'alongside of the new official
government they [the workers] must establish simultaneously
their own revolutionary workers' government, whether in the
form of municipal councils, or workers' clubs committees, so
that the *bourgeois* democratic authorities from the outset see
themselves supervised and threatened by authorities backed by

the whole mass of the workers'. All this tends to confirm the view that Blanqui influenced early Marxist precepts.

Did the two ever meet? Before 1848 there were common political associates. Karl Schapper, Wilhelm Weitling, Heinrich Bauer and Joseph Moll, members of the exiled German 'League of the Just', joined with, and fought under, Blanqui in the insurrection of May 1839. All of them knew Marx. Marx was resident in Paris between 1843 and 1845 and would have certainly been acquainted with the activities of the already legendary prisoner. Marx, expelled from Belgium, was back in Paris between March and April 1848, that is during the high tide of Blanqui's activity. He joined in the activities of the Clubs[1] and, significantly, posed identical arguments to those of Blanqui in issues involving the National Guard, taxation and universal suffrage. A personal meeting may have been casual, if at all. Nevertheless, Marx persisted in his admiration and respect for his great co-revolutionary. He followed his career with interest and consistently referred to Blanqui as the 'head and heart of the proletarian party in France'.

After 1848, the Blanquists who escaped to London allied themselves with the German contingent under Marx in forming 'La Societé Universelle des communistes révolutionnaires'. By July 1850, the society had split and an enraged Barthélemy, writing to Blanqui, called Marx a traitor and added 'les traîtres méritaient la mort'. Marx still maintained sporadic correspondence with various French Blanquists, whilst their leader was in gaol during the 1850's. In a letter to Engels (22nd April 1859) Marx voiced his satisfaction that the Paris workers were furious with the government's ignoble intent to transport Blanqui to Devil's Island. Freed by general amnesty, Blanqui crossed the Channel in January 1860 and arrived in London. Marx wrote later to Engels (6th June 1861): 'It is good that we again have contact with the genuine revolutionary party in France.' Did a meeting then take place? There is still no evidence either from the Marx/Engels correspondence

[1] See S. Bernstein, 'Marx in Paris, 1848: A neglected chapter', *Science and Society* III (Summer 1939).

or from current exchanges between Blanqui and his friend Dr Lacambre (21st April–May 1860) that it did.

Nevertheless between 1861 and 1870 the two-way communication continued through a third party. When Blanqui was rearrested for conspiracy Marx abused the 'canaille' press of England and Europe for their stand and helped collect funds for the launching of a propaganda sheet by Blanqui on his trial. During these years Marx was preparing *Das Kapital* and participating in the *International*, whilst Blanqui was either in prison or plotting in Belgium and Paris. A letter from Dr Watteau to Blanqui informed him that he had complied with the request of 'le vieux' to send Marx a copy of Tridon's *Les Hébertistes* (1864). A permanent contact was established through Marx's son-in-law, Lafargue. He acted as a go-between, and early in 1869 he informed Marx: 'Blanqui has the greatest esteem for you.' In June 1869 Marx spent eight days with Lafargue at the very time that Blanqui was making his clandestine excursions into Paris. The same year, Marx wrote of Lafargue's comment that Blanqui had defended and praised Marx's *Poverty of Philosophy*[1] and Blanqui defended Marx's *Kapital* against a highly critical review in *La Revue Positiviste*.[2]

It would appear that Engels' criticisms of Blanqui during the 1870's were not necessarily shared by Marx. Edward Vaillant, Communard exile who frequented Marx's company, held that Marx persisted in his opinion that Blanqui was the most profound French Socialist and the greatest revolutionary. This was the view taken by both Marx's sons-in-law, Lafargue and Longuet. When the imprisoned Blanqui was elected, Lafargue wrote and asked him to organize a French proletarian party 'le lancer à la conquête du pouvoir politique'. In the same letter he invites him to spend a well-needed rest in freedom at Lafargue's home in London. He ends: 'Marx, qui a suivi avec tant d'intérêt votre carrière politique, serait heureux de faire votre connaissance.'[3] There the case against their having met

---

[1] Marx/Engels, *Gesamtausgabe*, Dritte Abteilung, Band 4, p. 159.
[2] Blanqui MSS 9590, Pt 1, p. 64, Bibliothèque Nationale.
[3] Blanqui MSS 9588, Pt 2, p. 678, Bibliothèque Nationale.

rests. It underlines the consistency of Marx's attitude towards Blanqui. There is no record of Blanqui's reply. It seemed that Marx was always far more interested in Blanqui, than Blanqui was in Marx.

The intervention of Marxism on the French political scene did not mean the immediate supersession of Blanquism. After the death of Blanqui, to the early years of the twentieth century, the Marxist–Blanquist fusion was accepted as a continuation of the Babouvist tradition. It was Vaillant (1840–1915) who sustained this. Nevertheless, with the passing of 'le vieux' the revolutionary *élan* emanating from a conspiratorial *élite* rapidly declined. As the French radical left moved towards Marxism it was caught in the swell of parliamentary democracy and, as the trend continued, the old Jacobin Communism made its bow.

The other European state where conditions were favourable for social revolution was Germany. In spite of the failure of the Commune and Bismarck's attacks on German socialism, the workers were more fully organized and attained greater political strength than the French had ever done. They had learned to use the vote more effectively to advance their class interests. Engels, in old age, got the message. With his eye on the home-land (underneath there was always his sense of Teutonic pride in German example) and contrasting the movement there with the French experience, he wrote:[1] 'In France, where for over a hundred years, the ground was undermined by revolution after revolution, where there is not a single party that has not had a hand in conspiracies, insurrections and revolutionary activity of every kind . . . – even in France the Socialists are learning that they can gain no lasting victory unless they first win over the great mass of the people, i.e. in their case, the peasants. There, too, it is recognized that the slow work of propaganda and parliamentary activity are the immediate tasks of the party.' What had happened to that predestined course emerg-ing from the dialectic – the classic battle of proletarian versus *bourgeoisie*, which could only be resolved by clash of arms? He

[1] Engels, Introduction to *The class struggles in France* (1895 edition).

goes on, 'The irony of world history turns everything upside down. We, the "revolutionaries", the "rebels", we are thriving far better on legal than on illegal methods of revolt. The parties of order . . . are perishing under the legal conditions created by themselves . . . while we, under this legality, get firm muscles and rosy cheeks and look like living for ever.' Here is the ultimate rejection of Blanquist insurrectionism. He concludes, 'If we are not mad enough to let ourselves be driven into street fighting to please them, there is nothing left for them to do except to break through this legality so fatal to them.'

So here in western Europe the most sophisticated and indoctrinated Marxists became the least revolutionary. Germany, more than France, was developing ideal conditions for the final confrontation. Yet German workers, and later the French, had, contrary to the prognostications of the *Communist Manifesto*, gained, not lost, from a situation of maturing Capitalism. It was precisely because conditions existed in Russia analogous to those of pre-1871 France that the old Babouvist–Blanquist creed held fast. Lenin would make his *coup* in the name of a non-applicable ideology. We shall see how the great Idea, Utopian dream of an obscure Paris revolutionary, came to fruition in archaic St Petersburg.

PART II

Triumph in the East

CHAPTER 5

The Forerunners

Russia, in the nineteenth century, was predominantly a land of peasants. Their past and present was one dreary monologue of misery, frustration and oppression on a scale unknown to their western counterparts. The sensitive nerve in the body politic was serfdom. It had arrived belatedly and in so doing had reversed the social destination of its incumbents. In the fifteenth century there were both slaves and serfs, but the majority were still untied. Collective responsibility for taxes was imposed on groups of villages, and as long as this obligation was met the peasant had freedom of movement. In the sixteenth century, as western Europe became centralized, serfdom diminished. The reverse was true in Russia. As Muscovite rule tightened peasant freedom vanished. By the eighteenth century the process was complete. The land proletariat consisted of bonded serfs and state peasants. Both were liable to compulsory military service which might swallow up the most formative years of their adult life.

Centralization and serfdom meant that peasants were not only bound to government or landlord, but also to each other. *Mirs* – village communes – were government sponsored, and their institutional tasks were to guarantee peasant obligations to authority. In most parts they could periodically redistribute land holdings. This created the myth that a golden age of primitive communism had existed before the autocracy. Pre-Muscovite records do not substantiate this, but the myth persisted. The power of the *mir*, although limited and variable, could be harnessed for other ends. Nineteenth-century opponents of Tsarism would regard them as ready-made power points for revolutionism.

The Petrine monarchy bore heavily on landlord and peasant. But during the eighteenth century the burdens on the aristocracy diminished, whilst those on the peasantry increased. Peter I imposed a poll tax, not on those who could best meet it, but on the already impoverished peasant. In 1762, the nobles' obligation to serve in the army or administration was removed by edict. In 1767 the serfs were deprived of their final right of appeal against a vicious master. It was during this period, too, that forced service in the mines and the new factories was imposed; also decrees were introduced for rent payment for holdings by state peasants, and an increase of forced labour from two to three days a week, especially in the Ukraine. The most inhuman imposition was the law granting the landlords ultimate authority to select serfs for army training, which meant twenty-five years with the colours.

Passive and active opposition to the régime emerged from two main areas. One was among the possessors – the court, the nobility and the professionals. The impact of the Enlightenment was dramatic and durable. Catherine the Great had created the climate for questioning and research within circumscribed limits. It threw up a number of theorists on enlightened despotism, of whom the most significant was N. M. Karamzin (1766–1826). A noble from the central Volga region, he received his schooling in a boarding establishment in Moscow, where he joined a Freemasons Lodge centred round the publisher, N. I. Novikov. He did the grand tour of Europe during the turbulent years 1789–90. The French experience moulded his political ideas, and on return to Russia he founded the new literary sentimental movement. He brought out and edited the *Messenger of Europe*, the first of a series of monthly journals which became the main sounding board of literary and political discussion in the nineteenth century. He was eventually appointed official historiographer and produced a vast study, *A History of the State of Russia*, under the auspices of the, then, liberal-minded Alexander I.

In a *Memoir on Ancient and Modern Russia*, handed to Alexander in 1811, one detects the influence of enlightened constitutionalism, particularly that of Montesquieu. He reacted against the excesses of the Terror, losing his former optimism. He mourned the breakdown of his hopes: 'Where is the fruit of all that science and wisdom? Century of civilization, I no longer recognize you, plunged now in blood and flames, surrounded by murder and destruction, I can see you no more.'[1] Only a strong, centralized power could guarantee freedom. Anarchy would destroy it. But the sovereign power could only maintain security and stability through wise laws. The type of government was irrelevant, varying according to its suitability to the state concerned. Autocracy was suitable for Russia, since it had remained a working proposition for centuries. Reform and experiment outside the legitimate order could be dangerous, as France had shown. All this added up to an amalgam of enlightened despotism, controlled liberalism, the whole spiced with nationalism based on a traditional culture. Such Russophilism rejected change from below. This view was derived from another sector of the ruling class, which retained its Francophile commitment, and tried to import its radical example on the Russian scene. It was through them that the Jacobin Franco-Russian link was joined.

One of these early Radicals was the Southern nobleman Ya. P. Kozelsky (1727–93?). A graduate of the University of St Petersburg and later civil servant, he devoted much of his leisure time to academic treatises on politics and philosophy. He read and interpreted the works of the French 'Philosophes' and translated two volumes of excerpts from the *Encyclopédie*. Commenting on the philosophers he selected Rousseau as the 'high flying eagle' superior to all previous and contemporary thinkers. He repeated the old maxims of the 'philosophes' and, indirectly, proclaimed the rejection of autocracy. He argued for the direct participation of the common people in politics. The 'social contract' had caused man to lose his 'natural' freedom and equality, but in doing so had substituted the provision of moral and legal equality. The best form of government was an elected aristocracy in a representative republic, a notion

---

[1] Karamzin, *Correspondence, 1795.*

inspired by Rousseau's dictum on the Legislator. Property *per se* was to remain inviolate, though blatant inequality was to be rectified so that society would consist of the golden mean, that is, of peaceful hardworking people with a reasonably high standard of living. The body politic should be arranged so that neither the individual nor the state were a burden on each other. If rulers were unjust, vengeance meted out by the people was both just and natural. Education, rather than revolution was, however, a surer means of maintaining progress.

His views on economic problems were remarkable. Like his French counterparts he foresaw the Welfare State, but in equally vague terms. The wealth of a nation was a measure of its people's industry rather than its accumulated gold and silver. Price was a means of facilitating equivalent exchange and money tokens devised to measure price. Both the right and opportunity to work must be ensured. The eight-hour day was preferred, to enable workers to enjoy equal time off for sleep and recreation. The public and self-employed should render an account of their work annually to the legislature. No one must be allowed to be so in need as to accumulate debt. The individual who, through hazards outside his control such as fire or robbery, is reduced to need should be compensated by the state. Kozelsky also opposed all forms of imperial conquests, citing as an example the European carve up of North America, since this form of greed and aggression brought in its wake the criminal destruction of human beings.

The greatest of the early repentant noblemen, who is also classified as the 'first Russian radical', was Alexander Radish-chev (1749–1802).[1] The eldest son of a provincial noble, and master of 3,300 serfs, he spent his early childhood on his father's estate at Ablyazavo, where he gained first-hand experience of the conditions of the tied peasants. Between the age of eight and thirteen he lived with relations in Moscow, the most influential of whom was the curator of the new University, who gathered round him a group of highly motivated members of the intelli-

---

[1] See L. Kochan, 'Alexander Radishchev', in *History Today* (July 1964), and S. V. Utechin, *Russian Political Thought*, pp. 64–6.

gentsia. The young Radishchev shared the services of a private French tutor until he was thirteen. In 1762 he was selected for the Corps of Pages at Catherine's court, which operated as a training school for hand-picked sons of the gentry. In 1766 he was one of the twelve youths sent to the University of Leipzig, as part of a recent scheme for providing Russia with an élitist group of highly trained administrators. Leipzig gave him the opportunity to partake in study and discussions concerning the French Enlightenment then making its impact on German intellectual life. He became absorbed in the works of the great doyens of the movement including those of Rousseau and Mably. Their influence was irrevocable. He returned to Russia in 1772, imbued with liberalizing sentiments. In the hey-day of Catherine's reforming zeal, he ascended the rungs of promotion and finally emerged as Director of the St Petersburg Custom House. He was even accorded royal recognition for his services by receiving the award of Knight of the Order of St Vladimir. However, the Tsarina's approval was short-lived, for Catherine perceived the danger to autocracy emanating from the French Revolution and cut back on any projects associated with her previous reforming indulgences. She soon discerned that Radishchev was an 'enemy' agent.

Evidence of this was detected in his notes on Mably's *Observations sur l'Histoire des Grecs* (1773), where Radishchev substituted 'despotism' for 'autocracy' and added the ominous note: 'Autocracy is a condition that is most contrary to human nature. . . . We cannot grant unlimited power over ourselves. . . . If we live under the authority of laws, this is not because we inevitably have to do so, but because we find it to our advantage. If we give to the law a part of our rights and of our natural power, it is in order that they should be used in our interest; we make a silent contract with society about this. If it is broken, then we also are released from our obligation. The injustice of a sovereign gives to the people – his judge – the same (or an even greater) right over him as the right over offenders that the law gives to him. The sovereign is the first citizen of the society of the people.' This implicit rejection of the system coincided

with the great revolt of the serfs led by the Cossack Emelyan
Pugachev, whose motley bands of frontiersmen and escaped
peasants were ravaging vast areas from Perm to the lower
Volga. 'Burn, pillage, destroy . . . Seize the gentry, who have
enslaved you, and hang them, and let there be none left,'[1]
urged their leader. It was the French Revolution again, which
finally convinced Catherine that her doses of enlightenment
would prove fatal to herself, especially when the French Minister
Ségur was seen to be congratulated, after the news of the fall of
the Bastille, by her own grandson Alexander. Radishchev's
publication of his *Journey from St Petersburg to Moscow* (1790),
coming almost at the same time, roused Catherine to action.
She stopped the sale of the works of the 'philosophes' forthwith,
and broke off diplomatic relations with France – now recognized as the mortal enemy. 'Il faudra faire jeter au feu tous
leurs meilleurs auteurs, et tout ce qui a répandu leur langue en
Europe . . .,' she told Grimm. Radishchev was seized, tried for
incitement to rebellion, sentenced to death, but reprieved and
banished to Siberia for ten years.

Why was the *Journey* so dangerous as to warrant such ruthless
action against the author? It built up an objective picture of
Russian life in all its aspects; added to which it was the first
open and devastating criticism of the autocracy with prophetic
overtones. Radishchev foresaw the inevitable cataclysm. He
exhorted the nobility to 'go into the dwellings of [their]
brothers' and inculcate a spirit of love and equality. In the
long term it was in their interests to do so for only thus could
a universal uprising of desperate peasants be averted. The
national danger was the perpetuation of serfdom. It demoralized
and corrupted master and peasant alike. The narrator (the
Traveller) meets a peasant working in the field at high noon on
a hot Sunday and enquires why he is not resting. The peasant
answers, 'In a week, sir, there are six days, and we go six times
a week to work on the master's fields; in the evening, if the
weather is good, we haul to the master's house the hay that is

[1] The Chuvash tribe, from whom Lenin was descended, displayed unusual
ferocity in this uprising.

left in the woods; and on holidays the women and girls go walking in the woods, looking for mushrooms and berries. God grant that it rains this evening. If you have peasants of your own, sir, they are praying to God for the same thing.' The dialogue proceeds with the Traveller asking, 'But how do you manage to get food enough, if you have only the holidays free?' and the peasant replies, 'Not only the holidays: the nights are ours too. If a fellow isn't lazy, he won't starve to death. You see, one horse is resting; and when this one gets tired, I'll take the other; so the work gets done.' The Traveller is incensed at the terrible injustice perpetrated against the peasant folk. 'Tremble, cruel-hearted landlord, on the brow of your peasants I see your condemnation written!' He goes on to record episode after episode revealing the brutality of the master; the knoutings of wandering peasants; the raping of serf girls; and frustrated noblemen's daughters, unsought in marriage, ordering their male serfs to sleep with them. He finally warns the gentry of the consequences. 'All the hardened feelings of the slaves, not given vent by a kindly gesture of freedom, strengthen and intensify their inner longings. A stream that is barred in its course becomes more powerful in proportion to the opposition it meets. Once it has burst the dam, nothing can stem its flood. Such are our brothers, whom we keep enchained. They are waiting for a favourable chance and time. The alarum bell rings. And the destructive forces of bestiality break loose with terrifying speed. . . .' With prophetic insight he ends: 'The first demagogue or humanitarian who rises up to awaken the unfortunates will hasten the scythes' fierce sweep. Beware!'

Radishchev was rehabilitated in 1801, during the early reforming days of Alexander I, and was appointed to serve on the Commission of the Revision of the Laws. His own zeal unabated, he applied his antipathy towards serfdom to the subject at hand. This is exemplified in two major instances. One was over compensating the master whose serf had accidentally been killed. The Commission recommended an increase to the master; Radishchev opposed this and appended his own report suggesting that compensation should be due, not to the master, but to the deceased's next-of-kin. The other instance was his attitude in a discussion over the legal procedure for trying a suspect charged with rebellion, blasphemy or murder. The Commission instructed that such people had no right either to be presented with the charge or to challenge the judges. Again Radishchev rejected this and put forward the view that the accused had certain rights: to choose his own defence counsel or, if this were impossible, to be provided with one by the court, and to challenge his judges. He also maintained that the death sentence should not be ratified unless passed by a two-thirds majority vote in jury. His dissenting criticism was noble, but ineffectual. It was impossible for the unstable Alexander to sustain himself permanently on a diet of reform. The war against Napoleon and the post-1815 Metternich reaction put paid to that. But Radishchev had been dead long since.

For this passionately humane man was prematurely exhausted, not only as a result of his inability to influence change in the conditions of the peasantry. His personal life was burdened with debt and family quarrels. Melancholia set in, and at the point when he could no longer cope with the pressures and frustrations which beset him, he committed suicide (1802). His was a posthumous triumph. Subsequent Russian revolutionaries acknowledged him as their intellectual forerunner. He had, by inference, projected the idea of tyrannicide on to Russian radical thinking. He had extended Kozelsky's thesis on legal revenge and directed it towards the course of social revolution, in which the peasants could legitimately overthrow their masters by violence. Land could then become the rightful property of those who cultivated it and redistribution was valid under the text that 'it was good for equality'. This was the formula adopted by successive generations of radicals. Long after, in 1858, Herzen published the original edition of the *Journey* in London. He conceded, as did many of his Russian contemporaries, that Radishchev was the first martyr to immolate himself in the face of autocracy, on account of his persistent 'hatred of arbitrary power and his

valiant protest against serfdom'. In the broader view Radishchev had linked up the French experience with emerging
Russian radicalism; a link which would be welded tighter as
the tempo of revolutionary protest accelerated.

To the restlessness and frequent uprisings of the peasantry
was joined the opposition of a growing sector of the nobility
and professional intelligentsia. The latter were self-question-
ing, altruistic and, therefore, increasingly critical of autocracy.
The impetus to a dramatic reappraisal of the system was the
impact of the Napoleonic invasion in 1812. A united Patriotic
War had been won by the dogged resistance of peasant armies
led by sympathetic commanders. Many of the younger officers
had moved westward across Europe in the campaigns which
culminated in the defeat of Napoleon and the occupation of
France. The Emperor Alexander I was acclaimed as the prime
conqueror and his armies shared in his glory. Yet a France in
defeat would still conquer many of its alien occupants. The
young Russians were brought for the first time in contact with
the revolutionary *élan* which had permeated France since 1789.
This opened up the prospect of effecting socio-political change
in their own country and provided the motivating force for the
first élitist insurrection in 1825.

The officers returned to face with shame the Russian reality –
its inferiority and its backwardness. Yet they were also imbued
with a national pride conceived in victory, and in that moral
idealism which had once enthused their fallen idol, Tsar
Alexander I. They represented the young nobility united by a
sensitive compassion towards their suffering peasantry. Looking both ways they stood at the crossroads between the repentant noblemen and the future alienated intelligentsia – those
deserters or outcasts (*rasnochintsi*) from the nobility who, from
their concentrated introspection, evoked a passive revolutionism. The conspiracy of the Decembrists was hatched out
with astonishing inefficiency. On 14th December 1825 the
four crack regiments of the St Petersburg garrison refused to
take the oath recognizing the accession of Nicholas I. Not only
was the *coup* ill-planned, but the failure of the leader, Prince

Trubetskoy, to appear, and orders which never arrived, made
it a non-starter. The would-be insurrectionists were dispersed
with a whiff of artillery shot. The hanging of the five leaders was
universally acclaimed as the first martyrdom in the Russian
revolutionary movement. It was their ideas which proved the
more potent.

The Decembrists' thinking centred around two diverse
schools. The constitutional, and, therefore, more modest claims
of N. Muravyev (1796–1843) advocated the norms of democratic constitutionalism – a limited monarchy, division of
powers to offer checks and balances, full equality before the
law in a so-called just legislature (trial by jury, habeas corpus,
and the election of police officials) even though voting was
limited to property franchise. He declared himself for the
emancipation of the peasantry, but without their automatic
ownership of land. The influence and extension of Jacobinism
was demonstrated by the majority, whose spokesman was
Colonel Pestel. He wrote: 'Political news is spread everywhere . . . these events familiarized the mind with revolutions,
with the possibilities and opportunities of carrying them out.'
He conceived that each age had its own distinguishing feature:
'The present is distinguished by revolutionary thoughts.' He
openly asserted the debt he owed to the French Revolution:
'The majority of basic institutions introduced by the revolution
were retained and recognized as good things when the monarchy
was restored. . . . This made me think that the revolution was
apparently not as bad as it had been made out. . . .' But a
universal holocaust was dangerous: 'Terrible happenings in
France . . . made me seek a means of avoiding such a course.'
Hence the proposition that the 'societies decided to avert a
greater evil by a smaller one', that is, recourse to a military
coup by an enlightened conspiratorial minority.

The Jacobin wing demanded a republic. Pestel, the leader,
took his point of departure from Jacobin orthodoxy and moved
towards the Babouvist–Blanquist theme. In his *Russian Truth* he
offered a perceptive analysis of class trends in contemporary
Russia. 'The distinguishing feature of the present century is an

1. Maximilien de Robespierre

2. Jean Paul Marat

3. Noël François Babeuf

4. Auguste Blanqui

5. Karl Marx

6. Alexander Herzen, *photographed by Nadar*

7. Nikolai Chernyschevsky (*right*)
8. Sergei Nechaev (*below*)
9. Peter Nikitich Tkachev
   (*below right*)

10. Lenin

open struggle between the people and the feudal aristocracy, during which there begins to arise an aristocracy of wealth, much more harmful than the feudal aristocracy, since the latter can always be shaken by public opinion and is therefore to some extent dependent on it; whereas the aristocracy of wealth, owning this wealth, finds in it a tool for its intentions against which public opinion is powerless, and by means of which it makes the whole people . . . completely dependent upon itself.' He rejected property qualifications for voting and proposed national male suffrage. Russia was to consist of a fusion of nationalities, who would cease to regard themselves as traditionally separate entities. Its legislature would consist of a single chamber with the executive elected by direct vote and a constitutional court empowered to select the highest military commanders. Expropriation with compensation of part of landed property was to be operated from the centre. Part of the nationalized land was to be distributed gratis amongst a free peasantry and the rest bought and sold in open market to the highest bidder. Other political parties were deemed unnecessary since the government's function was to fulfil any of their individual 'legitimate' claims. The idea of a one-party state was a basic premise. The rising, though ill-planned and abortive, provided an example and an inspiration for future Russian insurrectionists. Under the repressive militarism of Nicholas I (1825–55) clandestine groups, re-formed both at home and in exile, mobilized their forces for an assault on the Tsarist autocracy.

Symptomatic of the reaction against brutal obscurantism was the growth and maturation of egalitarian ideas. This, as we have already seen, was always near the surface in the writings of the repentant nobles. Socialism, as a vague creed, emerged in the sixteenth century in Russia, when the two rationalist heretics, Bashkin and Theodosius 'the Squint', opposed slavery and declared it unlawful since it contravened the second commandment. Equality was valid since *all* were endowed with 'spiritual reason', and therefore private property must be renounced and communalized. Christians, who

H

eschewed power in this world, should, therefore, oppose the acceptance of state and even parental authority. Wars between Christians equated to fratricidal strife and should be rejected. In the eighteenth century the 'Runners' sect led by a soldier, Evfimy, preached that a communal patrimony was ordained by God and that private property was an evil responsible for immorality, tyranny and wars of conquest. Such were the unsophisticated manifestations of protest rising from the backward sector.

Direct action by rebellion was a recurrent feature in the vast provincial outback. The Pugachev débâcle was one of many. A massive force of hatred was building up and was reflected in the annual increase of serf outbreaks after the accession of Nicholas I. Decembrism had immediate repercussion in the countryside. In many areas the peasantry rose against their landlords, demanding land and freedom. Divov, Minister of Foreign Affairs, observed in his diary: 'There is talk of a few peasants' revolts. They are refusing to pay their due, saying that the late Emperor [Alexander I] had freed them. Such rumours were certainly the results of the fourteenth of December.' Intelligence chief Count Benckendorff confirmed that 'the serfs, encouraged by criminal promises and false hopes, had refused to obey their masters, and in many places, they had revolted'. The menace from the countryside, whether real or exaggerated, prompted the rigid Nicholas to deny officially that the late Tsar had issued any decree for emancipation or the abolition of feudal dues (12th May 1826) and to set up a secret committee to assess the peasant problem (6th December 1826). Landlords were forbidden to divide up families, or to sell serfs without allowing them continued use of their piece of land. This was intended to confuse the peasants, who would feel that although they were personally the property of the nobles, the land was irrevocably theirs. Nevertheless discontent grew and local revolts increased. The Ministry of Interior's statistics, though obviously an underestimate, reflect this. Between 1826 and 1830, there were 41 outbreaks, rising steadily to 172 between 1845 and 1849; the total number recorded between

1826 and 1849 being 417. In 1841 alone there were 1,622 actual and attempted assassinations of landlords. These were the incoherent outbursts of the *moujiks*. The more coherent and therefore more powerful voice of protest, sprang from within the ranks of the possessors themselves. The reactionary absolutism of 'the gendarme of Europe' focused against itself opposition from within and without the Empire. By 1850, 9,000 industrial factories employing half a million men were in existence, and with this the beginnings of the classic division between a *bourgeoisie* and an industrial proletariat. In the long run the *bourgeoisie* would prove the least effective in the overthrow of the régime. A conglomeration of peasants, nobles, intelligentsia and factory workers was mobilizing. Nicholas I had formally isolated the Tsarist bureaucracy so that it was held by the tenuous roots of a reactionary nobility, civil service and a secret police. A sharp, violent blow could bring the whole structure tumbling down. Preparation for that blow would be long and hard. The French Revolution of 1789 had initiated the first crop of Russian martyrs in 1825. France set a second example in 1830, and yet a third in 1848. Russian exiles would experience at first hand the barricades of the February and June days in Paris. It was then that the Jacobin links in the field of Franco-Russian revolutionary activity were joined.

CHAPTER 6

The First Elitists

The Russian autocracy fought back, not only with chains and the knout, but with ideas. A political doctrine, officially sponsored by the Tsar, was formulated as a countervailing force to disruptive westernism. A theory of Official Nationality was disseminated through government-controlled newspapers, circulars and reports under the jurisdiction of S. S. Uvarov (1786–1855), Minister of Education from 1833 to 1849. He argued that the Russian state could not survive to offer its unique contribution unless there was a universal submission to a trinitarian basis of government, namely Orthodoxy, Autocracy and Nationality. The first meant blind acceptance of the doctrinal 'truths' of the Orthodox creed, and, therefore, rejection of the current scepticism and rationalism emanating from western philosophers; the second, the rejection of the French 'philosophes' and the revolutionary aftermath; the third a link up with slavophilism to reassert the refusal to accept the western model. Uvarov privately refuted his own public assumptions. But his Machiavellian duplicity was not lost on those of the intelligentsia, who regarded the overthrow of Tsardom, in all its aspects, as both necessary and inevitable.

Slavophilism provided a stronger antidote to pro-westernism. Conversely it offered a prop to the *status quo*. Slavophiles conceived that Russia had a unique rôle to play, different and apart from the West. This was determined by its variance in anthropological descent and religious doctrine. The pundit of classical slavophilism, A. S. Khomyakov (1804–60), posed the argument that East and West presented two antithetical types. The East followed the principle of 'conciliarism' (*sobornost*), that is free unanimity in the pursuit of truth, which is ultimately realized within the Orthodox Church, whose precepts were mystic experience and instinctive action as opposed to rationalism. The West pursued the principle of necessity, which led it towards the path of fragmentation of man's spiritual forces – faith, reason and will. This was causative of the individual over-relying on an external authority founded on one of these forces. In turn this conditioned western society to the sociopolitical upheavals of the Reformation, *laissez-faire*, revolutions and constitutions, which were the direct result of progressive fragmentation. The Russian experience, on the contrary, offered as its panacea a harmonious society based on a Church which sought no secular power and the free communal life. But to conform with this, bureaucratic rule would have to go and free opinion be allowed, in order to assist the Tsar in performing his rule justly and efficiently – a task which had been freely entrusted to him by the governed. Above all, through conciliarism, Russia was gifted with its unique institution, the *mir*, unknown in the West. Most of the founding fathers of slavophilism were nobles from central or eastern Russia, Moscow-educated landlords and short-term government officials, who spurned St Petersburg as the centre of western corruption and hostility – the symbol of the alienation of Russia from its traditional roots. They shared, however, with the western oppositionists the idealization of the peasantry, which led them together into the 'go to the people' movement propounded by the Narodniki in the 1870's.

Western orientated opponents of the régime were represented by those 'intelligentsia of diverse ranks', who were steeped in Hegelian philosophy. Many were non-aristocratic professionals, passionately concerned with diagnosing and healing the ills of Russian society. One of the leading thinkers of these so-called Occidentalists was V. G. Belinsky (1811–48), who first submitted a vaguely materialist-based view of social development, which eventually led to socialism. He was a superb literary critic at a time when this medium had begun to be used as a cover for political criticism. His theories predominated at the

Moscow Stankevitch Philosophical Society, where many of his co-thinkers, including Bakunin and Granovsky, met. In general the Occidentalists were occupied with identifying Russia with the West through the proposition that Russia should either follow or imitate Europe. Russia, given political freedom, could utilize her vast latent resources in men and materials to equal and even overtake the rest of Europe rapidly. Although they also recognized Russia's 'individual genius', they felt that its national potentiality would only grow and mature under western influence. Europe was the finishing school, but Russians would not thereby lose their traditional identity.

The westerners were pushed into the forefront of discontent by the unrelenting pressure of autocracy. The publication in 1836 of Chaadev's 'A Philosophical Letter' in Moscow's bi-monthly review *The Telescope* helped to crystallize ideas in both Slavophil and Occidental camps. Chaadev, aristocrat and graduate of Moscow University, had served as a cavalry officer in the Wars of Liberation against Napoleon and had ended up with the allied occupation of Paris. French rationalist philosophy had impregnated his thinking and, on return to Russia, he joined one of the Decembrist organizations. He was abroad in 1825 when the outbreak occurred and the aftermath of severe repression drove him to write his *Philosophical Letters*. Handwritten, these were copied by friends and clandestinely distributed. In his printed article, 'A Philosophical Letter', he came out openly against Uvarov's Theory of Official Nationality. He weighed Russia against the West and found her wanting. It was a severe condemnation of a nation deadened by blind obscurantism. 'In Russia no one has a definite rôle in life; no one cultivates good habits for their own sake or follows a logical line of conduct; there is nothing to sympathize with or warm to; nothing is lasting, everything disappears leaving no impression on the outside world or on oneself.' He pursues this theme relentlessly. The Russian 'has no links with the past or future . . . He lacks mental balance and a sense of logic.' On the other hand in Europe 'everyone born in the West learns in his cradle, in his games, in his mother's caresses notions of duty, justice, law and order'. Whilst in Russia, 'cut off by our schism, nothing of what was happening in Europe reached us. . . . Whilst the entire world was building anew, we created nothing; we remained squatting in our hovels of logs and thatch.' To rectify this Russia must realize that she belongs 'on a social plane to the West'. Her hope for the future was to integrate with it or 'be swept body and soul into the maelstrom'. He concludes with the exhortation: 'Let us then do all in our power to lay the foundations of a new life for those that come after us. We cannot bequeath them what we ourselves have never possessed: beliefs, opinions based on experience, a strongly marked personality, and a philosophy developed in the course of a long, active, rich intellectual life. So let us leave them a few ideas, which, although they have not been handed down to us from one generation to another, will have at any rate some element of tradition, and therefore a little more force and value than our own thoughts.'

Chaadev's dramatic intervention stimulated both camps to look hard and critically at their own basic assumptions. Above all, it had a tremendous impact on the man who gave the revolutionary movement its first impetus. Alexander Herzen, then in exile at Viatka, recalled that the effect on him was like a bomb explosion. It was Herzen who took up the Occidentalist theme, added to it a generation of revolutionary experience on the barricades of western Europe, and applied it to the Russian scene. Lenin assesses him in this context. 'Herzen, who was inspired by the Decembrist Conspiracy and founded the Russian free press, hoisted the standard of revolt against Tsarist autocracy. And his deeds were not wasted. The revolutionary movement to which Herzen gave the first impetus, was taken over by the revolutionaries from the people, from Chernyshevsky to the heroes of *Narodnaya Volya*, who gave it body and strength and a razor edge. Herzen played a great part in the preparation of the Russian Revolution.'[1]

Alexander Herzen was born in 1812, the illegitimate son of Ivan Yakovlev, a Muscovite nobleman of ancient lineage, and

[1] Lenin, *To the Memory of Herzen* (1912).

an ex-Captain of the Guards, who preferred free love under *les droits de Seigneur* to legal marriage, and idleness to military responsibility. He, therefore, resigned early from the army and, during a tour in Germany, absconded with the sixteen-year-old daughter of a solid Stuttgart official setting her up at home as his chief mistress and housekeeper. Alexander was the product of their union, and his father treated him as a normal eldest son and favoured him. Yet Herzen appeared to have borne a chip on his shoulder for the 'humiliations and insults of his upbringing', as he put it, and assumed an ironical pose as a defence mechanism against real or imaginary insults. As his father treated him with indulgence, and as society was tolerant towards 'natural' children, he may well have exaggerated his early sufferings. In 1825 came the Decembrist uprising. It had a profound spiritual effect on him. Legend suggests that he and the younger Ogarev, standing together on the Sparrow Hills above Moscow, swore to dedicate their lives to the cause for which the five Decembrists had been martyred.

In 1829 he entered Moscow University, ostensibly to study mathematics and physics, but was soon caught up in traditional progressive student activities. Ogarev joined him there, and they formed the caucus of a westernist circle which enquired into idealist philosophy, notably Hegel and his school, and later Feuerbach. In 1834, he was arrested by the police for taking part in the alleged conspiracy of a student leader, Sokolovsky. This may have been no more than an illicit study group engaged in theoretical discussions on socialism, and the distribution of leaflets satirizing Tsarist rule. Herzen, although barely involved on the periphery, was dealt with severely. He was imprisoned for nine months, then banished to the provincial city of Viatka, where he was forced to remain as a petty administrator for three years. Before exile he had begun his famous love affair with his cousin Natalie, which exemplified the current romanticism in the Shelley–George Sand idiom, then the vogue among the young intelligentsia. Alexander was tall, handsome, debonair and, although engaged in a flirtation with a local invalid's young wife, was eager to consummate his wooing.

After a secret preliminary visit to Moscow on a forged passport, he and Natalie made plans to elope. 'Letters pale before union as stars before the sun. Quick!' she pleaded. The ardent lover responded. They stole away and were married in nearby Vladimir in May 1838.

Their passionate union was fulfilled, in all its intensity, but, in the romantic manner, was short-lived. In 1840, Herzen's father, possibly as an attempt to rehabilitate the son into his caste, got him assigned to a post in the Ministry of the Interior in St Petersburg. By temperament Herzen was unsuitable for dead bureaucratic routine, and did not hold this office for long. In a letter to his father he complained of police ineptitude in the case of six successive murders which had taken place near the Blue Bridge. The letter was censored, and Herzen's comments were reported to the Tsar. Herzen was not only dismissed from his post but was again exiled, this time to Novgorod for a year. This confirmed Herzen in his implacable hatred of the Russian autocracy. He returned to Moscow resolved either to partake in direct action against the régime or escape, if temporarily, to freedom in the West. The death of his father in 1846 solved his dilemma for him. A large fortune enabled him to make his choice. In January 1847, Herzen together with an *entourage* containing his whole household, left Russia. He never returned. Henceforth his life and his fortune were to provide a high capital investment from outside Russia for the revolutionary movement.

In March 1847 he reached the revolutionists' Mecca. Paris was in the twilight of the *bourgeois* monarchy, the antithesis of the once focal point of eighteenth-century philosophical rationalism, 'les droits de l'homme', and uninhibited *sansculottism*. He noted: 'Material interests have become the obsession of every class and have stifled all other interests. Great ideas, words that so lately shook the masses, making them leave home and kin, have disappeared, or are repeated, just as poets invoke Olympus and the Muses, or deists "the Supreme Being", from mere habit and politeness.' The Orleanist façade was symptomatic of a 'seventeen-year-old creed of crude egoism, of the unclean worship of material gain and tranquillity'. At this time, his observations were a little short-sighted. Heine could already smell blood in the streets. After six months, Herzen quit France, disillusioned, but the call of 1848 from Paris brought him back on May 5th – at the moment when *bourgeois* and 'proletarian' republicans were beginning to mobilize, and the clubbist leaders were re-echoing the call of '93. This time history was being played out in front of a more perceptive onlooker. He detected counter-revolution within the ranks of the Radical Left. He witnessed first hand the affair of May 15th. It was there, perhaps, that he saw Blanqui for the first time.

For it was then that the confusions of a revolutionary situation, when antagonisms were at times shaded or ill-defined, became clarified. Like the other contemporary viewer, Marx, he assessed the forces underlying the struggle in both class and ideological terms, and virtually drew the same conclusions. 'The people of Paris were prepared to do what Robespierre never dared . . .' that is, to carry the revolution through to a rationale finale in the interests of its artisan protagonists. Under whose leadership? Herzen suggested Blanqui. 'That is why the conservatives and the liberals of the old school fight with such fury against Barbès, Blanqui, Raspail. . . . On the other side was the Republic, not of Lamartine, but of Blanqui, a Republic not of words but of deeds; universal suffrage not merely applied pettily and stupidly for the election of a despotic Assembly, but for the whole administration; the liberation of man, the commune and the department from submission to a strong government using bullets and chains as methods of persuasion.'[1] The June Days confirmed this. On June 25th, while watching the fighting, Herzen was seized by a detachment of National Guards and would have been killed if his identity had not been established in time. He heard the firing squads across at the Champs de Mars, and observing the brutal ferocity of the National Guard wrote that 'the Cossacks and Croats were as meek as lambs' compared with Cavaignac's armed *bourgeoisie* on the rampage.

[1] Herzen, *Letters from France and Italy* (1848–9).

In retrospect, Herzen viewed with disillusionment and contempt the social reformists 'disguised as tribunes of the people'.[1] 'Louis Blanc never understood socialism; his well-known book *De l'Organisation du Travail* and a few brilliant phrases established his reputation.' In the futile Luxembourg Commission Blanc was merely 'the first priest and preacher in the new church, and its sessions no more than the solemn liturgies of an adolescent socialism'. It was Blanqui who emerged as the prototype of revolutionary socialism. He would be ruthless in dealing with obsolescent tradition. He alone was imbued with that revolutionary ardour and political imagination, which could both destroy and recreate. 'Blanqui is the revolutionary of our time. He has understood that nothing can be merely readjusted, but that the primary task is to pull down the existing structure. Gifted with remarkable eloquence, he roused the masses; all his words were an indictment of the old world. They loved him less than Barbès, but they preferred to listen to him.' This view was shared by the other great contemporary, Bakunin. When he thought of programmes, if at all, he 'thought in terms of a revolutionary dictatorship. He eventually accepted the methods of the French Revolution and of Babeuf, which he developed along lines parallel to Blanqui. His early anarchism only emphasized the negative, entirely destructive value which he assigned to the revolutionary dictatorship.'[2] As a reaction to the June Days both Herzen and Bakunin viewed the immediate solution in terms of a Blanquist *coup*, which would proceed to tear out the old order, root and branch. On the question of structure and direction of the post-revolutionary dictatorship they would both part company with 'le vieux'. Herzen's growing disillusionment with western revolutionism led him back to seek its fulfilment in Russia, and to assume an ambivalent approach to revolution as an idea. In 1851, he produced his *Russian People and Socialism* in which he expressed the feasibility of a unique form of Russian socialism blending the best of westernism with the slavophilist idealization of the *mir*. Herzen became more and more concerned with

---

[1] See also Chapter 3, p. 71 above.　　[2] F. Venturi, *Roots of Revolution*, pp. 61–2.

the concept of individual freedom as fundamental to value judgements on society or social movements. 'The liberty of the individual is the greatest thing of all, it is this and this alone that the true will of the people can develop.' In one sense he presaged the logical working out of Jacobin Communism. Socialism was not for him the grand finale in the socio-economic process. Any long-term curtailment of the liberty of the individual or of the minority would perpetuate violence as a measure for its rectification. 'Socialism will develop in all its phases until it reaches its own extremes and absurdities. Then there will again burst forth from the titanic breast of the revolting minority a cry of denial. Once more a mortal battle will be joined in which socialism will occupy the place of today's conservatism, and will be defeated by the coming revolution as yet invisible to us.' In spite of his theoretical oscillations, Herzen hammered home the Blanquist theme, which was adopted and reinforced by his friend and fellow exile, Ogarev, who concerned himself with organization, tactics and grand strategy, that is with the activist problems in a maturing revolutionary situation. It was Ogarev who was the consistent advocate of conspiratorial élitism. He applied the Jacobin approach to backward Russia, aiming at a voluntaristic secret conclave which would animate and direct the latent revolutionary consciousness of the peasantry.

Before analysing Ogarev's contribution to this movement from without, it is important to recognize that inside Russia similar groups were forming, almost exclusively student based. In the Universities of St Petersburg and Moscow ideas were being hatched, independently of those of the exiles, by intellectual circles fighting to keep radicalism alive in the oppressive atmosphere of military bureaucracy. The movement was not without its odd cranks and eccentrics. One such character was V. S. Pecherin, a semi-crazed poet, who had consumed Buonarroti's *Conspiration pour l'Egalité* with religious fervour. In his letters he described his elation on discovering it in a second-hand bookshop in Liège. His enthusiasm was short lived. He wandered across Europe seeking enlightenment, sometimes involved in, more often on the fringe of, refugee circles subscribing to some odd socialist Utopian creed. In 1840 he was converted to Catholicism; he visited Rome later, in 1859, but was repelled by the rigid autocracy of Papal rule, reminiscent of that of the Russia he had renounced. He ended up his days as chaplain in a Dublin hospital. In Russia socialist centres were also forming under the guise of literary clubs. The most notable of these was that of Petrashevsky, a disciple of the Utopians Saint-Simon and Fourier, as well as a great advocate of a peasant-based socialism. He attracted to him a côterie of intellectuals, most of whom had their social origins in the poorer gentry, and worked as journalists and civil servants. Members included F. M. Dostoevsky and A. A. Grigor'ev. They lacked the broad enervating culture derived from the European experience of their more fortunate contemporaries, Herzen and Bakunin. One important group leader, N. A. Speshnev, proposed 'Jesuitical' (conspiratorial) means of undermining authority, and formulated the triple weapons of conspiracy, propaganda and insurrection as indivisible in the destruction of the social order. Inspired by revolution abroad, Petrashevsky, in late 1848, essayed to convert his club, ostensibly formed for the study of foreign literature, into a training centre for revolutionists. The authorities caught on quickly; on 23rd April 1849, the police raided the club and arrested its leading members including Dostoevsky and Petrashevsky. A preamble to the charges brought against them was significant: 'The dangerous doctrines which caused disturbances and riots throughout western Europe and threatened to destroy the peace and well-being of the nations have unfortunately had a repercussion in our own country. A handful of nonentities, the majority of them young and immoral, has tried to ride rough-shod over the sacred rights of religion, law and property.' Nonentities indeed! Dostoevsky's four years in prison provided the background for a terrifying picture of suffering in his novel, *The House of the Dead*, which sustained and strengthened anti-Tsarist sentiments. At least one, Speshnev, had adopted the Babouvist principle, and transposed it on to the Russian setting.

After 1848, it was mainly outside Russia that imaginative

constructions in socialist thinking were taking place. It was still the Herzen–Ogarev partnership which constituted the exiles' centre for political exploration and criticism. Yet a dichotomy of views stemmed from them. Herzen, in the 1850's, was facing a number of dilemmas. He extolled Blanqui and his revolutionary *élan* yet rejected the 'democratic orthodoxy' to which the Jacobins clung, on the grounds that 'government is not an end, but a necessity'. A self-acknowledged Occidentalist, he now despaired of the West, and returned to Russia for the possibility of directing a course towards the point where the theoretical socialism of the West and the practical operation of the *mir* could meet and coalesce. Ogarev, on the other hand, was more concerned with means than ends, and his appreciation of the means led him to Blanquist techniques. Meanwhile a new generation of Russians were reacting against the liberal *mores*, which through sterile argument and vacillation had brought defeat in 1848. It was still suffering an intellectual paralysis, which rendered ineffectual any will to radical change. Inevitably youth moved towards the extreme; towards the immediate demands of activism and violence. In the short term this was the way of Ogarev; in the long term, through the Tkachevist school, it led to Lenin.

Nicholas Platonovich Ogarev (1814–77), the saint of Russian Jacobinism, was born in Penza, the son of a wealthy landlord. His early life resembled that of Herzen; they shared the same background of wealth and privilege. He was an epileptic, although the symptoms were relatively mild till his later years. A boyhood friend of Herzen, he was also involved in the Sokolovsky conspiracy and, as a result, was forced to live under supervision at his father's estate at Aksheno. The father, to divert his son's energies from the more dangerous pursuits of the mind, offered him a more pleasant indulgence of the flesh in the form of a beautiful serf-girl. Both mind and body were still unneglected, and he dedicated to her one of his most charming poems. Like his friend Herzen, he became a prisoner of the Romantic imagination. Two brief, but passionate affairs followed, both with cousins, neither ending in any permanent commitment. On 11th February 1836, at a ball given by the Governor of Penza, he found himself by the side of the Governor's niece, Maria Lvovna Roslavlev. This time it was the real thing. Ogarev recalls, 'Suddenly there broke from our lips the words, "I love you." This moment was recorded by the Angels in Heaven. . . .' This introduction worthy of Shelley was followed eight years later by a Byronic farewell. In 1838, still politically suspect, he petitioned the Governor (whom he also sent an advance loan of 5,000 roubles) for permission to travel south, to Pyategovsk. There he met a surviving Decembrist, Prince Odoevsky, who entrusted him with the aims and mysteries of the old conspiracy with such effect that Ogarev 'knelt before the crucifix and prayed that he might receive the crown of martyrdom for Russian freedom'. Circumstances accorded him the opportunity for more practical application of social principles. A year later his father died and he found himself heir to three estates scattered widely over Russia, containing in all 4,000 serfs. The largest, at Belo-omut in Ryazan, held 1,870 serfs, and Ogarev was resolved to apply his egalitarian convictions by liberating these, and granting them free ownership of the estate. Too many pressures, amongst which was his wife, forced him to modify the free grant to hired purchase by ten annual instalments. It was a lengthy operation. Delay was as much due to the suspicions of the peasants as to bureaucratic procrastination; but the agreement was eventually sealed and the liberated serfs never forgot their benefactor. When they heard of his death they collected together a fund to provide a yearly mass on the date of his death for the repose of his soul. This was continued until the early years of the twentieth century, and in 1914 descendants of the original serfs organized a special celebration at Belo-omut to commemorate the one-hundredth anniversary of his birth.

Consistent saintliness is always difficult to live with. His marriage disintegrated, and with it his property. By 1848 nothing remained of the original estate. He lost the second one at Uruchia to meet the legal claims of his wife; and made over the third, his original home Ashkeno, to his current mistress's brother-in-law who defaulted on his payments. Reduced almost to penury he approached his old friend Herzen for a loan of 45,000 roubles. It was granted and he bought over the owner-managership of a paper factory near Simbirsk, manned, not by serfs but by paid workers. Five years of normalcy, constant entreaties from Herzen, and the burning down of his factory probably by his own workmen, prompted him to join his friend. The death of his wife enabled him to legalize his relationship with his mistress, Natalie Tuchkov, and helped gain them a passport. In March 1856, the Ogarevs left Russia for ever. Herzen and Ogarev, reunited in London, added their intellectual skill and energy to the Russian underground. Together they provided a unique contribution to the mainstream of revolution. Both were preoccupied with the peasantry as the cause and means of transforming society. Herzen created Populism. Ogarev tainted it with Babouvism.

Herzen, the year before, on 27th February 1855, had addressed a meeting of revolutionary emigrés, which included Louis Blanc, Marx and Mazzini. He traced the link between the Decembrists and Petrashevskists, and proposed concepts, which were to have important historical derivatives. He suggested that in one way Russia was fortunate. She would not need to cover the ground previously trod by other countries. 'History is really unfair, and to those who joined it late, it gives the reward that comes from experience.' Here was the rudiments of the historical jump thesis, which was to be adopted by Chernyshevsky, and rationalized through to a maturer solution by Tkachev. Meanwhile the *Kolokol* (*The Bell*), the first Russian emigré journal, financed by Herzen with the two friends as major contributors, was projected on the Russian scene. It was smuggled into Russia and distributed throughout pro- and anti-government circles. It accorded advice on forthcoming peasant reforms by the new Tsar Alexander II to both legal and clandestine institutions, and was listened to. It shaped, and was shaped by, a changing Russia moving towards emancipation. It reached its apex of influence in 1861; thereafter it declined. The retrogressive nature of so-called reforms were sensitively reflected in the *Kolokol*. On 15th June of that year it already perceived them as 'a new serfdom' whilst the 'Tsar had cheated the people'. By then the day of Herzen and Ogarev was over. They were convinced themselves that they were too far away to assess the situation and so guide their compatriots. Lenin's earlier observations on Herzen are still valid. But Herzen's championship of the Poles in 1863 put paid to his standing within Russia. In the long term Ogarev's contribution to the partnership was to be more telling. In 1860 Ogarev had already sounded the call 'to go to the people'. 'We must train schoolmasters, men who can preach learning to the peasants; travelling schoolmasters, who can spread useful and applied knowledge from one end of Russia to the other.'[1] It became the journal's war-cry in late 1861, when universities had been closed as a result of student riots and conspiracies. It was his view that any movement aiming at a social transformation of society must be led by a secret *élite* (apostles) consisting of experts in various intellectual fields, who would conduct the planning and execution of a revolution 'as if they were one person'. The caucus would draw up and issue general and day-to-day orders which would be disseminated under central direction. Russia's massive size would require the setting up of provincial centres situated at the most convenient rendezvous amongst the most revolutionary elements such as the intelligentsia (universities and seminaries), the army (at the headquarters of the most discontented units), and the peasantry (at central fairs and markets). Front organizations were to be set up as a cover for the central directors, with members operating according to the degree of initiation. Those involved in carrying out minor tasks were 'the unconscious agents', who 'act in the sense of the society without the need to know of its existence'. Ogarev ultimately accepted the strategy of a universal insurrection based on peasants and workers, which was needed to transform society. Post-revolutionary terror was inevitable for the maintenance of revolutionary power. Tactically he sponsored 'the utilization of legal facilities', that is infiltration by

'Letter to a fellow countryman', *Kolokol* (1st August 1860).

party agents into high official posts. He agitated amongst dissentient minorities, such as the Cossacks and Poles, who were raw material for anti-Tsarist activity, and propaganda demanding their independence was kept up at high pressure. Not for nothing was it said that Buonarroti's *Conspiration pour l'Egalité* was a major contributory influence on Ogarev's thinking.

The 1861 Serf Emancipation act had an all-round catalytic effect. The Liberals and Constitutionalists seeking change under the auspices of an enlightened Tsar applauded the move as the harbinger of a coming Utopia. Their optimism was short-lived. Instead of removing, it aggravated peasant discontent, and during its application sparked off a more formidable period of fermentation and unrest, against which the rôle of the new revolutionary must be set. Social relationships between landlord and peasant worsened. Serfs were freed, not, in the main, for altruistic motives, but in order to ensure a more profitable return than the exaction of day labour. Under the new laws owners were to be compensated for the land granted to peasant holders at that moment in time and not for loss of labour dues. The peasant had to pay a redemption fee, through the commune, arranged over a period of 49 years. Prices were set by arbitrators elected by the government, and these were fixed so high that it appeared that the landlord derived income for loss of labour as well as land. In permanent debt, tied to the commune, where was this promised freedom for the peasant?[1] The peasant's suspicion was confirmed by the preservation of his status, as a member of an inferior caste, marked out for discriminating laws and impositions. The complicated wording, neglect of translations into the local vernacular and, in any case, inadequate production and distribution of copies of the manifesto enhanced the tension born of insecurity.

Economic factors piled up the pressure. Village control under local bureaucracy and redistribution of holdings hindered agricultural improvement. The wasteful strip system still

---

[1] The state peasants fared better. They obtained larger holdings and more favourable terms. The 800,000 registered males in the Imperial Estates got the best bargain.

prevailed and, in most villages, continuity of ownership by family inheritance was absent. Output, after emancipation, proved inadequate to meet the demand of a rapidly increasing population. Whilst peasant numbers rose from 50 to 80 million between 1861 and 1905, their land holdings in acres increased by a mere one-tenth. Debts mounted with their failure to keep up redemption dues, and, in spite of some government aid in first deferring and later part-cancelling debts, the poverty and depression of the peasantry meant a permanent source of revolutionism.

The loosening of social bonds then had been to a great extent illusory. One positive outcome was the emergence of a new intelligentsia. These, as Tkachev observed, 'were from another class of people . . . intermediate between those who have a solid economic basis and those who by no means possess one'. A rapid intake of this 'proletariat of thought' (a title imposed on these impoverished students), occurred in the universities during and after the end of the Crimean War. In accord with the new liberalization policy, by 1861 the universities were no longer the exclusive conclaves for young noblemen. That year 370 of the thousand students at St Petersburg could not afford to pay their admission fee. In Moscow they apparently constituted the majority: ragged and hungry, they slept in public parks or shared overcrowded lodgings and even cupboards.[1] A first generation of undergraduates, they were the new *déclassés* – neither aristocrat nor peasant in the normal social cleavage – with built-in psychoses inherent in many such groups. They provided the revolutionary fervour, turned the universities into a political battlefield, where they fought the bureaucracy to a standstill. They were a growing force to be wooed by both literary and political writers, who, whilst engaged in spreading their message, could never afford to ignore them. They conceived diverse ideas, through which some common threads may be detected: nostalgia for the 'simple' peasant life, antagonism towards a European corrupted aristocracy, an overbalance

[1] V. S. Eshersky, 'The University of Moscow in 1861', in *Works concerned with Russian History* (M. 1900).

in favour of slavophilism, and the glory of self-sacrifice. Through 'scholarly' research into the laws and customs of their rural past, they purported to reveal the lost Arcadia and the uniqueness of Russian tradition and culture as opposed to the West. The humane and imaginative insight of Turgenev and Dostoevsky was contemptuously derided as irrational and the writers dismissed as Tsarist sycophants. Unstable and rootless themselves they sought a mythical stability in the peasant mass to whom they attributed imaginary virtues. They were ready to 'go to the people', to respond to this call from Herzen and Ogarev, yet rejecting both as men of the past. On the periphery of these future *Narodniki* extremists spawned their exclusive doctrines. But all would grant their allegiance to a common prophet who, with the eclipse of the Herzen–Ogarev school, became a source of inspiration to the revolutionary intelligentsia. He was N. G. Chernyshevsky. In more ways akin to his contemporary, Auguste Blanqui, than any other Russian insurrectionist, he too shared the martyr's crown in his unremitting self-sacrifical devotion to the cause of revolutionary socialism.

One of the new men of the social 'intermediates', Chernyshevsky also served as a vehicle of continuity between new and old. He was born in 1828, the son of a priest, at Saratov, a town in the border lands which provided a meeting point between Russia proper and colonial territory, and where time had brewed a volatile admixture of Tartar and German. Here, too, free Cossacks roamed, almost at will, constantly joining battle against Tsarist forces operating as a spearhead for eastern expansionism. Cossacks were natural allies to the border intransigents of the past, notably Stenka Razin and Pugachev. Groups of *Raskolniki*, breakaway sects from the Orthodox Church as far back as the seventeenth century, still persisting in their independence from state institutions, flourished along the banks of the Volga. It was a wild, lawless land, a training ground for rebels. It nurtured Lenin.

In his reminiscences, whilst imprisoned in the St Peter–Paul fortress, Chernyshevsky recalled the harsh conditions of the peasants of his youth: the constant struggle for existence against brigands, Kirghiz slave traders, wolves and cholera, in which drunkenness offered the only escape. He always showed compassion towards chronic drunkards and *Yurodivy* – holy men inspired with mad revelations. In their fantasies he perceived the search for the true reality – the rejection of the artificial and the sophisticated, who battened on the ignorance of these simple primitives. His intellectual groundwork was prepared under the guidance of his father. One of the 'people of good sense' he had amassed an enormous library, which he made available without reservations to his son. The father's taste was catholic. His volumes ranged from theological treatises on the mediaeval saints to secular compositions such as language primers, and borrowed editions of contemporary literature as varied as the novels of George Sand and the political journals of Belinsky and Herzen. He had already begun to receive an education in the round when he entered the University of St Petersburg. It was also an honourable admission by a wise father that his son was not cut out for the priesthood.

In his diary (July 1848) he revealed that he was more and more convinced by the ideas of the socialists whilst following the events in France. Through wide reading of western philosophy he assured himself that Russia had contributed very few ideas in the past, but faced the opportunity of creating something unique in the future. Current observations on political developments in Paris drew him further towards revolutionary socialism. Applied to the Russian situation it meant the instigation of a peasants' revolt. The problem was one of organization: to bring together in one upsurge the *Raskolniki*, the peasants of the *obshchinas*, and disaffected government officials. He met the Petrashevskists in December 1848 and judged their vocal postures, their ineffectual liberalism, as noise in a talking shop. He observed in his diary: 'I do not like gentlemen who say "Freedom, freedom" and then restrict this word to laws without carrying it into life; who are prepared to abolish laws which speak of inequality but not to touch a social order in which nine-tenths of the population are made up of slaves and proletarians. The problem is not whether there should be a king or not, or whether there should be a constitution or not. It is, rather, one of social relations, and lies in the fact that one class should not suck the blood of another.' He was drawn to the proposition that only a dictatorship was capable of implementing movement and change. For a short term, he too passed through the harsh reappraisal which, like Herzen, led him to Blanqui. Disillusionment with the events of 1848–9, and the triumph of counter-revolution throughout, caused a revulsion from any form of authoritarianism, any form of imposition from above. 'Far better anarchy from below than from above.'

A feeling of impotence at the centre drove him back to his native Saratov, where he was offered a schoolmaster's post. He married and, like Blanqui, warned his wife of the consequences of being tied to a man like himself. 'Only a spark is needed to set everything alight. . . . And if the fire starts, despite my cowardly nature, I shall be incapable of not taking part. . . . And how will all this end? Forced labour or hanging.' It was absolute commitment or nothing. The Bishop of Saratov's enquiry into suspect methods in Chernyshevsky's teaching prompted him to get back to St Petersburg to write and undertake research for a thesis. Under the guise of the usual literary criticism he became the main contributor to the journal *Sovremennick* (*Contemporary*). He drew attention to the problem of serf-emancipation. By skilful analogy his articles escaped the censor and he pressed through his views on social revolutionism. Chernyshevsky, like Herzen, was already questioning whether socialism could be achieved in Russia before capitalism matured; he saw the *obshchina* as the base for change, as security for the peasant under a future agricultural collectivism. He had also reached the conclusion that Russia must learn from the European experience to 'skip all the intermediate stages of development, or, at least, enormously reduce their length and deprive them of their power'.[1]

An ultimate break, not only with the Liberals but with Herzen, was precipitated by the Tsar's emancipation project. The bitter scepticism of his writing roused the antipathy of the

---

[1] *Selected works on Economics*, Vol. 1, p. 718.

other contributors. The young Tolstoy poured scorn on him for his bad manners, and accused him of being one from whom 'opinion is spreading that to be worthless, bitter and nasty is something very beautiful'. Herzen described him as an *agent provocateur*. In June 1859 the two met in London. Chernyshevsky had come direct to his mentor to tell him the reasons for his tactics, and to explain the actual political situation within Russia to the outsider. There was little response either way. Both dug their heels in. Chernyshevsky left after four days even more disillusioned than before. His analysis was crystallized in a 'Letter from the Provinces' published in *Kolokol* soon after his visit in London. The author is unknown but believed to be one of his disciples. It points out the error of trusting reforms bestowed charitably from above. It warns that the price of liberation would be high due to regional committees drawn from the nobility issuing 'terrifying sums' which would lead to the peasants being worse off than before. Overburdensome mortgages on land payments would produce less security, more destitution. It advises *Kolokol* that 'only the peasant axes can save us. Let your bell sound, not to prayer, but for the charge. Summon Russia to arms!'

The 'Emancipation' proved his point. Doubly so since the Third Force put him first on the list for proscription (April 1862). They planted their own agents in his household and both his doorkeeper and cook were in their pay. It was only a question of time before his predictions on his own fate would be made true. The opportunity came, through a letter, sent by Herzen with a traveller, to ask Chernyshevsky's associate Serno-Solovevich to come and print the *Sovremennik* in London. A police agent there informed St Petersburg. The traveller was seized on the border, and the letter found and used as a pretext to arrest both Chernyshevsky and the proposed recipient. Chernyshevsky had anticipated this. At the last moment the enlightened governor of St Petersburg, Prince Suvorov, advised him to leave Russia. He refused. Like Blanqui he had committed himself absolutely. In him, too, was the unquenchable spirit of the professional revolutionary: an almost fatalistic resignation to a future of perpetual imprisonment – a price he was destined to pay for the belief in the rectitude of his ideals.

Between July 1862 and May 1864 he was a prisoner, without trial in the St Peter–Paul fortress. He adapted himself to the proposition that it would be a long stay. Here he created his most influential work through the medium of a novel *What is to be Done*. Its heroes are the new impoverished intelligentsia – 'the proletariat of thought' – centred in students' communes where they live sharing all property. They are enjoined in self-educative conspiratorial groups to do battle against the autocracy. The novel abounds in romantic sentiment and he affects the Utopian socialist dreams conjured up from his youth. Yet it was precisely this flavour that appealed to generations of future revolutionaries. Chernyshevsky himself ceased to be actively involved. In May 1864 he was sentenced to 'civil execution' and despatched to Siberia to suffer forced labour in a number of penal settlements. He was there for nineteen years, even refusing a free pardon in 1874 if he signed an appeal for mercy. In July 1883 agreement between *Narodnaya Volya* and Tsar Alexander III allowed him to transfer nearer home to Astrakhan, in return for suspension of terroristic acts during the coronation. By 1889 he was so ill that the authorities sanctioned his return to his birthplace, where he died four months later. His novels and his earlier works had made him more than a myth. It was during his absence that the most formidable army of youth had mustered in the ranks of *Zemlya I Volya* (Land and freedom) against the Tsarist régime. They marched forward under the banner of Chernyshevsky.

CHAPTER 7

Populists, Jacobins and Nihilists

The failure of emancipation brought the young rebel intelligentsia to the people. The first short-lived *Zemlya I Volya* registered direct contact with the Russian villages, gave magnanimous support to the Polish insurgents, and broke its back on both.

The outstanding philosopher of the movement was Nikolay Serno-Solovevich (1834–66) who was arrested with Chernyshevsky. He was the son of a successful civil servant recently ennobled by the Tsar. As a young man in St Petersburg he joined the circle of Maria Vasilevna Trubnikova, whose father was an exiled Decembrist. She gathered round her a group of young radicals who engaged themselves in study groups and discussions in European politics and literature. Their programme included the works of international revolutionists such as Proudhon, Lassalle and Herzen. Nikolay soaked himself in socialist ideas particularly those derived from Pestel and the French school. In a poem 'Confession' written later in the Peter–Paul fortress he tells of his early rejection of personal privilege and authority. Yet during the 'reform' period, after a journey across Europe, he decided to join the civil service in order to undertake active work in the land transference projects. Documents passed through his hands which opened his eyes to the obstructionist methods of the bureaucrats, to the whole façade of the so-called emancipatory process.

His indignation and cool effrontery took him straight to the Tsar. In September 1858 he approached the all-highest himself as he was strolling in his garden at Tsarkoe Selo and handed him a thesis on 'the general situation of the State, which was far from excellent'. The Tsar accepted it gracefully and even praised its proposals. 'In it [the young generation] there is much that is good and really noble. Russia must expect much from it, if and only if it is properly orientated.'[1] The Tsar's optimism was short-lived. At Kaluga, where Nikolay was sent that year to be secretary for the local organization in charge of peasant matters, his experiences destroyed his faith in a 'Socialist Tsar'. Here, too, he followed Chernyshevsky's commentaries and discoursed with local ex-Decembrists. He left his job. After short-term dabbling in writing for a financial journal (in which he propounded state over private investment through the issue of interest-bearing Treasury bonds backed by royal property) he went abroad to gather evidence for his opinions. He met Herzen and Ogarev in London. They got on splendidly and with Ogarev he conceived a new programme that could really 'liberate' the peasantry. Its slogan, first uttered by Ogarev, was *Zemlya I Volya* – Land and Freedom. Serno-Solovevich returned to Russia with the new programme contained in Ogarev's *What the people need*, and in St Petersburg became the central figure from which a variety of groups evolved. They owed allegiance to a newly-formed caucus named after Ogarev's slogan. It was secret and organized conspiratorially on the basis of groups of five, each of whom had to recruit a maximum of five others. Every group leader would only be acquainted with his own group plus four others of the group he had to enlist. The whole idea smacked of Buonarrotism, and was said to be instigated by Mazzini in advice offered to Ogarev. Serno was the founder. He sparked off the whole process. Early arrest did not assuage his own revolutionary fervour. Exiled to Irkutsk (1864) he was the leading figure in an insurrection planned in west Siberia amongst the peasants and Polish exiles. His death in 1866 probably saved him from the executioner.

Chernyshevsky joined as one of the top directors. By 1861 the most dynamic elements in the radical opposition were members

[1] M. Lemke, *Essays on the Liberation Movement of the 'Sixties'* (1908, 2nd edition), p. 43.

of, or connected with, the organization. Contributors to the *Sovremennik* such as N. Utin (who later tried to form a Russian section in the First International) and young Peter Lavrov were all involved, with Chernyshevsky as their guide and mentor. Nikolay Serno-Solovevich had put his finger on the vital problem. 'The people is courageous but that is not good enough to give the signal to take the initiative.' From both these leaders emerged a duality of approach: the attempt to 'go to the people', that is, to the peasantry, and rouse them to action; and to organize effectively a minority leadership which would lead to a successful revolutionary conclusion. The latter was transformed by Tkachev into a moral necessity. The younger Alexander Serno-Solovevich sounded the final break with the London *emigrés*. Chernyshevsky had opened the eyes of youth to political realities. Self-sacrifice and violence are inalienable weapons of special appeal to the young. The vague Populism of *Zemlya I Volya* was replaced by clear-cut aims and directives. A nine-teen-year-old student manifested a new breakthrough to the old creed. He was P. G. Zaichnevsky (1842–96). He gathered round him a group of young extremists pledged to follow through the Jacobin Communist idea to the ultimate limit.

His early years followed the normal pattern of the intelligentsia from the petty nobility. He was an outstanding student at this school in Orel, so that he gained easy admission to the mathematics faculty of Moscow University. He was soon more absorbed in radical politics than in his academic specialism and became printer and distributor of banned literature, specifically those of Ogarev, Herzen and Proudhon. Profits accruing from illicit sales were kept in a communal bank and used to subsidize poor students. All members contributed to a pool – the wealthy in cash, the poor sold their possessions or offered money derived from writing articles. From the proceeds they founded 'The First Free Russian Press' and produced Ogarev's pamphlet on the Decembrists on wooden type. This quickly wore out and was replaced by metal. The crude machine was hidden during a police raid, after which it was successfully transferred to Ryazan. It was here that they launched their inflammatory manifesto *Young Russia*. Its creator was already in prison. Its conception took part in a prison cell and the proofs were smuggled out with the help of a police guard.

The activist theme was pre-eminent. Missionary preaching by the intelligentsia was not enough. These 'natural proletarians' as leaders must 'stimulate armed revolt'. In a letter to a close friend, Argiropulo, Zaichnevsky said: 'There are two ways of putting oneself at the head of the People's movement; either like Louis Blanc, by infiltrating into the masses, spreading pamphlets among the workers, denouncing competition, business and everything that morally oppresses and kills the worker: or like Barbès, by putting oneself at the head of every movement and making one's name the name of every popular party. . . . With us in Russia at the present moment Louis Blanc's method is not feasible. That leaves the way chosen by Barbès.'[1] He called for a 'revolution, a bloody and pitiless revolution, which must change everything down to the very roots', declaring that 'we will go further, not only than the poor revolutionaries of 1848, but also than the great terrorists of the 1790's'. That liberal caution which pauses at the brink, affords security for the enemy and must be rejected. The object is the utter destruction of the régime and its replacement by 'a federal republican union of regions', with national and regional assemblies elected by national suffrage. The national assembly would be responsible for determining foreign policy and collecting internal revenue. Other than these, local control would be exercised by regional bodies. Regions would be divided into *obshchinas*, with the *mir* administrating the allocation of strips to those living inside and outside its jurisdiction. Land was to be retained for a fixed period then reallocated from the centre.

Taxation would be regulated so that its weight fell on the rich. 'Social' factories would replace private concerns and these 'must be run by people elected by society and give society an account of the work done in them, within a given time limit.

[1] A. Smirnov, 'For a biography of P. E. Zaichnevsky', in Krasnyy Arkhiv (1936), No. 111, Letter to Argiropulo.

We demand the creation of shops, in which the price of goods will correspond to their real worth and not to the whim of a merchant hoping to enrich himself as quickly as possible.' A rational approach to the problem of national minorities within Russia evidenced the need for 'complete independence of Poland and Lithuania, which more than any other region have shown their desire not to remain united with Russia. We demand that each region be given the chance of deciding by a majority vote whether or not it wishes to form part of the Russian Federal Republic.' Young Russia was, more than anything else, concerned with the means of fulfilling their programme. The distinctive élitism, as propounded by Blanqui, was unmistakable. After the revolution political change would be forcibly initiated by the revolutionary vanguard. 'We are indeed firmly convinced that the revolutionary party, which (if the movement is successful) will be the head of the government, will have to retain for a time the present system of centralization. This will certainly be necessary as regards politics, if not the administration, in order to be able to introduce as quickly as possible the new foundations of society and the economy. It will have to take the dictatorship into its own hands and stop at nothing. The elections for the National Assembly will have to be carried out under the influence of the government, which must at once make sure that the supporters of the present régime do not take part – that is, if any of them are still alive.' The vanguard would spring exclusively from the students and other members of the intelligentsia. The call to action ends with an uncanny prophecy: 'The day will soon come when we will unfurl the great banner of the future, the red banner. And with a mighty cry of "Long live the Russian Social and Democratic Republic" we will move against the Winter Palace to wipe out all who dwell there.' It goes on to propose that 'with full faith in ourselves and our forces, and in support of the people and in the glorious future of Russia – which destiny has ordained shall be the first country to realize the great cause of Socialism – we will cry "To your axes", and then we will strike the imperial party'. A Churchillian note rings out in the finale. 'We will destroy them in their houses, in the narrow streets of the town, in the broad avenues of the capital, and in the villages. Remember that, when this happens, any one who is not with us is against us, and an enemy, and that every method is used to destroy an enemy.'

The manifesto may be considered as the first breakthrough of the Jacobin approach to the transformation of a vast primary producing economy, wherein social aims were derived from agrarian roots (that is from the *obshchina* and *mir*) rather than urban experience. In this context Zaichnevsky and his party followed traditional Populism in basing his revolutionary army on the peasantry, in contradistinction to Babouvism which derived its ultimate strength from a city proletariat. *Young Russia* was more realistic in its choice of troops. Even with expanding industrialization a town proletariat was developing which was only one stage removed from the soil. This new proletariat was an urbanized peasantry.

Zaichnevsky was tried and transported to Siberia in January 1863. For six years he lived in the Irkutsk area, where he continued his studies and made contact with the Polish exiles. He returned to Penza in Russia in 1869, where he immediately set up a conspiratorial organization composed of students and local militia men. The police were on the alert and he was hounded from place to place until he returned to his home town, Orel, in 1872. Here he resumed his underground activity; his recruits mainly derived from the young intelligentsia. He ceaselessly spurned overt activism – such as mass meetings and individual terrorist acts – and had no confidence in spontaneous mass action on the premise that the masses were 'always on the side of the *fait accompli*'. Naturally he was rejected by the main body of the Populists. After 1875 it was logical for him to direct his support towards the small Tkachev group, to whose precepts he remained loyal for the rest of his turbulent career. He suffered two more periods of banishments to Siberia as a result of his continual involvement in conspiracies. During his last exile he contributed articles to the local *Eastern Observer* on European working-class movements.

His last trip to Russia was sanctioned in 1896, when he returned to die that year in Smolensk. His influence, together with that of Tkachev, on the direction along which the course of Russian revolutionism would travel, was vital. One of his women disciples became an Executive member of Narodnaya Volya. Four others later joined the Social Democratic party and in the great schism naturally chose the Leninist faction. In S. Mitskevich's view[1] both he and Tkachev are afforded the highest place in the foundations of Bolshevism. In *Young Russia* he found the ideas and slogans which were used in the implementation of Bolshevik method.

Spontaneous outbursts and abortive plots such as those of the Kazan students and Karakazov's attempted assassination of the Tsar (1866) accentuated reactionary policies which, in turn, drove the rebellious to greater extremism. As the reform period petered out, revolutionary passions of frustrated youth were bursting 'to carry things through to the end'.[2] This found expression in the review *Russkoe Slovoe* the mouthpiece of D. I. Pisarev and the *enfants terribles*, who were also obliquely influenced by Bakunin's liturgies on destruction. A name derived from Turgenev's *Fathers and Sons* was applied to them and which they welcomed. It was Nihilism.

The credo of revolution *per se* and the justification of any means employed to effect it reached its ultimate in the violent activism of Sergei Nechaev. In this 'proletarian of thought' there met and fused the diverse revolutionary currents which flowed from the extremist groups. Their common bible was *La conspiration pour l'Egalité*. One aspect of Nechaev was his attempt to inject Buonarrotism into the Russian setting. He had no need to 'go to the people'. He was already one of them. For Nechaev was born in Ivanovo in 1847 the son of a painter and peasant woman. Ivanovo was then a small, uninspiring provincial city which was undergoing a rapid expansion in textile production. Nechaev's formative years were spent amongst

[1] Article, 'The Russian Jacobins', in *Proletarskaya Revolyutsiva* (1923), nos. 6–7 (18–19), pp. 3–26.
[2] A. Coquart, *Dmitri Pisarev (1840–1868) et l'idéologie du nihilisme russe* (Paris 1946).

country peasants and he was to see, at first hand, the industrial proletarianization of many of them. A bright, imaginative lad, he reacted strongly against his dull environment. A small free private school run by a writer V. A. Demetev may have provided him with the opportunity for a primary education. Early on, he was in correspondence with the writer N. F. Nefedov, ten years Nechaev's senior, the son of an affluent peasant who was studying at Moscow University. Nefedov fed Nechaev with books and Populist ideas and influenced him in his decision to leave his home town. Nechaev was not without ambition for the finer things of life. 'Reality without any refinement hits me so hard, that I have to leap into the air . . .' he wrote to his mentor. In August 1865 he arrived in Moscow, but failed at his studies to qualify as a teacher and departed for St Petersburg. Here he practised as an unqualified schoolmaster. He observed the reaction to the attempted assassination of the Tsar by Karakazov. This sparked off a personal involvement in the revolutionary movement, in which he was resolved to play a leading part.

In 1868 he entered the university as an external student and absorbed himself in the study of the revolutionary tradition emanating from the Babouvist school. He became a member of Z. K. Ralli's group which was motivated by Buonarrotism. Here he made first contact with Tkachev and joined a co-ordinating committee, which set its aim at the organization of a clandestine all-Russian students' movement to overthrow Tsarism. He co-operated with Tkachev to produce his first written *Programme of Revolutionary Action*. They expressed a common appreciation of the society they were attacking, and the means by which it could be destroyed. The revolution was 'a law of history' but it was first necessary to unite and organize oppositional power to make that revolution possible. A large group of 'revolutionary prototypes' would form the vanguard of attack after the masses had been indoctrinated with a revolutionary *élan*. A time schedule was prepared. The formation of a central caucus based on Moscow and St Petersburg was to be finalized by 1st May 1869. Agitation and propaganda would thenceforth be disseminated throughout provincial towns, and amongst the peasantry during autumn and winter. 19th February 1870, the ninth anniversary of the edict for peasant emancipation, was the date set for the outbreak of universal revolution.

The Programme proposed that the Russian organization would also link up with its European counterparts. With this in mind, he managed to slip through a police net, and on 4th March 1869, using a false passport, crossed the frontier to make his way to the Mecca of revolutionary exiles – Switzerland. At Geneva he hastened to meet up with Bakunin, then at the height of his prestige. Hence follows a bizarre tale, perhaps the greatest tragicomedy in the whole of Russian revolutionary history. To enhance his own stature Nechaev informed Bakunin that he had just escaped from the Peter–Paul fortress, where he had been imprisoned as a leader of an all-Russian student movement. He had come as delegate of its powerful central committee which was planning a full-scale insurrection from its headquarters in St Petersburg. Bakunin, the master of bluff when it came to inventing imaginary revolutionary societies which he was supposed to command, was completely taken in by the cool young fanatic. So was Ogarev. The latter, convinced that Nechaev was spokesman for a tremendous new student upsurge, in two appeals[1] called on them to strike or leave the universities. Bakunin took up the same theme in his call: 'A few words to our young brothers in Russia' issued from Geneva (1st April 1869). Nechaev had used Bakunin's own weapons against him. His charm and passionate commitment to the Russian cause penetrated to the heart of Bakunin's sentimentalism; and Ogarev, already degenerating into alcoholic stupor, was an easy prey to both. Only Herzen retained a healthy scepticism. Later on meeting the young 'hero' he quickly saw through the act. But Ogarev, urgently spurred on by Bakunin, published a poem on Nechaev, which, when distributed throughout Russia, helped to exaggerate the importance of the young confidence trickster.

---

[1] 'Oh, Russian students the police is beating you', *Appeal to Russian students* (April 1869).

K

Bakunin, roused to a new frenzy by the 'Boy', collaborated with him to produce a spurt of pamphlets and proclamations which were smuggled into Russia. The result was two remarkable documents. One, issued on 12th May 1869, and handed to Nechaev by Bakunin, declared 'The bearer of this is one of the accredited representatives of the Russian section of the World Revolutionary Alliance No. 2771'. It was sealed with the title 'European Revolutionary Alliance, Central Committee', and signed 'Michael Bakunin'. It was a spontaneous piece of mutual make-believe to heighten the impression that a (non-existent) Russian organization was now irrevocably linked to a (equally non-existent) European Revolutionary movement. Who was deceiving whom? The second document was certainly more real and important, not only for the insight it gives us into the Nihilist mentality with its single-minded dedication to Revolution *per se*, but for the strategy and tactics to be employed in its fulfilment. It was the *Catechism of a Revolutionary* which Nechaev smuggled in on his return to Russia. The stamp of Buonarrotism is there; but it is the 'Conspiration' *in extremis*. The 'revolutionary prototype' is portrayed with a terrifying familiarity.

The revolutionary is a man set apart. He has no personal interests, no emotions, no attachments; he has no personal property, not even a name. Everything in him is absorbed by the one exclusive interest, the one thought, one single passion – the Revolution. In his innermost being he has, not only in words but in deeds, broken every bond with the present-day society and with the whole civilized world, including all its laws, customs, conventions and morality. If he continues to live in it, he does so as its implacable enemy for the sole purpose of destroying it. He scorns all doctrines and renounces culture and learning, leaving these to future generations. He knows one science only: the science of destruction, and to master it he now studies mechanics, physics, chemistry and perhaps medicine. For the same purpose he pursues day and night the vital science of human beings, their habits, the parts they like to play, and the interplay of social behaviour in all the strata of this foul world order. He despises public opinion. He despises and hates the prevailing moral code in all its manifestations. Anything assisting the triumph of the revolution is for him moral, anything hindering it is immoral and criminal. He knows no mercy for tsardom or generally for the whole set-up for society, and he expects no mercy for himself. Between them and him there is an unceasing and relentless war to the death, open or underground and he must steel himself to withstand torture. Stern to himself he must also be hard towards others. All the gentle and enfeebling sentiments of kinship, love, gratitude and even honour must be suppressed in him by the single cold passion for revolution. For him there can be only one delight, one reward, one satisfaction – the success of the Revolution. In the unflinching pursuit of merciless destruction he must be prepared to perish himself or to destroy with his own hands everything standing in the path of the revolution. The true revolutionary is by his very nature immune from romanticism, exaltation, rapture. Even personal hatred or revenge are forbidden. Revolutionary fervour has become an everyday habit with him, but it must always be combined with cold calculation. At all times and everywhere he must do what the interest of the revolution demands, irrespective of his own personal inclinations.

A strict revolutionary hierarchy must be maintained. The controlling body would consist of the 'true' revolutionaries, who must use their auxiliaries of the second and third rank as so much expendable material to be consumed by the cause. The hated society consists of six groups which must be attacked or used and discarded according to expediency. The top-layer – the powerful and intelligent – must be assassinated. The second group – the powerful and unintelligent – should be allowed to continue because their stupid reactionary behaviour sustains the revolutionary 'motif'. The third – those of high rank but devoid of both intelligence and competence – must be used as pawns. They are easily blackmailed. 'We must get hold of their dirty secrets and so make them our slaves.' The fourth – the opportunistic politicians and 'progressives' – must be undermined from within. This could be devised by planting agents who would play on compromising them to such an extent that they would be forced to act with the revolutionaries in destroying society. The fifth – the armchair revolutionaries, those who merely talked and scribbled – must be manœuvred into revolutionary action, when the weaklings amongst them will be destroyed. The final group was that of women, who could be of inestimable value provided that their revolutionary comprehension was proven in 'deed and without rhetoric'.

The insurrection aimed at is defined in Bakuninist terms. Statism of any kind is rejected. 'The only revolution that can save the people is one that destroys every established object root and branch, that annihilates all State traditions, orders and classes in Russia.' The *élite* were instructed to draw close to those elements who were natural revolutionaries. They were the outlaws who 'ever since the foundation of the State of Moscow have never given up protesting, not just in words but in deeds, against anything directly or indirectly tied to the State; against the nobility, the bureaucracy, the priests, against the world of guilds and against the *kulaks*. We must ally ourselves with the doughty world of brigands, who in Russia are the only real revolutionaries.'

Nechaev proceeded to live out in practice his own portrayal of 'a revolutionary prototype'. Cash was needed and there was legitimate loot around for the wary. He smelt out a potential source in the legacy of a landowner called Bakhmetiev. He had been a wealthy crank, who, converted to some vague form of egalitarianism, sailed off to a Pacific island to form a Communist colony and disappeared. During his journey out he had stopped off at London and deposited £800 in the joint hands of Herzen and Ogarev to be used for propaganda within Russia. The old partners, imbued with that *bourgeois* morality so despised by both Nechaev and Bakunin, had retained the capital sum intact whilst only using the interest. Bakunin and his 'Boy' saw in this a means of financing their own joint enterprises. They pestered the sick Ogarev, who in turn begged Herzen to release the money. Herzen, also now tired and old, reluctantly gave in. Half of the cash was handed over to Bakunin who in turn passed over a diminished sum to Nechaev.

Nechaev could now return to Russia with an enhanced reputation. Was he not Russian representative for the European Revolutionary Alliance, signed up by the master revolutionary himself? He was also joint author with Bakunin of pamphlets and tracts which he carried with him. Above all he had a supply of ready cash. In August 1869 he left Geneva, made his way back to Russia through the Balkans, and with the aid of some young Bulgarian Bakuninists crossed the Russian frontier without incident. He centred his headquarters in Moscow, where he assembled a small group of off-beat youths, who were to constitute the hierarchical caucus. Amongst them was Peter Uspensky, the fallen son of a nobleman, a university drop-out, who had set up a conspiratorial centre in Cherkesov's bookshop, from which he controlled a number of revolutionary cells. Together with Nechaev he founded *Narodnaya Rasprava*, and the group quickly penetrated into the most active sectors of the University, particularly the School of Agriculture. Here they were joined by Nikolay Dolgov, who began a long and turbulent revolutionary career at this time, and who brought into the organization a number of new recruits amongst whom was the ill-fated Ivan Ivanovich Ivanov.

The organization began to assume the old Buonarrotist concept of groups of five, each group apparently divorced from the rest to prevent police infiltration. All had to undertake propaganda work in their immediate *milieu*, and for this purpose a supply of clothing was distributed, from officials' uniforms to peasants' smocks. All owed absolute submission to Nechaev, who was the Supreme Commander. It was the duty of the subordinates to carry out any order of his, however terrible, without question. Members were enjoined to spy on each other in order to root out deviationists. Nechaev laid down that all conspiratorial activity would be geared to the aim of instigating a mass insurrection on 19th February 1870. True to the *Catechism* Nechaev conceived individuals as so much capital expenditure to be employed in the service of the Revolution. Those who dared to hinder its course would be ruthlessly eliminated. It was this conjecture, applied to Ivanov, which gave rise to an appalling murder.

Ivanov, who belonged to a summit group of the organization, refused to submit to the dictates of Nechaev. Things came to a head when Ivanov opposed the distribution of literature in the students' canteen, on the basis that if this were discovered the police would shut down the kitchen and poor students would be deprived of their cheap meals. His error was in making his views known to other members of the organization. Nechaev was resolved to make this a test case in order to consolidate his authority and to bind the hierarchy irrevocably to his person by involving them as accomplices in murder. On 21st November 1869, Ivanov was instructed to meet his comrades at a cave in a secluded part of Petrovsk park in order to help dig up a printing machine hidden there at the time of the Karakazov incident. There he was set upon by Nechaev and three others and almost strangled. The *coup de grâce* was delivered by Nechaev himself, who shot him in the back of the neck. The body was weighted with bricks and dumped in the nearest pond.[1] Four days later, whilst Nechaev was away in St Petersburg, the corpse was discovered. The police soon gleaned that this was a political murder, in which the *Narodnaya Rasprava* was involved, and widespread searches and arrests of suspects were made. All evidence pointed to Nechaev as instigator of the crime.

Nechaev was surprised at the hue and cry which followed; and was well informed that the Third Department was out to get him. He learned that members of his organization were either rounded up or under constant surveillance. He disappeared. The police built up a picture of the elusive leader, which assumed exaggerated proportions. This was fostered by Nechaev himself, who had already created his own myth. During the three intensive months in Russia he had adopted various disguises and pseudonyms within his own organization which enabled him to fabricate stories of the superhuman courage and genius of the unknown chief. All forces were mobilized to seize him – quickly. For unless he was brought to bay, the police reasoned, the organization would continue to have cohesive direction.

Russian agents abroad were alerted and an army of spies went into action. Bismarck even instructed the Prussian police to join in the hunt. There was no sign of Nechaev. But he was

[1] This crime was the subject of Dostoevsky's novel, *The Devils.*

around. In early January 1870 he reappeared in Geneva. Ogarev informed Bakunin, then living in Locarno, that his protégé had returned. Bakunin, in a letter dated 12th January 1870, urged his 'Boy' to join him in his backwater where he would be safe. Nechaev accepted the offer. The big bluff continued; however, this time Nechaev faced the old anarchist, no longer as an apprentice, but as a co-partner and revolutionary with an equally international reputation. False scents and trails were laid to bamboozle the police. A letter appeared in Bakunin's periodical *Progress*, purporting to have come from Nechaev inside Russia, in which he declared that, whilst under arrest on the way to Siberia he had been rescued by the organization and was now under cover. In the same issue Bakunin questioned the existence of Nechaev, accusing the Tsarist government of using him as a blind for other nefarious activities. Meanwhile, amongst the *emigrés*, Nechaev continued to boost the myth of a still active revolutionary committee and organization operating inside Russia. Money was needed. Bakunin was commissioned to translate Marx's *Capital* into Russian and received an advance of 300 roubles. He had hardly begun when Nechaev pressed him to concentrate his time and energies on the Russian movement where the revolution could break out at any moment. Bakunin pleaded that he was being harassed by his publisher. Nechaev took care of that. The publisher received a threatening letter from 'People's Retribution' warning him to stop pressurizing Bakunin as he was committed to more important activities. Bakunin knew nothing about it. But two years later Marx used the letter at the Hague Congress to malign Bakunin and obtain his expulsion from the First International.

There was an alternative source of funds. The remaining half of the Bakhmetiev legacy was now controlled by Ogarev, who instructed the deceased Herzen's children to bring the money to Geneva, where, in their presence it was received by Nechaev on behalf of the Russian Committee. Nechaev was then able to continue his universal mission of propagandizing himself and his 'organization'. A pamphlet, *The People's Retribution No. 2*, was issued to reaffirm the existence of the Committee, as well as informing its readers that from a telegram sent by the Governor of Perm to the secret police it was confirmed that Nechaev had died on his way to the Nerchinsk mines. It lauded the character of the 'dead' hero, setting him up as an example to be followed by the true revolutionary. He was the first to print the *Communist Manifesto* in Russian, and claimed that its precepts had been adopted by the organization. In succeeding publications he outlined his view on the egalitarian *communauté*, in which the Babouvist components are self-evident.

All private property was to be expropriated and transferred to public ownership. Communal dwelling places were to be installed, where all shared feeding and sleeping accommodation. The Committee would impose Trade Unions, and membership was compulsory for workers in all concerns. Those who refused to join would starve. 'Such people will remain without means of existence and left with only two alternatives – to work or die.' Union officials would evaluate production and send reports to a central organization which, in turn, would analyse supply and demand and impose overall direction on the economy. Shifts of emphasis in the various factors of production would be employed and control would be such that it would effect the allocation of the individual's work and consumption. State education only was free to all children, who must follow a balanced academic and practical curriculum. Like Babeuf, Nechaev envisaged his Committee as an all-powerful body regulating the citizenry from the cradle to the grave.

True to himself he proceeded to play out the rôle he prescribed. He soon got the measure of the old crew of *emigrés* which included a periphery group of Marxists led by N. I. Utin. Here he suffered his first setback. They refused to surrender control of their paper *The People's Cause* to Nechaev. Utin rejected his claim to be *bona fide* representative of the Russian cause. Nechaev's rejoinder was that they were '*bourgeois* who protected ownership instead of promoting the revolution'. He turned and dealt with the less resilient section.

Switzerland was becoming too hot for him; he was branded for a civil crime which could mean forced extradition. Tsarist agents and Swiss police were closing in and 19th February 1870 had come and gone. It was time to get out. He had to secure himself a guaranteed *entrée* elsewhere. Bakunin could be used for that. He and other members of his circle discovered that compromising documents had been filched and evidence pointed to Nechaev as the thief. He disdained to deny it. Since Bakunin refused to recognize his absolute authority, the *Catechism*'s principle of 'he who is not with us is against us' had to be applied to him. So Nechaev departed for London with the the necessary letters of introduction.

Nechaev's chameleon-like qualities were no better demonstrated than when put to the test in England. Bakunin's warning letter to his friends seemed to have fallen on stony ground. Yet it is remarkable both for its appraisal of the character of Nechaev, and the dangers accruing to a movement which places power into the hands of the Nechaevist. The analogy bites deep when reckoned against subsequent experience during and after the culmination of the Russian revolutionary movement.[1]

> It is . . . true that Nechaev is one of the most active and energetic men I have ever met. As soon as it is a question of what he calls 'the cause', he knows no doubts, no fears, and is just as pitiless to himself as to others. . . . The revolutionary organization having been destroyed in Russia, he is now trying to form one abroad. . . . He is convinced that in order to create an active and invulnerable organization, he must pursue a Machiavellian policy and employ Jesuitical methods: violence for the body and deceit for the mind.
>
> As soon as he penetrates into your circle, what will he do? At first he comes with a pack of lies in order to win your sympathy and trust. But that will not satisfy him. The divided sympathy of men, who give the revolution only part of their activity and still maintain other human interests such as love, friendship, family or social obligations, is not sufficient for him. In the name of 'the cause' he will, without your realizing it gain power over your whole personality. When you are out, he will open your drawers

[1] Y. Steklov, *M. A. Bakunin*, Vol. III, p. 542.

and boxes and read your letters; if he finds anything that could embarrass you or your friends, he will steal it and hide it in order to use it later against you and your friends, and when we all together unmasked him, he was bold enough to reply; 'Yes, that is our system. We consider all people who are not completely at one with us as our enemies and are obliged to deceive and decry them. . . . 'All personal connections, all feelings of friendship, all ties of a private nature are for him an evil that must be destroyed, because they are a force outside the control of the conspiratorial organization and lessen its hold upon you. . . .

At the same time Nechaev is a force, because of his enormous energy. I parted company with him with regret, because our task demands a lot of energy and one rarely meets a man who possesses so much of it. . . . His last idea was to organize a band of thieves and robbers in Switzerland in order to get money for revolutionary purposes. I saved him by forcing him to leave the country. He would only have brought ruin upon himself and us.

Bakunin points out that only the in-group is bound by any 'normal' morality.

Truth, mutual trust, real solidarity exists only among a dozen people who make up the *sancta sanctorum* of the society. All the rest serve as a blind, soulless weapon in the hands of these dozen men who have reached an agreement among themselves. It is allowed, indeed it is even a duty to cheat them, to compromise them, and in cases of necessity to have them killed.

But Nechaev survived, indeed flourished, during his short stay in London. His new journal '*The Community*' was provided with sufficient local funds to continue his propaganda. In his first issue he supplied an appropriate rejoinder to Bakunin, now interred amongst a generation of revolutionary 'has-beens'. The liberal radicalism of the great talkers of the Herzen set was dismissed as a hot-house flower 'which, splendidly blossoming on the artificial temperature of a secure living standard, quickly withered away at the first touch of the cold air of reality'. They were no longer of relevance. His own generation, 'the proletarians of thought', had taken command of the revolution. Justifiably so, since they alone knew suffering and oppression at first hand. 'Before our eyes, our brothers died of hunger; our ears were full of the crack of the whip with which our fathers were beaten, and of the screams of our sisters sold by their mothers for a piece of bread. The flame of revolt runs in our blood.' Bakunin and his *petit-bourgeois* Swiss artisans are treated with derision: 'They are querulous windbags and not fighters for the cause of the people. . . . The life of a suffering worker they know only from hearsay. . . . Diamond cutters, watchmakers, draughtsmen, and other providers of luxuries for the over-fed and idle beneficiaries of the present social order, they have no incentive to be real fighters. They are not compelled by the driving power of necessity to put an end to the present intolerable situation.' On this recognition, he informs Bakunin that 'there can be no more clashes between us, as I am convinced that you will never again appear as an active force in the Russian revolution!'

Yet Nechaev still had the audacity to press his claim in the second issue for the residual interest on the Bakhmetiev fund estimated at 1,410 francs 50 centimes. There were no more pickings from that quarter, but Nechaev managed to survive for two years of travelling to and fro, particularly during the Franco-Prussian war. No evidence has come to light as to whether he was involved in the Paris Commune. He could well have been, and the Russian historian B. Nikolaevsky[1] implies that it was during a sojourn in Paris that he planted the idea of Russian Jacobinism amongst fellow *emigrés* in Paris who included both Tursky and Tkachev.

The Russian government, frustrated in its attempt to capture the elusive leader, decided to stage the first open public trial of the rank and file. This was in accord with European counter-revolutionary policies following the recent Paris Commune. They also held a trump card. The Third Department had decoded the *Catechism*. It would reveal to both liberals and revolutionaries the criminal inhumanity of the Nechaevist creed. The trial opened in St Petersburg on 1st July 1871 with

---

[1] B. Nikolaevsky, 'In memory of the last Jacobin, G. M. Tursky', *Katorga i ssylka* (1926), No. 11.

79 young people indicted on a charge of conspiracy to over-throw the government. The overall result was a greater indict-ment of the accusers than the accused. Nechaevism was exposed, but brilliant defence counsel deftly separated the opposing motivations of leader and led within the 'conspiracy'. The public was convinced that not only were the rank and file innocent dupes, but their end cause was both moral and just. For the youths' conscious energies had been directed towards winning students' rights to free unions and discussion, to collect mutual aid funds and an end to the degradation of police supervision. As an experiment the trial proved both a farce and a danger to the autocracy. Of the 79 only the four men involved in the murder received heavy sentences – seven to fourteen years hard labour in Siberia. The rest were treated mildly. A police agent, in his report, saw clearly that new revolutionary conspiracies could well be sparked off by such 'open' trials since Nechaev's ideas were now widely dis-seminated. Although reasonable people would reject his evil methods, unfortunately 'reasonable circles form a passive mass, while revolutions have always been made by a minority which seizes power by way of systematic coercion!'

In one major respect police measures had proved fruitful. Nechaev had been publicly exposed as an imposter and a killer. Bakunin, his pride wounded by his own further humiliation, told Ogarev, 'We have made fine fools of ourselves by being taken in by Nechaev's lies! How Herzen would have laughed at us, were he still alive. . . .' In the short term revelations at the trial besmirched the name of Nechaev. Socialist revolutionary leaders would reject him for nearly a decade. Abroad he roused both the pity and contempt of the *emigrés*; pity because they were at least safe from extradition. He was not. Diminishing means of subsistence forced Nechaev to return to Switzerland, in spite of a magnanimous warning from Bakunin that the place was swarming with Russian agents.

The last act was played out in high melodrama. After a short stay in a previous hide-out in La Chaux-de-Fonds, Nechaev returned to Zurich in August 1872, where he had left, as security for unpaid rent, a case containing documents stolen from the Bakuninists. They could be used for blackmail. Here he was located by a so-called Secretary of a Slavonic Section, an ex-Polish insurrectionist Adolf Stempkowski, who was really a Tsarist spy. Perceiving that Nechaev was destitute, he offered him the possibility of aid by certain fellow *emigrés*, who would meet him in a beer house at Hottingen on the edge of the city. Nechaev came, and was promptly seized by Swiss police. In spite of an abortive attempt by young Russians to free him, he was, after a quick hearing, despatched to the Bavarian frontier, where he was handed over to Russian agents.

The government was resolved that it would not repeat the same mistake twice. His indictment would be based only on the civil charge of murder. The trial would be quick, to last one day, so that publicity was kept down to a minimum. On 8th January 1873 the hearing was held in Moscow and recognized as being farcical. Again the proceedings boomeranged against the authorities. Determined to ignore the political issue, it was deliberately thrust upon them by the defendant. The picture emerged of a brave self-willed martyr, hurling defiance at both judge and prosecutor. 'It is degrading for me to reply . . .! I have ceased to be a slave of your despot! I have told the investigator in St Petersburg that you can take my life but I shall keep my honour!' The time-lag between the trial of the Nechaevists and their leader was long enough to modify general opinion. Questions were being asked: Why had the government been afraid to reopen the political issue? Why had the accused acted fearlessly against his accusers? It was as though he was convinced of his deliverance. Was there a conspiracy yet in existence whose members were still actively involved in carrying through the Nechaevist programme? Individual reappraisals turned into a universal reassessment of the affair; and it gained momentum when a decree of the same year recalled thousands of young students home from overseas.

In the end the legend was self-created. At the parade of 'civil execution' he again publicly fulminated against the autocracy. Contemptuously spurning the services of a priest he cried,

'Before three years are over their heads will be hacked off on this very spot by the first Russian guillotine. Down with the Tsar!' The Tsar responded accordingly: no Siberia for Nechaev. There must be no possibility of escape. He underlined the order that 'the more prudent course is to keep him *for ever* in prison'. Number one enemy of the State disappeared into cell number five of the Alexeyevsky dungeon in the St Peter–Paul fortress. Though confined in an impenetrable gloom, Nechaev lost none of his relentless ferocity against the authorities. Like Blanqui, then undergoing his final long incarceration, his indomitable will persisted against the monotony and degradation. Perhaps his last years were sustained by a primitive nobility. At first he asked for and received everything. He knew why. The government was convinced that his clandestine organization remained unimpaired. They would in turn attempt to buy him or wear him down until he talked. The tragicomedy was enacted with the prisoner's obstinate silence convincing his gaolers that the conspiracy was still in existence. For neither bribe nor torture could break him. Nechaev exercised his will over his guards, who first listened and then were beguiled by this fascinating captive who spoke their language and dared to express openly the inner longings of the oppressed. In 1875 a general was sent to his cell to order the prisoner to confess. Nechaev, in a frenzied rage, struck him. But the authorities could do nothing as it would expose a senior officer to ridicule if the truth leaked out. Externally the Nechaev affair appeared to be forgotten. The main character seemed to have vanished from the face of the earth. It was dramatically reopened when a letter conclusively proved to have been written by him appeared at the headquarters of *Narodnaya Volya*, verifying that he was still alive and actively committed. Nechaev had managed to make contact through the guards with a new prisoner, Stepan Shirayev, who was a leading terrorist. When faced with the problem of liberating him, he stuck courageously to the letter of his own *Catechism*. He was of lesser importance to the main task in hand. They were to go ahead and concentrate their energy on killing the Tsar. On 1st March 1881 the assassination was carried out. The subsequent reaction bore heavily on the prisoner. The neighbouring cells were soon filled with the condemned leaders of the terrorist organization. To keep them alive was an unnecessary expenditure. Rations were cut to starvation level and Nechaev was included with the rest. After eighteen months of incredible suffering he succumbed to the effects of dropsy and scurvy on 21st November 1882.

Nechaevism did not die with its founder. Though Nechaev had been ostracized for his ruthless will in the maintenance of the revolutionary objective, it was precisely this quality that provided the basis for the terrorist groups born out of the second 'go to the people' movement of the 1870's. The Ukase of 1873, which ordered all Russians to leave Zurich under threat of outlawry, added to the ferment inside. In liberal Switzerland young *emigrés* and students completed their education in revolution. Here the influences of Bakunin, Lavrov, the Commune and the International met and blended to sustain heterogeneous groups inflamed with a quasi-religious fervour. They returned as missionaries bringing the socialist revelation to the Russian peasantry. Young men and women (for women's claim to equality provided the movement with its most dedicated and self-sacrificing elements!) went forth to labour with the masses in factories, fields and workshops. The disease spread to the older folk. Doctors, officials, judges were not the least ardent in the crusade. They spoke openly and fearlessly, as much to test their own moral courage as to propound the new message. 'Rigorism was elevated into a dogma. For several years indeed even absolute asceticism was maintained . . . among the youth of both sexes.'[1] Informers – voluntary and professional – moved in easily for the kill. After the 'mad summer' of 1874 Count Pahlen, Minister of Justice, proclaimed that 770 people had been seized and tried, of whom 158 were women. He expressed special concern about the aid rendered to the Populists by reputable officials and landlords. Arrests and imprisonment were of no avail. The movement was a tidal wave that swept relentlessly towards the borders. After the initial setback, mass

[1] 'Underground Russia', *Stepniak*, p. 30.

indoctrination was rejected. It was replaced by a system of 'colonization' (*poselenia*) in which underground groups were concentrated in particular areas or districts. This was the first step back to the conspiratorial activism of Nechaev.

The government provided a further impetus when they again made recourse to public trials (1877–8): first the great trial of the 50 of the Society of Moscow, followed by the trial of the 193. The authorities had learned nothing and forgotten nothing. Their intentions were twofold: to frighten sections of the *bourgeoisie* and the intelligentsia with the 'red peril' so as to realign them with the monarchy; and to punish the subversives severely to discourage the rest. Both failed. The calm bearing and noble altruism of the accused won universal sympathy. The timing of the trial was wrong. It coincided with the peak of opposition against the government over their conduct in the Russo-Turkish war. Thus instead of alienating the intelligentsia from the revolutionists it drew them closer together. But the Christian-like martyr was finished. The new terrorist of the *Narodnaya Volya* bore greater resemblance to the Nechaevist than to his saintly predecessor. The Movement was again redirected along the lines of a 'Revolution *sui generis*, carried on, however, not by the mass of the people or those feeling the need of it, but by a kind of delegation, acting on behalf of the mass of the people'.[1] The professional revolutionary was back in business. Their groups remained small and exclusive according to the Machiavellian dictum that 'the many ruin them'. Secret operations were very expensive. Continual changes of disguise, lodgings (from which a quick exit was vital and which meant abandoned furniture etc.), the cost of raw materials for explosives, and transport needs to facilitate rapid movement, meant money. The larger the organization, the greater the expense, and the easier its penetration by government agents. That the 'few were not enough' balanced itself out by blood letting – that is through arrests and executions as the organization over-extended itself. In the short term *Narodnaya Volya* paid off. It culminated in a successful regicide. But the system survived it. For the

[1] 'Underground Russia', *Stepniak*, p. 264.

terrorist it was a process of self-immolation on the altars of the autocracy. A more sophisticated approach was required; that is an ideological basis for action as well as a reappraisal of strategy and tactics derived from historical experience. Nechaev had provided the new revolutionary prototype. But he could never reconcile the irreconcilables – his practical élitism and theoretical libertarianism. His old comrade, Peter Tkachev, would point the way. It was he who would fuse and solidify into one cohesive whole the old Russian Blanquist tradition with its new Marxist formula and transmute them into the most challenging political force that confronted the autocracy.

L

CHAPTER 8

Tkachev

In the 1920's a great debate took place among Soviet historiographers to evaluate the influence of nineteenth-century revolutionaries on the foundation of Bolshevism. Three major characters emerged in the general debate as bearing genuine Communist potential. They were Nechaev, Zaichnevsky and Tkachev.

In his *The controversies over Nechaev* Aleksander Gambarov declared Nechaev 'one of the earliest forerunners of the great upheaval which was finally brought to conclusion . . . in October 1917', and extolled his 'undoubtedly brilliant anticipation of the character and content of the contemporary Communist movement'. To enhance his thesis he attempted to justify the Ivanov affair and the other Nechaevist aberrations, by employing arguments which could not be corroborated by existent evidence. B. P. Koz'min in a reasonably objective analysis considerably modified the pronouncements of Gambarov and other eulogists. In *History and Fantasy*[1] he first looks backwards and accords due homage to Nechaev when this subject is reviewed against his contemporaries and successors:

> Nechaev's invincible energy, his hatred of any kind of exploitation, his devotion to the revolutionary cause, the strong influence of his personality on his associates, his manly behaviour in court, his many years of suffering in the Peter–Paul fortress, the tenacity with which he sought under the most unfavourable circumstances to secure his liberation, an attempt which was unsuccessful for reasons beyond his control – all this guarantees to Nechaev one of the most prominent places in the gallery of Russian revolutionaries and makes it unnecessary to gloss over the shortcomings

[1] *Pechat i Revolyutsiya*, Book 6 (1926), pp. 96–108.

which he undoubtedly had and to attribute falsely to him merits which he actually did not have.

The tone changes. As Stalin's rule tightened it became impolitic to enhance Nechaev's reputation. It was too near the bone for Stalinist comfort. Koz'min then brought emphasis to bear on the less salubrious side of Nechaev's activities; and rejected Gambarov's portrayal on the grounds that it was impossible to disprove that Nechaev did not resort to scandalous methods and that Gambarov's thesis was morally dangerous since it accorded to Nechaevism a normal form of revolutionary activity.[1] It was less easy to reject those features of Jacobinistic Blanquism which related to the organization and tactics assumed by Lenin. In this context the significance of Tkachev was irrefutable. Yet here too the debate was discontinued and a conspiracy of silence ensued.

Like Blanqui, Tkachev has, until recently, been the neglected figure in the gallery of revolutionists. Yet he emerges as the connecting link in the Franco-Russian chain of conspiratorial élitism which stretched from Babeuf to Lenin.

Peter Nikitich Tkachev was born in 1844, the son of a petty nobleman in the small town of Vilikye Luki. After the premature death of his father he was despatched to boarding school in the capital, where he was soon caught up in the storm of political ideas that raged in St Petersburg at the time. The journal *Sovremennik* introduced him to radical ideas, and in 1861, on entering the university, his involvement in student propaganda and demonstrations led to his first imprisonment, from October to December, in the Kronstadt fortress. He had already adopted political aims and direction in favour of the Jacobin view as distinct from the current theories of the Constitutionalists and intellectual Populists. His political development thenceforth must be measured against the background period of fermentation engendered by the great emancipation edict of 1861. Conspiratorial action and leadership in

---

[1] Collection ed. by B. I. Gorev and B. P. Koz'min, *All-Union Society of Political Prisoners and Exiles* (Moscow, 1932), pp. 168–226.

student riots brought him under the surveillance of the Third Department.

In 1862, although recently released from gaol, he once more threw himself into revolutionary activity. In a pamphlet, *What We Want*, he set out an egalitarian creed appealing to the peasantry for the 'need for speedy revolution'. Action, not words, was the maxim. The police responded. Tkachev, recognized as the author and a source of disaffection, was seized, tried, and imprisoned for three years. Released before the sentence had expired, and undeterred by the consequences, he returned to underground conspiracy. In 1866 the student Karakazov made an abortive attempt on the life of Alexander II. This provided the police with another opportunity to round up all the enemies of the state. Tkachev was hauled in for questioning; but there was no evidence to connect him with the would-be assassin. It was during this period that he emerged as a talented writer on diverse subjects – from economics to contemporary literature – but with a common underlying theme of political analysis and criticism, introduced by indirect or analogous propositions as a safeguard against police censorship. In the Nihilistic journals *Russo Slovo* and *Delo* he worked out his political ideology.

In a variety of articles, arguments were mustered and directed towards some contemporary political objective. In criticizing positivism, Tkachev suggested that there could be no comparison between nature and society since 'the laws of organic and inorganic development are eternally uniform and cannot be modified or avoided – on the contrary, the laws which govern society are always the product of society itself, i.e. the results of human will and human calculations. They are born and die with society.' In an essay entitled 'Science in Poetry and Poetry in Science', he attacked Social Darwinism on the grounds that it offered a justification rather than a criticism of events. Natural and historical selection worked in reverse since society's final aim was the abolition of the struggle for existence. Mankind, on the contrary, was drawn to combine, and therefore to offset natural selection. By rationalizing in these terms he drew up a 'formula for progress' which he conceived as a realistic critical appraisal based on an economic interpretation of history. This drew him to Marxism. By 1865 he had already discovered Marx, and was indeed the first Russian, before Plekhanov, to accept Marxist teaching on economic materialism. In a commentary in 1864 his view of Dankwardt's reforms in the methodology of civil law reflected the basic tenet of Marxism.

> He [Dankwardt] was the first to show, or, rather point out the close link between the economic and juridical sphere of social life; he has shown that civil law is only a determined reflex of a people's economic life.

This is reinforced the next year when he mentions Marx directly for the first time.

> It [economic materialism] has been transplanted into our press – like everything else worthwhile in it – from the culture of western Europe. As early as 1859 the well-known German exile Karl Marx has clearly and exactly expressed it. . . . The idea has now become common to all thinking and honest men, and no intelligent man can find any serious objection to it.

The disciple is won over completely by 1869 in an article in *Delo*:

> I maintain that all events in the intellectual and spiritual world correspond in the last analysis to events in the economic world and to the 'economic structure' of society, to use the expression adopted by Marx. The development and tendencies of economic principles condition the development and tendencies of political and social relations, and even leave their mark on the intellectual processes of society, on its moral ideas and its political and social conceptions.

His Marxist interpretation was mature enough before his days of exile to regard materialism as a 'spur that inspired direct practical action' towards the ultimate end – egalitarianism, which is the fulfilment of the whole historic process.

But his egalitarianism transcended mere economic considerations. It was all-embracing. Tkachev's Communist man was ultimately to achieve that standard level of physical organic equality akin to the 'uniformity in nature' posited by Mably. His ideal was the true reality, which he regarded as being quite attainable since it was the rational view put into practice. He applied these principles to economic problems rejecting all *bourgeois* hypotheses emanating from the free workings of supply and demand.

> The problem will be solved . . . when everyone is uncondition-ally equal, when there is no difference between anyone either from the intellectual, moral or physical point of view. Then they will have an exactly equal share in the returns of production, and any special valuation of their work will become utterly super-fluous.

This rendered the idea of 'to each according to his labour or to his needs' useless, for this could only be feasible in an attempt to marry together the two antithetical principles of socialism and capitalism, an attempt that was bound to fail. Only people who were equal both physically and intellectually could bring about absolute parity of distribution. Only under socialism which defers to common educational systems and living con-ditions, could this be possible.

Who were the raw material for revolutions? What were the tactics and strategy to be employed? In 1867 he suggested in *German Idealists and Philistines* that the peasants were the most authentic force since 'they were unaffected with the romantic dream of the knights, nor the nebulous dreams of the scholas-tics. They saw life as it really was.' His arguments matured further in his translation of Ernest Becker's *The Problem of the Workers in its Contemporary Significance and the Means to Solve it* (1869). The Nechaevist infection was potent and it directed him more firmly along the road taken by the Jacobin, Zaich-nevsky. Here his mode of using analogous themes to solve current political problems is most striking. He admitted that, although the inert mass of peasants was in constant destitution, he had little faith in their starting an egalitarian revolution when the peasantry's '*forma metitis* and . . . way of life is closer to the primitives'. He posed the insoluble dilemma facing both workers and peasants: without political control they could not

protect their material interests but were unable to gain that
control while still in a position of economic oppression.

Hence peaceful change for them was a chimera. The only way
out was violent revolution – a revolution which, in normal
Marxist terms, would be out of context, since it would tend to
leapfrog the *bourgeois* state of development. Clearly this conception is of historical importance in an analysis of the roots of
Leninism; for Tkachev is emphatic in this declaration:

> Under the normal order of things political control belongs to
> those classes who dominate the economic sphere . . . but the
> normal order can be temporarily interrupted . . . and then the
> vicious circle can be broken. It is absurd to expect a natural
> transition from the old régime to the new one, because the two
> are based on diametrically opposed principles. Everybody ought
> to know that this transition requires a certain jump and every-
> body must prepare for it.

Pushed forward in time, this general argument could well be
employed to justify the Bolshevik seizure of power. For by
1869 Tkachev had already clarified his views on the means of
effecting a successful revolution. The peasants could achieve it,
provided certain safeguards were met. Since they could not
organize themselves, a select few, a conspiratorial *corps d'élite*
of professional revolutionaries, would do this for them; for they
alone could bring aim and direction to the enterprise. Thus
Tkachev rejected Lavrov's and Bakunin's concept of popular
education, that is, preparation through learning, which would
mean delay or reliance on the 'popular genius' to effect automatic action when the time was ripe.

Tkachev insisted that the revolutionary vanguard was the
master key to any revolutionary situation. Tkachev had assessed,
as early as 1864, 'the insuperable difficulties which face us when
we make any personal attempt to draw nearer to the people
and to make clear to ourselves . . . what are their requirements
and wishes'. He attempted to discover, through a critical study
of the economy, how the people's latent force could be activated.
In his calculations there were 50 million peasants and half a
million employed urban workers. Of the latter he deduced that

each received 35 roubles per annum in money value against the gross industrial production, as against 2,200 roubles accruing to each industrialist, that is a percentage comparison of 1·5 per cent to 98·5 per cent. Yet the workers and peasants together paid 22 per cent of national taxes whilst the minority consumed 97 per cent of the national income. The revolutionary potential was there; primarily among the peasantry, since a mature urban proletariat was not yet in existence. The vanguard, therefore, must come from the intelligentsia. They would provide the source of both the *élan* and extremism which successful leadership requires. But he foresaw obstacles in the way of creating such a revolutionary *élite*. There was the current trend of successful writers being 'kept' by leisured parasites who patronized them to enhance their own status in the field of cultural demand. Many were being absorbed in the expanding economy, which was hiving off the intelligentsia into techno-logical and commercial projects. With a stake in the Establish-ment, many of the would-be leaders were thus removed from the social war. On the other hand the uncompromising residue could contribute the most selfless and dedicated partisans to the revolution. For only a minority, a very small minority, would achieve self-fulfilment in the cause. But the enlightened few must not rely on a spontaneous outburst from below. 'Taken as a whole the masses do not and cannot believe in their own strength. They will never on their own initiative begin to fight against the misery that surrounds them.' By 1868 Tkachev had spurned 'the idealization of the uncivilized masses' as 'one of the most widespread and dangerous illusions'. Instead of 'going to the people' as peaceful missionaries it was the duty of the vanguard to spark off and lead an insurrection there and then, in order to direct the workers and peasants along the historical 'jump'. Any idea of a peaceful transition was Utopian nonsense.

Among the café intelligentsia and student societies he expounded his theories and there found a kindred spirit in Nechaev. They co-operated in the issue of *A Programme of Revolutionary Action*.[1] Within the Ralli group he issued his own

[1] See p. 132 above.

manifesto *To Society* ostensibly to publicize student demands. It is certain that he went most of the way with Nechaev's ruthlessness. (Tkachev's sister notes this trait in him when she records that as a young student he once advocated the extermination of all above twenty-five years of age as they were beyond redemption for the making of the new society!) He was arrested in March 1869 long before the Nechaevist 'conspiracy' blew up. Again imprisoned he was finally brought up for trial with the Nechaevists, accused of being the author of *To Society* and sentenced to sixteen months' imprisonment. The secret police were resolved to put him out of the way once and for all by ordering his banishment to Siberia on completion of the sentence; but he managed to obtain permission to return to his birthplace. In December 1872 he succeeded in escaping abroad, with the help of the Populist Chaikovskyist group. No longer suffering the frustrations of imprisonment or stagnation in the provinces, he finally realized his ideas in the freer atmosphere of western Europe. Here he came under the influence of the greatest revolutionary of them all – Auguste Blanqui – and his disciples, the Blanquist exiles who had survived the Paris Commune. Within Russia Tkachev had become an isolated figure in the radical movement. During his period of forced incarceration and exile the Populist creed had overshadowed all else. Discredited by his association with Nechaev (a stigma that was to mark him always!) he also personified an outmoded sect which propagated the conspiratorial idea. Tkachev regained confidence in his credo among the *emigrés* in Zurich and in France. First he co-operated with Lavrov in his journal *Vperyod (Forward)*, but the latter's gradualist theme and opposition to so-called premature *coups* soon led them to part company. A conflict of temperaments was also reflected in their contributory articles. In his first short essay Tkachev brought a wealth of recent experience to bear on his impressive analysis of socio-political conditions inside Russia at that time (1874):

> The *obshchina* is beginning to dissolve; the government is doing everything possible to destroy it once and for all. Among the

peasants a class of *kulaks* is growing up, who buy and hire out the land of the peasant and nobles, a sort of peasant aristocracy. The free movement of landed property from owner to owner becomes less difficult every day; the widening of agrarian credit, and the development of monetary transactions, increase each day. The gentry are compelled willy-nilly to bring in improvements to their agricultural systems. Such progress is usually accompanied by a development of national industry and an increase in town life. And so in Russia at this time all the conditions are there for the formation on one side of a very strong conservative class of peasants, landowners and farmers; and on the other side a *bourgeoisie* of money, trade, industry – capitalists in fact. As these classes come into being and grow stronger, the situation of the people will inevitably grow worse, and the chances for the success of a violent revolution will grow more and more problematical. That is why we cannot wait. . . . Do not let us allow any postponement, any delay. Now, or perhaps, very soon, never.

By halting capitalist maturation Russia could avoid the chaos and suffering of a *laissez-faire* economy experienced by the West and leap straight into socialism. He recognized, on these terms, the dangers of Lassalle's 'bloodless revolution' which he ascribed to all western-working class movements and the dangers inherent in the dogmatic application of Marxism, that is the paradox that as western radicals adopted a rigid acceptance of historical materialism they became less revolutionary. Tkachev expressed openly a conclusion reached later by Lenin, although Lenin never accepted this as a basic criticism of the Marxist creed. Tkachev elucidated his argument in his article 'The Aims of Revolutionary Propaganda in Russia' (April 1874) when he finally split with Lavrov. It subsequently called forth criticism from Engles that no incoherent uprising could ever constitute a social revolution.[1] He condemned Tkachev's naïve speculations which brought forth a sharp response. Tkachev questioned how far such criticism would affect the Germans if it were received from a Chinese or Japanese, who had learned German and had never seen Germany. A pointed thrust was made directly at Engels when he continued the analogy on the lines of the Chinese or Japanese 'who had never

---

[1] Leipzig journal, *Volkstaat*, Nos. 117 and 118 (1874).

read anything published there, and who had conceived the idea of teaching German revolutionaries from the height of their . . . majesty what they ought to do'. He justly asked why Engels pontificated on the Russian movement developing on western rather than on independent lines, as this 'clearly offended the fundamental principles of the programme of the International'; and went on to inform him of the peculiar problems influencing the Russian situation. 'We have no urban proletariat, we have no freedom of the press and no representative assemblies' and therefore there was little prospect of 'disciplined trade unions, conscious of the conditions under which they lived and the means to improve them'. Yet the possibility of a mass insurrection was greater in Russia than in the West. At this stage he offered the argument that the *obshchina*, Russia's unique institution, provided the instinctive Communist ethos. But he had already rejected the potentiality of a revolutionary take-off from here. In the 1870's the *obshchinas* were already undermined. He perceptively conceived of a situation which could result in the downfall of the system.

> Two or three military defeats, simultaneous peasant revolts and an open rising in a town during peacetime will be enough for the government to be completely isolated and alone, deserted by all.

It was the duty of the *élite* to anticipate such a situation, to help it on, and reap the advantages therefrom.[1]

Engels repeated his argument[2] on the basis of applied Marxist doctrine, yet Marx himself adopted a contrary view evolved from a less dogmatic, more fact-finding approach:

> In order that I might be qualified to estimate the economic development in Russia today, I learnt Russian and then for many years studied the official publications and others bearing on the subject. I have arrived at the conclusion: If Russia continues to pursue the path she has followed since 1861 she will lose the finest chance [i.e. of escaping capitalist development] ever offered by history to a nation, in order to undergo all the fatal vicissitudes of the capitalist régime.[3]

---

[1] *Offener Brief an Herrn. Fr. Engels* (Zurich, 1874).

[2] 'Russia and the Socialist Revolution', in *Volkstaat* (25th April 1875).

[3] Marx to Editor of *Otyecestvenniye Zapisky* (December 1877).

In the joint preface to the Russian edition of the *Communist Manifesto* (21st January 1882) disciple and master then seemed in accord in exploring the possibility of the *obshchina* passing immediately into the highest Communist form of landed property and jointly proffered the categorical imperative. 'The only possible answer to this question today is as follows: If the Russian Revolution becomes the signal for the worker's Revolution in the West, so that one supplements the other, then the present form of landownership in Russia may be the starting point of an historical development.'

By 1885 Engels had completely reversed his opinion in favour of the Tkachevist theme. In a letter to the Russian revolutionary Vera Zasulich (23rd April 1885) Engels views with anticipation a Blanquist-led insurrection at any moment:

> What I know or believe about the situation in Russia impels me to the opinion that the Russians are approaching their 1789. The revolution *must* break out there in a given time: it *may* break out there any day. In these circumstances the country is like a charged mine which only needs a fuse to be laid to it. Especially since March 13. [i.e. 1st March 1881 old style and date of assassination of Alexander II.] This is one of the exceptional cases where it is possible for a handful of people to *make* a revolution, i.e. with one small push to cause a whole system, which (to use a metaphor of Plekhanov's) is in more than labile equilibrium, to come crashing down, and thus by one action, in itself insignificant, to release uncontrollable explosive forces. Well now, if ever Blanquism – the phantasy of overturning an entire society through the action of a small conspiracy – had a certain justification for its existence, that is certainly in Petersburg. . . .

Although he believed that such leaders would be swept away in the explosion he ended with a summary of conditions within Russia already confirmed by Tkachev.

> There where the position is so strained, where the revolutionary elements are accumulated to such a degree, where the economic situation of the enormous mass of the people becomes daily more impossible, where every stage of social development is represented, from the primitive commune to modern large-scale industry and high finance, and where all these contradictions are violently held together by an unexampled despotism, a despotism which is be-

coming more and more unbearable to the youth in whom the national worth and intelligence are united – there, when 1789 has once been launched, 1793 will not be long in following.

Lenin would disprove Engels's prognosis that the revolutionary 'flood' would soon 'rob [the *élite*] of their illusions'. And Tkachev would be more than vindicated.

Meanwhile Tkachev had joined forces with his Jacobin co-exiles Kaspar Tursky and Karl Yanitsky to found a new journal (November 1875) *Nabat* (The Tocsin) which appeared sporadically for five years. Although one of the many aspiring reviews of the time, it must be considered now as having major historical importance. For its contributors and agents included the French Blanquists in exile, E. Granger, E. Vaillant, and Eudes of the Commune. It was, therefore, one of the first joint sounding boards of western and eastern Blanquists, wherein their common postulates and experiences first met and fused. Tkachev, with an eye constantly on the Russian scene, brought to bear his own version of action. He posed the two main problems which faced the 'true' revolutionary – the time to strike and the means to be employed.

He drove home his formula repeatedly. The time to do battle was there and then. The revolution must be precipitated 'not in a remote future, not some time, but NOW, at the present juncture'. Constant discontent under Tsarist oppression was the permanent built-in regulator for insurrection. However, it was an illusion to suppose that isolated groups or factions could make and sustain a revolution. It was the prime duty of the *élite* to use their intellectual and spiritual power to 'combine the existing revolutionary elements that would lead to the immediate, inevitable explosion. They did not wait for events to make it propitious; they chose the moment to strike . . .' The conquest of state power would be carried out through 'centralization, severe discipline, speedy decision and unity in action'. It was the activist minority who would force political awareness upon the masses, stimulating them into action by arousing popular passions, which 'destroying and crushing everything in its way and always acting unaccountably and unconsciously' would smash the existing system in an orgy of destruction. The determined *élite*, taking advantage of the chaos they had brought about, would seize the centres of power. The revolutionary energies of the led would be used to tear out the roots of the old society; and the leaders, directing the final operation, could organize rebuilding on the social rubble. Finally, under an umbrella of terrorist power, the *corps d'élite* could re-educate the masses in the principles of socialism. To start with education first, as a means of bringing about an uprising, was to begin from the end.

Broadly defined measures were laid down for the creation of the new society. Tkachev suggested an elasticity of approach, with a gradual advance by trial and error towards egalitarianism. This could be implemented along the following lines. He partly meets Marx's hypothesis that the existing *obshchina*, founded on the basis of private property, could be transformed over a period of time into a communal one for which the criteria would be collective effort and use of the means of production. Starting with rural change there would evolve the gradual expropriation of *all* means of production which would be communalized. The parasitic middleman in the exchange process would be destroyed by the introduction of necessary controls. All efforts would be applied to the abolition of physical, intellectual and moral inequality amongst men through compulsory social education founded on equality and inspired by love and fraternity. The family, rooted in man's egoism, woman's subservience and child slavery, must be ended. Finally Tkachev again parallels Marx's dictum on 'the withering away of the state' by declaring for the strengthening of collective self-administration with the gradual elimination of the state's central functions. Like Marx and Engels[1] he attacked the Anarchists' anti-Statism *per se* on the assumption that it was

---

[1] Engels's letter to Van Patten (18th April 1883):
The anarchists put the thing upside down. They declare that the proletarian revolution must begin by doing away with the political organization of the state. . . . But to destroy it at such a moment would be to destroy the only organism by means of which the victorious proletariat can assert its newly conquered power, hold down its capitalist adversaries and carry out that economic revolution of society without which the whole victory must end in a

impractical in the early post-revolutionary stages. Anarchism presumed the establishment of absolute equality *immediately*, but this could only come about through the ruthlessness of dedicated leaders, who would constitute the authority to implement such equality.[1] He rejected the Bakuninist fiction of educating the people since it involved delay and delay meant danger. Tkachev focused the dilemma which constantly bedevilled Anarchist precepts:

> Any organization presupposes a centre, and instructions of general significance. Whether it is founded on federal or central-izing principles – i.e. whether it has at its centre dictators holding all the power or merely delegates representing local groups with restricted mandates – any organization is always authoritarian and, therefore, anti-anarchist.

Therefore he asks the pointed question. How could one ORGANIZE ALL the peasants, artisans etc., against the Tsarist bureaucracy if one insists that any authority is evil? Against this he confirms the justification for a controlling *élite* dedicated to the destruction of the present superstructure. This was in accord with the primary stages of Bakuninism. After victory comes the point of divergence. The leadership 'by making use of its force and its own authority . . . can introduce new pro-gressive Communist elements into the conditions of the people's life, and free their existence from its age old chains and bring life to its dried and petrified forms'.

His general thesis was particularly applicable to Russia. The strength of the revolutionary lay in the intrinsic weakness of his opponents who were disunited groups of nobility, clergy and merchants. State power was lodged in the Tsarist bureaucracy, which had neither roots in any class, nor base in the economic structure of society. It virtually floated in mid-air. The demo-lition of the state order could be easily effected. A quick,

---

new defeat and in a mass slaughter of the workers similar to those after the Paris Commune.

Does it require my express assurance that Marx opposed this Anarchist nonsense from the first day it was put forward in its present form by Bakunin?

[1] Pamphlet *Anarchy of Thought*, a collection of critical essays by P. N. Tkachev. *Nabat* publication (London, 1879).

powerful *coup* would bring it tumbling down, without the danger of the complications inherent in western society, where *bourgeois* institutions, already well entrenched, could prove a more formidable obstacle. In the first issue of *Nabat* Tkachev restated his view that these advantages might be short-lived since the development of the *bourgeoisie* was already accelerating and threatened the prospects of a successful revolution. He warned that 'tomorrow might become moderate, prudent and sensible. So hurry! Do not let this moment pass.' He continued to place little faith in the prolongation of revolutionary fervour among the peasantry. Hence his directive for a revolution from above and outside the rural masses was argued from a realistic appreciation of their limitations. They were phlegmatic, slow to chide, and had to be pin-pricked into action. He had previously made the point with prophetic foresight.

> If they see that the terrible power before which they used to tremble and abase themselves is disorganized, disunited, helpless, defiled and they do not need to be afraid of anybody or anything, then the repressed feeling of bitterness and the demand for revenge will break out with irresistible force.[1]

Naturally lazy, however, they would soon tire of destruction and lapse into torpidity. At this stage the revolutionary *élite* would have to drive them in order to complete the operation, and after the old system was purged force them to create the new.

He deduced, rightly, that government-sponsored village improvement was capitalism's attempt to expand into the countryside. In the fifth issue of *Nabat* (1876) he had already labelled the Populists 'reactionary revolutionaries'. He scorned their attachment to worn-out adages. He pointed out that their futile attempts to create workmen's and agricultural co-operatives would certainly lead to change, but not to revolution. The change, for the worse, would be to expedite the introduction of *bourgeois* institutions in the western mode. Always scorning the trite and senseless reference to a mysterious

---

[1] Lenin, exhorting the Bolsheviks in July 1917 to prepare to seize power, made a speech which was an almost word-for-word replica of this.

popular genius attributed to the *moujiks*, Tkachev was finally moved to argue that the revolutionaries should concentrate their attention on the developing factory proletariat. They were already mobilizing as a united force against capitalistic exploitation. Economic conditions in the countryside were proving less and less conducive to practical organization. ('One must be extremely naïve to imagine that propaganda and agitation of a few dozen young men can maintain and develop institutions which lack economic soil. . . .') Tkachev was observing the western experience transplanted into Russia. The urban workers could provide the phalanx for the vanguard. But it was the Jacobin *élite* who must spark off the revolution at once, since even 'policemen believe in long-term revolution'!

Sensitive to the socio-economic transformation within Russia, Tkachev's political attitude moved towards those areas where the ideas of Blanqui and Marx coalesced. Economic materialism and the class struggle had been received and accepted from Marx. Above all else in the pages of *Nabat* is indelibly underlined the political Blanquism, derived as much from the disciples (associated with *Nabat*) as from the oracle himself. Tkachev stresses forcibly the Blanquist creed – the minority *coup*. By 1878 he was uncompromising in this view, and in words that might have been written by 'le vieux' himself he took his final stand:

> It is essential that all our revolutionaries, whatever they call themselves, forget and throw away at the earliest possible moment all the federal Utopias, and turn once again to the old centralized organization which has been tried more than once. In that lies force, and in that lies salvation.

In 1880 we find him contributing to Blanqui's *Ni Dieu ni Maître* although there is no evidence to date that the two great revolutionists ever met. On the death of the master, in a moving funeral oration[1] published in Blanqui's journal, he acknowledged the Frenchman as the tutor of socialist insurrection and the debt owed to him by the 'true' revolutionaries of Russia. 'To him, to his ideas, to his abnegation, to the clarity of his

---

[1] *Ni Dieu Ni Maître* (9th January 1881). Tkachev was too ill to attend in person.

M

mind, to his clairvoyance, we owe in great measure the progress which clearly manifests itself in the Russian revolutionary movement.' Tkachev may have been over-eulogistic at such a time although Tursky in his own chorus at the graveside made similar emphasis of the impact of Blanqui's reputation on the Russian autocracy. 'It is just because the Tsarist government recognized the international significance of those principles which Auguste Blanqui so eminently represented, that it prohibited in Russia even the mention of his name. . . .'

The legacy of Nechaev drove Tkachev and the Jacobins into the political wilderness for nearly a decade. The failure of *Zemlya I Volya* forced the radicals back towards clandestine activity. In Geneva the *Rabotnik* (Worker)[1] printed a 'Letter of a French Worker to his brothers in Russia' by L. Khalin in which reference is made to Babeuf and the *Manifesto of the Equals*. The writer also remarked on the new centres of revolutionism arising from the urbanized peasantry, that is those deprived of land and forced into the factories. His main call was for class warfare led by an urban vanguard. Plekhanov in his personal recollections discerned the emergence of an *élite* of worker revolutionaries, who in the latter part of the 1870's were drawn into the core of *Narodnaya Volya*. To diminish the danger of *agents provocateurs* infiltrating into workers' groups there was deliberate separation of function between leadership and rank and file. The failure of the 'movement to the people' meant a complete reappraisal of tactics. It directed the most active and committed towards the Tkachevist line. Zhelyabov[2] voiced the lessons of his time. 'We have tried in different ways to act on behalf of the people. At the beginning of the seventies we chose to live like workers and peacefully propagate our Socialist ideas. The movement was absolutely harmless. But how did it end? It was broken only because of the immense obstacles in the form of prison and banishment with which it had to contend. A movement which was unstained by blood

---

[1] Dated January 1875.
[2] Odessan revolutionary who became the soul of *Narodnaya Volya*. Greatly admired by Lenin.

and which repudiated violence was crushed.' By 1879 the lesson was learned. So the 'dreamy idealist of the previous lustre' moved towards a 'violent revolution by means of a conspiracy. . . . In this spirit I did what I could to found a single centralized organization, made up of autonomous groups but acting according to a common plan in the interests of a common purpose.' By 1878 public demonstration was abandoned. The wheel had turned full circle. Conspiratorial groups had moved back into place. But they had added a new dimension – individual acts of terror against leaders of the régime as a means of destroying the state. Tkachev opposed concentrating on terrorism alone as it would dissipate the leadership's scarce resources; but the return to clandestine, centralized organization gave him sufficient optimism to found a new political group, 'The Society for the Liberation of the People'. There is no record that it had any direct influence on events inside Russia. But the list of terrorists include many of those who were, or had been, associated with Tkachev.

The first act of assassination was carried out by Vera Zasulich, who was previously involved in the Nechaev affair and had known Tkachev in her youth. On 28th January 1878 she shot the brutal governor of St Petersburg, General Trepov. She was freed in open court. In the south terrorism became more prominent as armed resistance was adopted by the Central Committee of *Zemlya I Volya*. It was in this area that the Tkachevists, who had returned from exile, operated, and these included the most dedicated professionals. Two remarkable women were involved in direct action. Elizabeta Nikolaevna Yuzhakova had taken part in the Paris Commune, had worked with Nechaev in Switzerland and later joined the *Nabat* group; Galina Cheryavskaya was a Tkachevist who took a leading part in *Narodnaya Volya*. In the same group was N. Vitashevsky (a neo-Jacobin) who had tried to contact Tkachev in Switzerland. Over all these was the stern leadership of I. M. Kovalsky, prototype of Tkachev's revolutionary: fanatical sectarian, ruthless, poverty-stricken and self-sacrifical. He was certainly a member of Tkachev's secret 'Society for the Liberation of the

People' whose aim was to penetrate into other organizations and eventually control them. The execution of a local bandit Lukyanov[1] prompted Kovalsky to issue a manifesto declaring that if the punishment for robbery and murder is death, it should also be applied to those who rob and oppress the people. On the 30th January 1878 armed police raided the headquarters which housed the press and Kovalsky resisted with gun and dagger. He was with difficulty disarmed, and later an armed attempt to rescue him failed. He was tried and shot on the 2nd August 1878. His execution signalled the conversion of the Populist movement to terrorism which in turn gave birth to *Narodnaya Volya*.

In April 1878 the centralization of *Zemlya I Volya* was carried out under Alexander Mikhailov. A caucus of professional revolutionaries (*kruzhok*) assumed supreme command for terrorist operations. The individual had to submit unquestioningly to its decisions, and by a majority vote it could select and order a member to carry out a sentence of execution. The holding of private property was strictly forbidden. Communalism was absolute. To prevent police infiltration a rigid code was to be adhered to before admitting newcomers. Each would-be applicant underwent a close scrutiny of personality to ensure his reliability. Five of the central circle had to guarantee him and at least two-thirds of the members had to vote acceptance. Each member of the supreme leadership would also be a member of a local group, which carried out assignments in a given area. The idea of 'communion' prevailed, that is the central caucus was empowered to control and co-ordinate all activities and distribute funds. It was also elected by a two-thirds majority and consisted of from three to five members who exercised control for an unspecified period. These provided the elements of a permanent élitist group with unlimited directive power.

The organization looked back on, and drew extensively from, the experience of both Nechaev and Tkachev. Among its

---

[1] *Nabat*, Nos. I and II of 1878, wrote that he had been a volunteer in a Slav uprising and an ex-member of the Garibaldini.

methods of operation was 'to approach and even merge with those whose religious or revolutionary natures make them hostile to the state'; to establish relations and links with industrial workers, and also with liberals 'so as to exploit them for our purposes'. Article 9 of its secret memorandum confirms the Machiavellian principle adopted by Nechaev that 'the end justifies the means' to the exclusion of those means which might harm the organization itself. Ultimately its leadership was committed to the complete destruction of the State through a systematic annihilation of top government officials.

On 4th August 1879 General Mezentsov, head of the Third Section, was stabbed to death. The government responded with brutal reprisals as terrorist acts continued. This forced greater centralization on the conspiratorial body, which to ensure maximum safety, moved to the towns, notably St Petersburg. Here the students and factory workers provided them with militant recruits. An abortive attempt on the Tsar's life by Solovev (2nd April 1879) prompted the enforcement of the ukase of April 5th, which imposed martial law on six 'infected' areas under the rule of military governors. Between June 17th and 21st, under the guise of respectable citizens on a holiday spree, the terrorists met at Lipetsk. The majority agreed to the continuation of a centralized hierarchical party, who would act as shock troops preparing to seize the centres of power. Naming themselves the 'Executive Committee' they adopted the title *Narodnaya Volya* (The People's Will), whose voluntaristic representatives they claimed to be. Their political doctrine was crystallized in their official publications. It revealed marked agreement with Tkachev's prescription. They directed attention to the main enemy – the Bureaucratic State. The policy of the autocracy was 'literally planned with the aim of generating the *kulak*. . . . Remove this oppression [i.e. that exercised by the State] and at a single blow, you will remove nine-tenths of the likelihood of a *bourgeoisie* being formed.' They warned that the State was trying 'to get support from the *bourgeoisie* and like the most zealous midwife it is doing whatever it can arrange for the little monster of the people to have a happy delivery'. If the *bourgeoisie* were allowed to mature, it would inevitably replace the autocracy. In that event, it 'will of course be able to keep the people in slavery to a far greater extent than happens today. And it will find more efficient methods for paralysing our activities than the present government which is unable to go beyond the prison and the gallows.' Therefore it was the primary task of the revolutionaries to smash the state so that the power of the *bourgeoisie* was still-born. The time for action was immediately, 'before it is too late, while there is a real possibility that power can in fact pass to the people. Now or never; that is our dilemma.'

It was the extremist Jacobin wing which influenced the Executive Committee along this course. In the eighth review V. D. Lebedeva emphasized that the revolutionary party would not relinquish power to a democratic representation of the people until a complete destruction of the State had been carried out. A *Zemsky Sobor* (i.e. Constitutional Assembly) would then be brought in, with the party acting out its Jacobin rôle until local autonomy could be finally arrived at. *Narodnaya Volya* failed partly, as Tkachev feared, because it associated the destruction of powerful individuals with that of the State. They managed to assassinate Tsar Alexander II on 1st March 1881, but Tsarism survived; indeed it was strengthened by the violent and successful reaction which followed. It finally put paid to Tkachev's hopes. He was convinced at the time that both Russia and western Europe were ripe for revolution, and had transferred his printing press to Russia, where he made little headway. The 'Society for the Liberation of the People' had hardly begun to operate, and there is little evidence that it ever did. Tkachev was by now prematurely worn out by frustration and despair, and the futility of his attempts brought on mental illness. In 1886, after terrible suffering, he died in a lunatic asylum.

It will be argued that Lenin's guide to action is fundamentally derived from the tradition of Jacobin Blanquism translated into Russian terms by Tkachev. During the free discussions of the 1920's great play was made on the elements of Blanquism

in the formulation of Marxist–Leninism. B. I. Gorev, a Menshevik, writing about Auguste Blanqui[1] on the eve of a break
with his own party, poses the three organizational and tactical
features of Blanquism which are equated with those of the
Bolsheviks; the idea of a conspiratorial party, the seizure of
power, and the dictatorship of the revolutionary vanguard
after the seizure of power. This brought upon him the threats
of a self-titled 'orthodox' Leninist writing under the pseudonym
of 'Sineira'. Gorev, accused of being a Revisionist and Bernsteinite, promptly replied quoting Lenin's own *One step forward,
two steps backwards!* 'A Jacobin, indissolubly linked with the
organization of the proletariat, conscious of its class interests,
is a revolutionary Social Democrat!' The discussion was continued by S. Mitskevich and N. Butarin. In his article 'The
Russian Jacobins'[2] Mitskevich emphasized the relevance of
two historical phenomena in the Russian revolutionary tradition – the launching of Zaichnevsky's *Young Russia* in 1862, and
Tkachev's ideology. Here, he declared, were the ideas and
slogans used in the implementation of Bolshevism.

In *Young Russia* Mitskevich saw the 'basic precepts of the
October Revolution'. He argued that Zaichnevsky's propositions had included the following: 'A federated socialist republic
on the basis of self-determination'; the idea of revolution as the
only prerequisite for Socialism; the demand for the organization of socialized factories and trade, nationalization of land,
the confiscation of the riches of the church, the public education
of children; the necessity of a strictly centralized party, which,
after the revolution, 'would, as soon as possible, lay the foundation of a new economic and social order'; and which, with the
help of the dictatorship, would regulate elections to a national
assembly in such a way that would not include proponents of
the old order. Two of Zaichnevsky's predictions were fulfilled
as a result of the October Revolution: First, it was Russia's
fate to establish Socialism; second, that all former oppositional
parties would unite against the social revolution.

[1] *Auguste Blanqui*, Moscow State Publishing House (1921).
[2] *Proletarskaya Revolyutsiva* (1923) Nos. 6–7 (18–19), pp. 3–26.

Mitskevich accorded to Tkachev's *The task of revolutionary propaganda in Russia* a prime source of Bolshevik activism. Although Tkachev was seen as a Utopian in stressing the possibility of a revolution in his own lifetime, yet 'it is an irrefutable fact that the Russian Revolution to a significant degree proceeded according to Tkachev's idea, with the seizure of power at an appointed time by a revolutionary party which has been organized on the principle of strict centralization and discipline. And this party [i.e. Bolshevik], having seized power, is working in many respects as Tkachev advised.' In opposing the 'pure' Leninist, Butarin, Mitskevich concluded his defence thus: 'Let Comrade Butarin not tell me that they [The Russian Jacobins] were not genuine proletarian socialists. I know that, but I also know that it is necessary to think dialectically and not to limit oneself to saying, yes, yes, no, no. The Russian Jacobins were the forerunners of Russian revolutionary Marxism but they were not yet revolutionary Marxists.'

Stalinism closed the debate. Lenin had already been canonized. Only the saints could be held to work under divine inspiration. Henceforth it would be heresy to question doctrine, and an Inquisition would deal with those who did.

CHAPTER 9

Prelude to Revolution

The ascendancy of Lenin marked the culminating point in the Franco-Russian revolutionary experience. The complexities observed in Lenin's character, and in his manœuvres towards power, were as much a result of his close reading of the whole of the revolutionary past as of immediate tactical considerations. In Russia more potent ingredients were stirring in the political brew. Tkachev had been observing the emergence of the bare nucleus of an urban proletariat. Lenin's ideas matured in the climate of rapid industrialization: of an expanding working-class movement into the major centres and a more sensitive polarization of opposing social forces. Events were thus moving to his advantage. He was fully cognizant with the possibilities; they could be read in the text of the nineteenth-century 'revolutionary handbook'. His sharp intellect, iron will, and an intuitive sense of opportunism did the rest. All these enabled him to transform into reality the great Idea generated by the western Babouvists.

The last twenty years of the century saw a duality in government policy. On the one hand there prevailed a more efficient containment of political opposition. The new Tsar Alexander III (1881–94) was resolved that, unlike his father, he would die in his bed. The '*Okhrana*', a special secret police, was set up and succeeded in penetrating all sectors of political activity. Student organizations underwent closer supervision than ever before. Spies and *agents-provocateurs* provided additional tools in securing police control. Censorship was resumed and there was established a more extensive scrutiny of literary publications. Open dissent becoming less possible, the greater was the propensity towards clandestine organization. The roads leading to Siberia were clogged with those aspirants of open intent. By the early twentieth century it was reasonable to suppose that the smaller the repository for party secrets, the greater the possibility of survival.

On the other hand Alexander III pursued his father's belief in economic expansion. Emancipation, which had freed labour on the land, brought waves of peasant migration into the towns – a flow of cheap labour in the classical mould. Recurrent capitalization of land and industry accrued from government compensation. Reinforcement of local areas of specialist production was facilitated by foreign capital such as oil in the Caucasus, coal, iron and steel in the Ukraine, textiles in the capital towns. Increased grain output and export meant an increase in railway building,[1] which in turn stimulated demand in the heavy industries. Foreign capital was attracted by the prospect of high interest rates, special government protection and high import tariffs. The Franco-Russian political *rapprochement* in the 1890's furthered the range of external investment funds.[2] Industrial concerns were controlled by foreign managements, who were naturally concerned with quick maximization of profits. Home entrepreneurs could only compete by reducing the most costly factor of production – labour. A large pool of urbanized peasantry was available, facilitating assault on wages. The hired town labourer was clearly subjected to the most brutal form of exploitation. Tkachev's, and Lenin's, raw material for the vanguard of insurrectionism was becoming clearly defined.

The old *malheureux*, the rural peasant, up to 1917 and beyond still constituted the major force of discontent. Those who remained in the *mir* were still subject to the strictures of immobility. Taxation and repayment loans, having been removed from the sole authority of the landlords, were now under the collective jurisdiction of the commune. Built-in

---

[1] The Trans-Caspian railway was completed between 1883 and 1888; the Trans-Siberian railway between 1891 and 1904.

[2] Russia was the largest recipient of French capital – 7 milliard francs by 1900.

deficiencies arising from the strip system continued to prevail. Primitive husbandry meant a rural pauperization, sustained by old techniques and equipment; and therefore no hope of improvement derived from rationalization and economies of scale.

Absentee-landlordism was rife. The town-orientated gentry had always used their peasant labour and land produce to pay for the sophisticated life in town. This was subject to increasing costs. Few invested the proceeds of Emancipation payments in modernizing techniques. The failure of repayments on loans from state and private creditors meant the transfer of property to more resourceful owners, i.e. the land shark, the *kulak*, or the more business-minded noble entrepreneur. Between 1861 and 1905 landholding by the gentry fell from 50 to 25 per cent of the total farming area. Moral and financial bankruptcy were not far apart. The *moujik* was always there on the receiving end of all oppressive and injudicious acts. The changeover to indirect taxation squeezed them dry. Only violent revolution could relieve them of their overwhelming burdens. Only then would the land be theirs.

By 1900 under Count Witte, the modern go-ahead Finance Minister, industrialization was speeded up. He demonstrated that central organization and administrative efficiency could go hand in hand, provided that there was a well-trained Civil Service. Russia adopted the Gold Standard in 1897. Maximization of external investment was effected by high tariffs. Discriminatory taxation in favour of large-scale corn producers boosted grain exports. Again, those who could least afford to subsidized those who could. Income was derived from the poor peasants' needs – sugar, tobacco and alcohol.

The rapid growth of factory plant brought its natural concomitants of a new *bourgeoisie* and an urban working class. Class conflict was naked and vicious. Such was the speed of transformation that monolithic structures mushroomed. By 1900 a compact proletarian army of 3,000,000 was mobilizing in the towns. The more advanced centres lay in Poland and the north, where specialist industries had been located for generations. Much of this had resulted from the westernizing implications of the reforms of Peter I. Skilled artisans in St Petersburg were always in the forefront of the movements of protest and revolt. Here was the traditional training centre for an *élite*. Elsewhere the old domestic system was merging into small-scale industry. In eastern Poland and the Ukraine, areas which included the Jewish Pale, minor industrial manufactories such as leather, clothing, matches and shoes generated battalions of militant artisans. In Vilno (the 'Jerusalem of Lithuania') and Lodz highly intelligent and articulate groups of Yiddish-speaking workers formed the activist elements of the revolutionary movement. Restrictive laws bound the Jews to the ghettos where they suffered both political discrimination and economic exploitation. Marxism and Social Democracy soon flourished in the Pale. The first Jewish Socialist party, the Bund, was founded there in 1897, and *Paole Tsione*, a Socialist form of Zionism, was first expounded there. The more rapid the industrial growth, the greater the areas of social misery. New recruits to the revolution were added as a result of terrible housing conditions, the iron discipline of the factory and government protection of employers tending to perpetuate low pay.[1] It would accord with both the Marxist and Tkachevist theses that the motivating force had arrived. The radical intelligentsia diverted their attention from the rural peasantry and concentrated their energies on agitation and propaganda amongst the urban proletariat.

Marxism had come early to Russia.[2] Many of the *narodniki* had proclaimed themselves converts. *Das Kapital* had first appeared in Russian translation in 1872, and had been passed by the authorities. It was considered dull and unreadable, apparently not applicable to the Russian situation, and, therefore, harmless. But enlightened academics, such as Sieber, quickly caught on to its potentiality. Theoretical discussions and learned commentaries appeared in safe journals. They may have raised a yawn in the headquarters of the *Okhrana*,

---

[1] Some progressive labour laws were passed but these applied only to large factories, i.e. those employing over twenty people.

[2] See Chapter 8, p. 153 above.

but they provided a new creed for the students and the intelligentsia of the 1880's and 1890's. 'Nearly everyone became a Marxist,' commented Lenin dryly in 1902. The first important Marxist circle, 'The Emancipation of Labour', was founded in 1883 by G. V. Plekhanov (1856–1918) amongst the Russian exiles in Geneva. Plekhanov had defaulted from *Narodnaya Volya* over the question of terrorism. He argued for long-term evolutionary processes against the minority voluntarism and terrorist act. Posing a Marxist interpretation he conceived of a large Social-Democratic party evolving with capitalist development, which would accelerate the maturation of the *bourgeoisie*, and, at the same time, enhance proletarian strength and consciousness for the final take-over. His tactical proposals, in view of his own divorcement from the realities of the situation within Russia, were, at least, questionable. In Russia, independent Marxist groups had sprung up, involved in day-to-day contact with workers, and forced to vary tactics according to actual situations. To them action derived from broad abstract theory was absurd. By 1900 the build up of a mass Social-Democratic Party was made impossible. This was due to effective counter-measures by the police. The workers were more concerned with 'economic' means for gaining maximum concessions from their employers, such as industrial strikes in boom periods. The tragicomedy was that they were aided by the police, whose top official, Zubatov, proved himself to be a successful Trade Union organizer by employing agents in workers' organizations. These led workers' demands and the employers were forced to acquiesce. They, therefore, provided a successful challenge to Social-Democratic influence until one of Zubatov's unions sparked off a series of mass strikes in the south in 1903, and Zubatov was sacked. All this added to the frustrations and disillusionment which forced the young revolutionists to put first things first; and top priority was concentration on a compact internal organization to guarantee leadership in the prolonged struggle. The way led back to Tkachev. In this context the emergence of Lenin and a disciplined élitist party was inevitable.

Vladimir Ilyich Ulyanov was born in Simbirsk (1870) in the central Volga region near the wild lands traditionally associated with Pugachev and the *Raskolniki*. His father had become provincial director of schools in 1869, and his mother had also been a schoolmistress. Against a cultivated background and the repressive period of the 1880's, all five children were converted to revolutionary ideas. His elder brother, Alexander, was nineteen when he was executed in 1887 for his part in a plot to assassinate the Tsar. Alexander's group were the descendants of the People's Will and associated themselves with the methods of conspiratorial action in overthrowing the autocracy. They also proclaimed themselves Marxists. Alexander wrote from prison that the differences between his group and the Marxist Social Democrats seemed 'very insignificant and only theoretical. . . . We place greater hopes on the immediate passage of the national economy to a higher stage, and attributing a greater independent significance to the intellectuals, consider it necessary and expedient to embark at once on a political struggle with the government.' This was not lost on the young Lenin. He rejected his brother's terrorism but retained the view that political activism was the first consideration in the fight to destroy the autocracy. The manner of his brother's death helped to convert him into a permanent revolutionary.

The young Ulyanov was an excellent student at the local high school. His headmaster spoke of him as 'the pride of the school' and took a special interest in him. His good work at school must have carried more weight than the fact that he was the brother of a recently executed terrorist. It is an irony of history that the same headmaster's son, Alexander Kerensky, would in 1917 be deprived of supreme power by his father's protégé. Lenin managed to gain a place in the law faculty at Kazan University in August 1887. On December 4th of the same year he was expelled as a result of a students' 'riotous assembly'. It was officially reported by a member of the local board that his behaviour and background 'gave reason to believe him capable of unlawful and criminal demonstrations of all kinds'. He was exiled to Kokushkino – his mother's estate.

Here he read extensively into the revolutionary literature of the past. We know that he was drawn to Chernyshevsky, whose novel *What is to be Done*, in Lenin's words, 'turned me upside down'. From the writings of Chernyshevsky he built up an image of the revolutionary man, in certain ways akin to that of Nechaev: one imbued with an iron will, coldly dispassionate in his appraisal of revolutionary possibilities, absolute in his dedication. Only through and by him could 'revolutionary democratism' (i.e. a socialist workers' republic) be created. He also conveyed a lucid comprehension of social antagonisms in the current dialectic. Liberal reformers were contemptuously written off. Lenin never forgot that his own family's 'liberal minded' friends had abruptly cut them at the time of the attempt on the Tsar's life. In October 1889 Lenin was living in the family home at Samara where he joined a revolutionary circle headed by Skliarenko, natural son of a Dr Popov, who kept a massive library of revolutionary books and journals, amongst which were the works of Marx and Tkachev. It was at this stage that Lenin was converted to a Marxism which was was not without its Populist flavour. In fact the Tkachevist commitment to conspiratorial voluntarism was to become the overriding feature in Lenin's own appendage to Marxist ideology. At Samara Lenin also made friendly contact with prominent Jacobins, notably M. I. Golubev's wife Yasneva, a devotee of Zaichnevsky. It was a long-term friendship. After 1904 she became a Social Democrat allying herself to the Bolshevik faction of the party.

In 1891 Lenin took his law examinations at St Petersburg University, and gained a first-class diploma with the highest marks in all subjects. In January 1892 he practised as an assistant in Samara; but not for long. The next year he parted company from his family, who went to live in Moscow, whilst he made his way to St Petersburg to begin his life-long career as a professional revolutionary.

Officially Lenin remained a member of the Bar in order to disguise his involvement in the revolutionary underground. In 1894, he wrote and illegally distributed his first major treatise

What the Friends of the People are in which he rejected residual Populism in favour of a purely Marxist party. He attached himself to Stepan I. Radchenko's group of 'elders', who conducted study circles for the political education of local workers. Lenin soon became impatient with this slow, and apparently, unrewarding means of agitation and desired to spread his wings further and faster. In May 1895 he went to Switzerland to seek advice and printed literature from the Plekhanov group. His return to Russia coincided with that from exile of Julius Martov, a Jewish Marxist, who was moving in the same theoretical direction as Lenin. Both were convinced of the necessity of a central Marxist party. Both pressed their own groups to merge, resulting in 'The Union of Struggle for the Emancipation of the Working Class' in St Petersburg. Its members are considered as being the founding fathers of the Russian Communist Party, although the importance of Martov has, significantly, been overlooked in official Soviet historiography. But it was Martov who seemed to have impressed on the rest the policy of widespread agitation amongst strikers and more direct involvement with the day-to-day struggles of the workers. Specialization of function was introduced. The Radchenko family controlled funds. Fourteen members formed three major committees for the purpose of undertaking agitation in the three centres of industry in the capital. Lenin was responsible for the production and distribution of literature. In that year of labour troubles the concentration of propaganda among strikers earned the group a reputation far beyond its real influence. The police moved in. On 9th December 1895 most of the leaders, including Lenin, were arrested. Martov avoided the round-up till January 6th, which gave him sufficient time to proclaim that the caucus of the party remained intact and would continue its activities.

Lenin suffered his first term of imprisonment of over a year. Whilst in prison he maintained a clandestine output of leaflets and manifestos by the use of *ersatz* ink (milk) and containers (bread) which could easily be disposed of. In February 1897 he was given three days of freedom before his despatch to Siberia. So was Martov. They spent them together with

Martov's family in a large flat in St Petersburg. To the end, in spite of later antagonism and bitter mutual recriminations in political debate, Lenin's affection for his Jewish comrade of the golden years of struggle remained inviolate. Martov's brother Vladimir paints a sympathetic picture of the relationship between the young men:

> On the first day that Lenin came . . . he stayed overnight with us to talk his fill with Iulii [Julius] alone, for whom he showed great sympathy and respect. They would not even go to bed but talked into the morning. This night very likely marked the beginning of the close personal relations between them while in exile. . . .

There is a wealth of evidence relating to Lenin's constant regard for his old friend. In the hard winter of 1919–20 Lenin found time to select and order the services of a top Moscow doctor for Martov, who was ill. B. Nicolaevsky recalls[1] hearing from Rykov, that at a meeting of the Politbureau during the winter of 1922–3 Zinoviev was pressed by Lenin to raise the question of money for medical aid for the ailing Martov. Rykov added, 'Even Stalin did not protest and he hated Martov.' Lenin insisted on getting news of him. Krupskaya writes in her reminiscences: 'Vladimir Ilyich was seriously ill when he said to me once sadly, "They say Martov is dying too".' His compassion towards an old friend, even when they were politically alienated, is one quality of Lenin which appears to have escaped even his critical admirers. His successor could never be accused of the same 'weakness'. Lenin would often divide his attitudes towards the man depending on whether the situation was a political one or not. He would trounce an opponent in debate, pour upon him all the violent polemic which he could muster, and afterwards greet him with kindly humour; it is fair to add, provided Lenin was the victor.

Lenin was sentenced to exile in Siberia at Shushenskoe in the Yenesei region for three years (February 1897–February 1900). In some ways it was a curious punishment, the main hardships

---

[1] B. Nicolaevsky, 'Pages from the Past', in *Sotsialisticheskii vestnik* (July–August 1958), p. 151.

N

being the normal hazards of climate and territorial isolation. He could send and receive mail and all kinds of literature by post, and publications of any kind were tolerated provided they met the censor's requirements. He was, therefore, able to study at leisure and complete his major work, *The Development of Capitalism in Russia*, and an important pamphlet *The Tasks of the Russian Social Democrats* in which he outlined a basic programme of Marxist Social-Democratism. In May 1898 he was joined by Nadhezda Krupskaya, who, after being seized by the police, asked to be exiled to Shushenskoe. Lenin married her. He was fortunate to have acquired a life-long companion, and posterity a shrewd chronicler.

Certain events within Russia and Germany forced Lenin to adapt his Marxist views to accord with the changes which were taking place within Russia proper. In September 1899 E. Bernstein's revisionist treatise *The Bases of Socialism and the Tasks of Social Democracy* reached Lenin. Bernstein questioned the inevitability of revolutionary violence as the final outcome of the class struggle. His conclusions were drawn from the German situation, and were akin to Engels's observations, although Engels never discarded revolution as an ultimate necessity. concentration on workers' 'economic' activities, such as Trade Unions, and the strengthening of the organization of 'legal' Socialism in the fight for higher standards within a free capitalist society was the choice he offered against so-called rigid adherence to outmoded doctrine. Within Russia the publication of *Credo of the Young* by an ex-Social Democrat, Elena Kuskova, revealed kinship with the Bernsteinite heresy. Lenin mustered his forces to combat both. Amongst the exiles he read his public denunciation and the printed record reached Plekhanov in Switzerland. He published it as 'A Protest by the Russian Social Democrats' in *Rabochee Delo*. Lenin thundered against the homebred reformist: 'The Credo merely reveals a desire to obscure the class character of the struggle of the proletariat, to weaken the struggle by a meaningless "recognition of society" and to reduce revolutionary Marxism to trivial reformism.' Lenin feared that the necessity for revolution might be swallowed up in the morass of revolutionary inertia if the 'Economists' were heeded. His attacks on Bernstein and Kuskova obliged him to work out a counter programme. It must be centred round the hypothesis that the inevitability of revolution was inviolate; and that this could only be brought about by the organization of an intellectual *élite*, voluntaristically involved to bring political consciousness to the masses. It led him on to the most sophisticated pronouncement on revolutionary élitism to date.

Lenin's *What is to be Done* (published in March 1902) was the outcome. It was the high-water mark of revolutionary directives. It was not only an ardent 'appeal for organization' (Krupskaya); it laid down the strategy and tactics to be employed by a Jacobin Communist party. Lenin had made a realistic appreciation of the situation. Past and present experience decreed that it was ludicrous to compare possibilities within Russia and those of central and western Europe where a popular Social Democracy could legally arise. In an autocratic state the movement must be organized subterraneously through trained professionals. The Russian situation was such that no revolutionary party could succeed without a stable caucus of leaders to preserve continuity; the more widespread the organization the greater the need for central direction. 'In a country given over to the rule of a single individual, it is better to limit the number of members of such a body. . . . The more limited the number, the more difficult it will be to seize such an organization.'

Lenin rejected the Economists. 'Economism' or economic response was not the only situation in which the masses could be roused to political action, since 'all and sundry manifestations of police tyranny and autocratic outrage, in addition to the evils connected with the economic struggle are equally "widely applicable" as a means of "drawing in" the masses'. The Social Democrats must infiltrate everywhere to arouse discontent and focus opposition on the autocracy. 'We must have "our own men" among Social Democrats everywhere, among all social strata, and in all positions from which we can learn the inner springs of our state mechanism. Such men are required for propaganda and agitation, but in a still larger measure for organization.' Since 'the growth of the labour movement is outstripping the growth and development of the revolutionary organizations' it was more valid that the party must be small in number, well disciplined and trained in conspiracy. Lenin argued that the active and widespread participation of the masses would not suffer. It would provide an increasing number of professional revolutionaries from its ranks; agitation and propaganda would be more effectively disseminated and the source would be held more secure to enable a constant feed-in of illicit literature. His overall plan of attack was made in Tkachevist terms relative to the contemporary social conditions, that is with an expanding, though still minimal, restive industrial proletariat. But his reservations on an immediate call for attack were sensible. The ground was to be prepared by first gathering and organizing, then mobilizing, permanent troops. Insurrection there and then would be doomed, since at that juncture 'the crowd is not ours'. Success could only come from an 'attack . . . made by regular troops and not by a spontaneous outburst of the crowd'. The disciplined vanguard could then take its rightful place at the head of the crowd. In his discussion Lenin condemned the naïve application of Tkachev's ideas as interpreted by L. Nadezhdin who, in *Rabochee Delo*, argued against fundamentals of tactics and durable programmes.

> Apparently he [Nadezhdin] has forgotten the well-known epigram which says: if an original historical event represents a tragedy, the copy of it is only a farce. The attempt to seize power, after the ground for the attempt had been prepared by the preaching of Tkachev and carried out by means of the 'terrifying' terror which really did terrify, was majestic, but the 'excitative' terror of a little Tkachev is simply ridiculous and is particularly ridiculous when it is supplemented by the idea of an organization of average workers.

Finally Lenin argued for a central newspaper (he was already involved in the production of *Iskra*), which would obviate uneconomic diffusion of effort through unco-ordinated local broadsheets, and replace them by a more rational means of propaganda with the maximization of effect. It would also entail a minimum call on the short supply of able journalists in the party. A newspaper could both estimate the right moment and sound the *nabat* for universal insurrection.

By 1902 Lenin had become convinced of his own rectitude. This feeling was linked with an unshakable belief in the historical rôle of the Russian revolution under his leadership. In *What is to be Done* he pointed out the universal as well as the national significance of a Russian triumph, seeing it as the summation of all that had gone before in the world revolutionary tradition and foreseeing in victory a Russia launched on her mission of international revolution:

> History has set before us a task to be accomplished in the near future which is far more revolutionary than all the immediate tasks of the proletariat of any other country. The fulfilment of his task, the destruction of the most powerful bulwark of European and (we may even say) of Asiatic reaction, would surely make the Russian proletariat the vanguard of the international proletarian revolution.

By 1902 Lenin had spent some time out of Russia, had experienced the free air of Europe, and launched, together with the Swiss exiles, the newspaper *Iskra* (The Spark). It was not long before he fell out with the rest of the editorial board which was presided over by the equally intractable Plekhanov. The depository of truth could not reside in two such people at the same time. Lenin *knew* that he had it. When the printers of *Iskra* declared that it had become dangerous to continue publishing in Germany, the first split came. Plekhanov declared for a move to Switzerland; Lenin for London. Lenin got his way. A large-scale industrial proletariat – the first and still the best defined in Marxist classicism – together with the leading *bourgeois* civilization was open to his scrutiny. The British Museum was readily accessible. He would follow in the steps of the master.

It proved a fruitful year. Lenin and Krupskaya arrived on

12th April 1902. Nikolai Alexeyev, a former member of the
League for the Liberation of the Working Classes, helped them
settle in their new home. He put Lenin in touch with Harry
Quelch, the English socialist editor of *Justice* and Isaac Mitchell,
the Secretary of the General Federation of Trade Unions. Both
offered invaluable assistance. Lenin applied, under the pseudonym of Dr Jacob Richter, for a reader's ticket to the British
Museum, enclosing a reference from Mitchell. Henceforth,
following the pattern of Marx, he would walk daily to the
library from his lodgings and spend most mornings reading
social and economic documents and writing *Iskra* editorials.
The paper was printed through the auspices of Harry
Quelch on the Social Democratic Federation's Twentieth-
Century Press, housed at 37a Clerkenwell Green (now Marx
House).

The language and habits of the English at first bewildered
him. In Siberia he had learned English by rote from books.
Together with Krupskaya he had worked on a translation of
the Webbs' *Trade Unionism* at Shushenskoye. In the practical
application there seemed little co-relation between the spoken
and written word they had studied. Lenin was resolved to
overcome this. He spent Sundays at Speakers' Corner in Hyde
Park closely observing the orations of Irish atheists (whose
accent, curiously enough, he found easiest to follow!), Salvation
Army Messianists and crazy sectarians. He reinforced his
knowledge by exchanging lessons with two Englishmen, obtained
through an advertisement in the *Athenæum*. His curiosity was
all-embracing. Krupskaya remarked:

Ilya studied living London. He loved going long rides about the
town on top of an omnibus. He liked the movement of this huge,
commercial city. The quiet squares, the detached houses with
their separate entrances and shining windows adorned with
greenery, the drives frequented only by highly polished broughams
were much in evidence – but tucked away nearby, the mean little
streets inhabited by the London working people, where lines
with washing hung across the street, and pale children played
in the gutter – these sights could not be seen from the bus stops.
In such districts we went on foot, and observing these blatant

contrasts in richness and poverty, Lenin would mutter through clenched teeth in English, 'Two Nations!'

Accounts of Lenin in London continue to provide us with fresh insights into Lenin's personality and his political manœuvrings. He saw the workings of the oldest capitalist society in the raw. In his response to this environment we can further evidence his sense of compassionate involvement with the 'dispossessed'. He soaked himself in the working-class atmosphere. He observed the late night turn out from pubs of drunken, worn-out women, many of whom showed black eyes from recent beatings. He visited workers' districts on pay-day evenings and noted the markets, congested with stalls lit by oil flares, where the poor brought their wares; the parks, where tired men sat and rested after a week's labour; the pubs and reading-rooms where they spent their nightly recreation. He later suggested that such reading-rooms should be set up in Russia as an aid to mass literacy. Newspaper advertisements were scrutinized for labour meetings, and this often led him into socialist churches, when services were followed by political lectures and discussions. In one of these, the 'Seven Sisters', the preacher used in his sermon the exodus of the Jews from Egypt as symbolizing the flight of the workers from the kingdom of capitalism into that of socialism, and a young man reading a paper on municipal socialism argued against the need for revolution to transform society. Lenin was unimpressed by these homebred socialists. He found them reserved and paro- chial. One of them was horrified to learn that Krupskaya had served a term in prison. A pupil of Lenin's, a Mr Raymond who was manager of a large bookshop, confessed that he had stopped preaching socialism on the pretext that it was predestined anyway, when the true reason was that his employer had threatened to dismiss him. As he had a wife and children to support he submitted. The same man, a native of London, was not as familiar with its environs as the newcomer. When Lenin took him to a workers' meeting in Whitechapel, Raymond saw for the first time the bizarre conglomeration of curiously garbed Jewish and foreign exiles who lived and worked in the ghetto. The East End was always a favourite haunt of Lenin. There he came to life amongst his compatriots and spoke at Jewish labour meetings. He often frequented a bookshop at 106 Commercial Road, which was stocked with contemporary revolutionary literature. It was kept by a colourful gigantic seven-foot-tall Siberian, sporting a huge black beard, called Petrov.

His flat at Holford Square, King's Cross, became a focal point of international activity. Martov and the veteran Vera Zasulich lived near by and came almost daily. Martov and Krupskaya undertook routine responsibilities in order to enable Lenin to pursue his work in the British Museum. Clandestine operations were organized under the overall direction of Lenin. In Zasulich's Sidmouth Street flat were housed presses to print passports ('handkerchiefs') forged by the deft professional, Peter Hergomenovich. It provided a temporary lodgings for revolutionaries in transit. It was also the liaison centre for *Iskra* agents and the clearing house for propaganda ('beer') on its way to Russia. Kalinin, whilst a factory worker in St Petersburg, was involved as a contact man for local distribution. Although little else finally arrived at the destination, Lenin's pamphlet *What is to be Done* was successfully transported from London and distributed throughout Russia.

Many of the great revolutionaries visited Lenin that year. Litvinov and Plekhanov topped the list. Relations between Lenin and Plekhanov were becoming strained. Both had ferociously criticized each other's articles in *Iskra* but had until then precariously maintained outward solidarity. Lenin, as an ultimate insurance in the struggle for party leadership, was already weaving a secret web of support behind the backs of his co-editors. Leninist agents within Russia were creating factions, which in turn manœuvred their own representatives into the position of elected mandates to the central congress of the party. In the autumn Lenin met Trotsky for the first time. After a gruelling examination Lenin recognized in him the personification of his own élitist brand of revolutionary. Together they interfused in the right proportions abstract theory and revolutionary practicality. Their qualities were to complement each other and prove formidable when the hour of decision came.

The first act in Lenin's bid for control of the Social Democratic party was performed within the hothouse atmosphere of the Second Congress held at Brussels and London in 1903. For three weeks, during the long hot summer, Congress played out its dramatic rôle. The debates revealed the polarization of two opposing forces: one led by Lenin, the other under his erstwhile comrade Martov. The organization and aims of the Party were the major points of conflict. Martov wanted to broaden its base to include any worker who volunteered to help 'personally and regularly under the guidance of one of the organizations'. Lenin's terms were more restrictive. He defined the party man as 'anyone who accepts the programme of the Party, supports it with material means and personally participates in one of its organizations'. Arguments turned into bitter antagonisms. As the dialogue continued it became evident that the rift between the factions was due to fundamentally divergent views on party structure. Lenin clearly emerged as the protagonist for an authoritarian élitism. This brought on his head the charges of 'Bonapartism' and 'Jacobinism'. Martov was more concerned with the formation of a western type Social-Democratic party based on a wider, looser association. It was an expensive luxury at that time, and Lenin's arguments were the more realistic. In clandestine operations it was necessary to minimize the prospect of 'blood letting' by keeping the organization 'little and good'. Past experience in the Russian underground movement had shown that 'it is almost impossible for us to distinguish talkers from workers. . . . We suffer severely from the presence of this evil, not only among the intelligentsia, but also in the ranks of the working class, and Comrade Martov's formula legalizes it.' Lenin's relentless logic in open debate, and timely lobbying of both waverers and supporters behind the scenes, secured him the victory. The Jewish Bund as a third force was ousted with the help of Martov. In turn Martov was manœuvred out of the editorial board of *Iskra* which then left Lenin and Plekhanov in control. A small overall majority opted for Lenin who in turn controlled the central committee. This was the historic split between Lenin's Bolsheviks (Majorityites) and the opposing Mensheviks (Minorityites)

London continued to provide the setting for momentous decisions which altered the whole course of Russian revolutionism. Lenin returned briefly to England in April 1905 to attend the Third Congress of the R.S.D.R.P. which was almost exclusively Bolshevik since the Mensheviks held their own meeting in Geneva. Here he tentatively called for a reunification of the opposing factions and an armed uprising under party leadership within Russia, which was then experiencing her first mass upheaval. More is known of his activities during the fifth congress also held in London (April–May 1907), in which Lenin was joined by Stalin, Litvinov and Gorky. The party met at the Reverend Swan's Brotherhood Church in Southgate Street, East London. The site was arranged through the intercession of George Lansbury, the I.L.P. Christian Socialist, and the journalist, H. N. Brailsford. It was an ill-fated attempt to paper up the cracks in party unity. Gorky paints a vivid picture of Lenin hurling his thunderous polemics at the opposition and recaptures the intensity of the clash of human wills played out against 'the bare walls of a wooden church . . . unadorned to the point of absurdity'. Otherwise Lenin renewed his happier associations with the East End. He was a visitor at the Anarchist Club in Jubilee Street, Stepney, which, although predominantly Jewish, offered food and hospitality to all local and foreign workers. One of the last surviving Yiddish Anarchists, now an old lady of eighty-nine, who voluntarily served meals at the club, recalls seeing Lenin there as 'a small, balding, taciturn man brooding alone at a table in the corner'. George Lansbury again came to his help by raising a loan from a rich manufacturer, Mr Fels, when the party was desperately in need of funds. The loan could not be repaid by the date due, that is, 1st January 1908, since funds were inadequate to meet the commitment. But Lenin kept his word. The loan plus interest was fully repaid by the Soviet Government in 1923.

Meanwhile his *raison d'être*, the first Russian Revolution, virtually caught him napping. (This was to happen again in February 1917.) The disasters of the Russo-Japanese war reached a climax with the Japanese capture of Fort Arthur in December 1904. Widespread anti-war sentiment combined with a plea for social and economic reform, were the motivating forces which directed a peaceful procession of workmen behind Father Gapon to the Winter Palace on 22nd January 1905. The ensuing burst of gunfire reverberated across Europe. Lenin heard the news in Geneva. He had spent the whole of the previous year in literary combat with the Mensheviks, had left *Iskra* and founded a new paper, *Vperyod* (Forward). The caucus of a Leninist Bolsheviki was taking shape. It included Olminsky, Bogdanov, Vorovsky and Lunacharsky, three of whom in their specialist rôles would become international figures after 1917. Lenin foresaw the uprising in the front page article of *Vperyod* (4th January 1905). 'A military collapse is now inevitable, and together with it there will come inevitably a tenfold increase of unrest, discontent and rebellion. For that moment we must prepare with all energy. At that moment one of those outbreaks which are recurring, now here, now there, with such growing frequency, will develop into a tremendous popular movement.'

Yet the timing caught him unprepared; and between January and October Lenin persisted in distributing a vast output of written exhortations to his personal followers and associated groups within Russia, whilst what the roused masses desperately needed was on-the-spot leadership. It was Trotsky who was performing this task, when Lenin was working himself into a state of verbal frenzy by the quiet waters of Geneva. Eventually Lenin set out to intervene with the ultimate aim of directing affairs. He arrived on November 8th to find St Petersburg turbulent but elated. On October 30th the Tsar had granted a State Duma, together with a new constitution and individual freedom of speech and association. Trotsky was the dominating figure in the Soviet of Workers' Delegates, which had arisen spontaneously out of local factory organizations. At first it appeared to Lenin, that this smacked of the 'Economism' which he had denounced in *What is to be Done*; but he soon perceived that such bodies could be made use of as a weapon against the autocracy. In effect they brought a fresh influx of workers into all party organizations, particularly that of the Bolsheviks.

However, during the course of the 1905 revolution events were outside Lenin's control. His most devoted followers were the secret police, who dogged his footsteps everywhere. An uprising in Moscow, led and inspired by his own Bolsheviks, lasted from 20th to 30th December. It passed him by. He had crossed the Finnish border on the 24th to escape police agents. The last dramatic moments of the Moscow affair ended in the workers' district of Presnaya, where the insurgents were blasted to pieces by the Semyonovsky Regiment, whilst the titular head of the insurrection, like his great predecessor of June 1848, Auguste Blanqui, remained the impotent outsider.

Lenin learned the lessons of failure. The October Manifesto had split the Tsarist opposition by offering scraps to the *bourgeois* parties, who then shrank back from further violence. The reforms brought no perceptible economic alleviation to the workers and they naturally sustained their revolutionary vigour. Lenin saw the situation as analogous to 1830 and 1848. 'The proletariat is fighting; the *bourgeoisie* is stealing towards power.' 1905 had 'awakened millions of workers and tens of millions to political life and political struggle'. More resolute, energetic and aggressive action might have swept the revolution on to its inevitable finale – the seizure of power by the masses under the direction of the élitist party. This was a restatement of the 'revolution in permanence' first proclaimed by Robespierre[1] and given its proletarian interpretation by Blanqui, which Marx adopted.[2] Trotsky and Helphand had also anticipated him.[3] The spontaneous formations of working-class delegates elected by workshop and factory – the Soviets – could be harnessed to the reins of the vanguard as a tactical strike

---

[1] See Chapter 1, p. 13.

[2] See Chapter 4, p. 83.

[3] In a pamphlet *Till the Ninth of January*, written by Trotsky, with a long foreword by Helphand (published in Geneva, March 1905), both concerned themselves with leading the proletariat to an immediate seizure of power.

force. The first task was to reaffirm and strengthen the rôle of his party and his own place in that organization. The Mensheviks would have to be removed and against them he ruled harshly, 'I shall always conduct a war of extermination.' Henceforth, he drove himself to the limit to become the accepted head of the all-Russian Social Democrats. By 1914 he had succeeded. A police report then noted: 'The Leninists ... have behind them in Russia an overwhelming majority of the underground social democratic organizations.' The party, by then, had realized the tactical fulfilment of the endeavours of generations of failed Jacobins.

Lenin repeatedly confirmed his association with both the western and Russian Jacobin tradition. In 1904, in *One step forwards, two steps backwards*, he had already answered Axelrod's accusation of Blanquism by openly identifying himself with it. 'These "dreadful words" – Jacobinism and the rest – are expressive of nothing but opportunism. A Jacobin who maintains an inseparable bond with the organization of the proletariat, a proletariat conscious of its class interests, is a revolutionary Social Democrat. A Girondist, who yearns for professors and high school students, who is afraid of the dictatorship of the proletariat and who sighs about the absolute value of democratic demands is an opportunist.' In 1905 in *Two Tactics of Social Democracy in Democratic Revolution* the theme is repeated and Marx is brought in to underline the validity of his argument.

> If the revolution gains a decisive victory – then we shall settle accounts with Tsarism in the Jacobin, or if you like, in the plebeian way. 'The Terror in France,' wrote Marx in 1848, in the famous *Neue Reinische Zeitung*, 'was nothing but a plebeian way of settling accounts with the enemies of the *bourgeoisie*: absolutism, feudalism and philistinism. Have those people, who in a period of a democratic revolution try to frighten the Social Democratic workers in Russia with the bogy of 'Jacobinism' ever stopped to think of the significance of these words of Marx?

He elaborated this further in Section 6 completely identifying the Bolsheviks with the Jacobins in the context of the 1905 revolution. It was an identification which would be restated in 1917:

The Jacobins of contemporary Social Democracy – the Bolsheviks, the adherents of the Vperyod (Vperyodovitsi) . . . or whatever we may call them – wish by their slogans to inspire the revolutionary and republican petty *bourgeoisie*, and especially the peasantry, to rise to the level of the consistent democratism of the proletariat which fully retains its individuality as a class. They want the people, i.e. the proletariat and the peasantry, to settle accounts with the monarchy and the aristocracy in a 'plebeian way', ruthlessly destroying the enemies of liberty, crushing their resistance by force, making no concessions whatever to the accursed heritage of serfdom, of Asiatic barbarism and of all that is an insult to mankind.

Before 1914 there were more long years in the wilderness. For Lenin it was a time of incohesion, of frustration and moments of despair. Gorky reports from Capri (1907), where Lenin visited him: 'Vladimir Ilyich Lenin stood before me even more firm and more inflexible than he had been at the London Congress. . . . Now he was in a quiet, rather cold and mocking mood, sternly rejecting all philosophical conversations and altogether on the alert. And at the same time there was in Capri another Lenin . . . a wonderful companion and lighthearted person . . . very gentle in his relations with people.' It was the same Gorky who wrote, too, 'I have never met a person who so hated poverty and suffering. . . . What I most prized in him was his tireless and inexorable detestation of poverty in all its forms, and his burning belief that poverty was in no way an inevitable part of life and that it must be done away with.'[1] Revolution alone could eliminate the disease. Inspired by the same sentiments as Blanqui, the resolution to bring it about became stronger as the prospects seemed to diminish. For during the lean years the Russian Social-Democratic leadership was irretrievably torn apart by factional strife. But these were the men in exile – the *emigrés*. Within Russia Lenin's agents were astir. Not only was Lenin presented there as the only possible leader available, but money was being accumulated for exclusive use by the Bolsheviks. So that the 'Tsar should pay for the Revolution' expropriation of funds was carried out

[1] Maxim Gorky, *Nicolai Lenin – The Man*, p. 5.

by bank robberies, in which some shady characters, such as Kamo the Tiflis robber (1907) were involved. Lenin was forced to pay lip service to party condemnation of such deeds, whilst surreptitiously receiving the loot as subscriptions for Bolshevik funds. At an all-Russian conference held in Paris (January 1910) called to conciliate the factions, it came to light that not only had Lenin direct links with participants of the Tiflis affair, but that he was holding the residue of the bank-notes, which he ostensibly agreed to destroy. He was also found to have manipulated the Schmidt inheritance into Bolshevik hands.[1] He was instructed to return this to the care of the Central Committee under the jurisdiction of Kautsky, Clara Zetkin and Mehring, who, in turn, placed it in the charge of a German bank. Up to 1914 it was used to finance the Russian exiles. When war broke out it was appropriated by the German treasury – a minor but additional subsidy for an Imperialist war!

More disturbing events, as far as Lenin was concerned, were taking place in the Russian countryside. Stolypin had become Prime Minister in July 1906, and was directing his attention to implementing widespread agrarian reforms. The peasantry, normally the least consistent and, therefore, the least reliable force in a revolutionary situation, was to be subjected to a centrally-directed experiment in land transference. Stolypin's first decree was to maximize land purchase by bringing all state and Tsarist land under the Peasant Bank. Land redemption annuities had ended with the revolution, which meant decreased government interest in the perpetuation of the *mir*. On 22nd November 1906, an act was passed allowing peasants freedom to leave the *mir* and the right to ownership of any land they tilled there. During the next four years further decrees were passed granting family heads sole proprietorship of their holdings, together with the right to either opt out or consolidate their strips. With joint ownership abolished an ever-increasing

---

[1] Nicolai Schmidt, a wealthy magnate killed in 1905, left his estate to the Social-Democratic party. Bolshevik agents married his two daughers to secure the inheritance.

number of peasants were forced into the labour markets of the towns. Government credit was offered to 'reliable' owners to buy more land from those willing to sell. The result was a growing 'kulakization' of the countryside, with the more efficient, thrifty and ruthless buying up and consolidating larger properties. 'We put our stake in the strong,' declared Stolypin. Certainly by 1917 half the land previously retained by the landlords since 1861 had been transferred to enterprising peasants either as leases or outright purchases. Tkachev's fears of capitalist expansion into the rural areas had proved valid. Lenin, too, recognized the dangers accruing from this. Tsardom was creating a new conservative vested interest in the land; and a new ally. Revolutionary potential among a now divided peasantry would accordingly diminish. But Stolypin's weapon proved double edged. The urban proletarianization of the peasantry was speeded up, as those who were evicted or bought out from their holdings left for the cities. But there was now no point of return since the lifeline with the land was cut for ever. An ever increasing army of dispossessed peasants in the towns balanced up the changing pattern in the fields. And even there the destruction of over ten million peasants and two million horses after 1914 delayed the consolidation of the new *kulak* classes.

Lenin spent most of his time in Paris, Switzerland and Poland up to the outbreak of war. In 1911 he set up a training school for Russian revolutionaries at Longjumeau outside Paris, and amongst his staff were Kamenev and Zinoviev, who specialized in teaching the history of the Social-Democratic party. His activities were well known to the Okhrana, whose spies had penetrated into Lenin's inner ring. They were responsible for the seizure of many Bolshevik agents, and their 'plants' effectively thwarted any organized attempt at undermining the régime. They were specially bemused with Lenin's splitting tactics, which neatly accorded with their own means of dividing, and, therefore, weakening the opposition. An extraordinary case was that of Roman Malinovsky, burglar and rapist, who was said to have taken part in the Moscow insurrection of 1905.

He was a born con man. He sold himself to the police and by cool daring and a persuasive tongue won the affection and respect of Lenin and other top Social Democrats. He managed to get himself elected to the Fourth Duma, where he not only joined the Bolshevik faction but also had the effrontery to read out the party programme at the opening session – after it had been suitably amended by the Okhrana! He even manœuvred a fellow spy, Chernomazov, into the post of editor of *Pravda* between May 1913 and February 1914, after instigating the arrest of Stalin. On the eve of war Bolshevik influence outside the Duma appeared negligible. But the reputation of Lenin transcended that of his party. He was already a myth.

August 1914 found Lenin in Cracow in Austrian Poland, where at the declaration of war he was quickly interned as an enemy alien, and just as quickly released through the intercession of Victor Adler, the leader of the Austrian Social Democratic party, one of those despised ones who had voted for war credits. For at the point of crisis the Second International had proved a double illusion. It had failed to prevent war, and when war came almost all its delegates voted to support their own governments in defence of the national interest.[1] Lenin rallied against these social 'chauvinists' who had betrayed the fundamental principle of the International by endorsing the mutual slaughter of working men, instead of directing arms against their own *bourgeoisie*. It confirmed his view that only he, and his own party, held the depository of truth, since the greatest Social Democratic party, the German, had failed the international proletariat. They had criminally repudiated the decision of the International Socialist Congress of August 1907 held at Stuttgart: that is to oppose all armaments and refuse to participate in their production, and if it proved impossible to prevent war, members should use the opportunity of the 'economic and political crisis brought about by the war to rouse the people and thereby hasten the abolition

---

[1] The exceptions were the Russian and Serbian Social Democrats. Also 14 members of the German Social Democratic party led by Karl Liebnecht unconditionally refused to vote for war credits.

o

of a capitalist rule'. In accordance with this dictum Lenin was resolved to transform the Imperialist war into a civil war, not only in Russia, but within all the other contending national states.

Lenin spent his last years in the quiet, idyllic backwaters of Berne and Zurich. The growing holocaust was already bringing other Socialists to rethink their original attitudes towards the conflict. The Italian Socialist Party initiated an international conference at Zimmerwald near Berne (5th to 8th September 1915), in which thirty-five representatives from anti-war groups in the belligerent countries attended. In a joint manifesto they declared that, far from saving democracy and liberating the oppressed, 'in reality they [the warmakers] are burying the liberty of their own nations as well as the independence of other peoples, there in the places of devastation. . . . The real struggle is the struggle for freedom, for the reconciliation among peoples, for socialism.' The meeting was not convened in order 'to lead in any way to the creation of a new International'. Here Lenin intervened. He was bent on severing all connection with the majority Social Democrats, the 'opportunists', who, in his view, would continue to betray the international proletariat. He put forward a tentative resolution for the setting up of a Third International. It was defeated. But he and eight of his associates managed to add a dramatic rider to the final manifesto: 'Civil war – not civil peace – that is our slogan.'

Meanwhile events inside Russia were moving to his advantage. Lenin planned to use the war for his prime objective – the destruction of Tsarism. Any means, any opportunity would be employed towards this end. Again at a second conference at Kienthal (April 1916) he appended an exhortation to the soldiers to end the war immediately: 'Lay down your weapons. You should turn them against the common foe – the capitalist governments.' With one eye on the terrible inflictions suffered by the Russian people as a result of inept leadership, his appeal for revolutionary defeatism coincided more and more with the growing demoralization amongst all sectors. His second weapon was his agitation for self-determination for all nationalities, which, if disseminated successfully amongst the subject peoples, would help undermine the weakening structure. But he seemed, even to himself, a voice crying in the wilderness. On the surface there was little response to his pronouncements. Far away in quiet Switzerland, there was very little news of home. Speaking to a group of Swiss workers on the Revolution of 1905, Lenin voiced his own pessimism. 'We, the old ones, may never see the decisive battles of the coming revolution.' It was January 1917!

The régime was already collapsing. Military defeats, a progressive dislocation of the country's transport and resources as a result of government inefficiency, *l'affaire* Rasputin, all added up to an explosive situation. The Tsar, in an act of monumental folly, assumed the Supreme Command in the field, which left his neurotic, capricious Tsarina virtually in control of the affairs of state. What was vitally necessary at the time was a stable, efficient direction in the hours of crisis. Instead a crazy 'ministerial leapfrog' ensued as one incompetent minister replaced another. It was as though the Romanovs were seeking their own destruction. In February 1917 they had not long to wait.

A long hard winter had brought on a coal and food crisis. In such a situation political and economic demands reach a crescendo. The 'little father' of the masses had, by now, committed the unpardonable sin – he had lost their confidence. On March 8th riots in bread queues were the signal for widespread disturbances in Petrograd. A great lock-out of the workers in the Putilov factory on March 7th had already brought in a nucleus of revolutionary potential. On March 9th an additional 200,000 workmen took to the streets, and by March 10th Petrograd was in the throes of a general strike. A forest of banners appeared demanding peace, bread, and an end to the autocracy. There was no repetition of 1905. This time, the Cossacks, militant defenders of the Tsar, had virtually gone on strike too. Except for a few desultory shots, which had helped stimulate revolt, they were soon fraternizing with the crowd. Everything now hinged on the activity of the city garrison. But inside rank and file reservists of the Pavlovsky regiment (which had brutally suppressed the Moscow rising of 1905) had turned their rifles against their officers and shot the Colonel. By March 12th the revolutionary *élan* had permeated the troops to such an extent that fully armed, they had 'gone over to the revolution'.

Out of the immediacy of near chaos, a people's order was being constructed rising spontaneously from the 'revolutionary creativity of the people', which, outside the official groups and parties, can be aligned historically with the First and Second Paris Communes and the 1905 Russian workers' organizations. Such were the *Soviets*, a new power structure, automatically brought into being by worker and artisan groups, a process almost identical with the revolutionary societies and municipal communes, which had mushroomed into existence during the great French revolution. They were, in effect, the people's councils, formulated by anarchists such as Bakunin, and the later anarcho-syndicalists, who saw them as the basis of a free federation of representative self-governing units.[1] Alexander Kerensky was himself vice-president of the Workers' and Soldiers' Soviet prior to his becoming Minister of Justice in the Provisional Government which was proclaimed on March 15th. The same day the Tsar abdicated. The dynasty fell without a whimper. Control had passed into two parallel and conflicting forces – the armed Soviets, and a caretaker administration pledged to continue an unpopular war.

On March 15th, too, Lenin and Krupskaya learned of the revolution from a Swiss newspaper. Lenin was convinced that this, at last, was his opportunity, and was determined to take control of events. Frustrated by lack of information he poured out a stream of directives to his party members within Russia in letters from afar, most of which were divorced from reality; understandably so since little news was getting through to him and his appreciation could merely be hypothetical. He was straining on the leash to get back. But return was impossible across the war-torn terrain between him and Russia. It was a suggestion of Martov which ultimately proved acceptable. He

[1] See Hannah Arndt, *On Revolution*, Chapter 6, Pt IV, pp. 259–85.

proposed a deal with the German government to allow the transit of the Russian *emigrés* across Germany in exchange for an equivalent number of Germans interred in Russia. The task of intermediary fell on Alexander Helphand ('Parvus'), who held the extraordinary position of an exiled Russian Marxist acting as secret adviser to the German Foreign Ministry. He convinced both parties of the mutual benefits accruing to the Bolsheviks and Germany alike if a large-scale political and military breakdown was engineered inside Russia. A separate peace would follow from the Bolsheviks pledged to revolutionary defeatism with a commitment to immediate peace.[1] Maximum German resources could then be concentrated on the Western Front. From the records in the Imperial archives, it is evident that the Germans were more in favour of the idea than Lenin. On April 9th the famous 'sealed train', accorded extra-territorial privileges, crossed the Swiss frontier into Germany. A chalk line across the floor separated Lenin's group from the rest of the train, and this division was scrupulously respected by the German authorities. On April 16th his connecting train steamed into the Finland Station. The years in the wilderness were over; and the exile was greeted with a reception which went beyond his wildest dreams. To the soldiers, sailors and workmen the legend had become a reality. He responded to their magnificent welcome on an ominous note: 'I greet you as the vanguard of the world proletarian army. The predatory imperialist war is the beginning of a civil war all over Europe.' For the emotional crowds who had come to greet their hero, the consequences of his arrival were soon to be made clear.

[1] On the politics and diplomacy of the 'sealed train' incident see A. B. Zeman and W. B. Scharlau, *The Merchant of Revolution – Alexander Helphand*, Chapter X.

CHAPTER 10

The Insurrectionists Seize Power

Lenin lost no time in making known to his party what his intentions were. In the bare Kshesinskaya Palace, now shorn of its glitter and period trappings, the top Bolsheviks met to hear their oracle. An air of jubilation quickly changed into one of baffled dismay as Lenin commenced his harangue. He smote them mercilessly. Had they not allowed themselves to be tied to the *bourgeois* traitors by blindly acquiescing in government policy? It was their bounden duty not to support but to destroy the Provisional Government and replace it by Soviet power. The Bolsheviks had infiltrated the Soviet organizations. The next stage was to mobilize them as a spearhead for attack. The material losses and deprivation suffered by the masses, as the war continued, would harden the antagonism already dividing the two centres of power. This would solve Lenin's dilemma. His attitude towards the Soviets was ambivalent. They provided a threat or a promise. On the one hand they could offer an alternative challenge to Lenin's élitist centralism. On the other hand, under Bolshevik control, they could be employed as the vital instrument in the seizure of power.[1]

The next morning, April 17th, he delivered his 'April Theses' to the Bolshevik delegates at the All-Russian Conference of Soviets of Workers' and Soldiers' Deputies. He outlined a comprehensive synopsis of the party's means and objectives.

---

[1] The Kronstadt rebellion focused the contradiction in so-called Bolshevik Soviet power, when the Kronstadt sailors rose against the Bolshevik dictatorship to demand a genuine Social Democracy. After ten days' bloody fighting the rising was finally crushed on May 18th, 1921, that is on the 50th anniversary of the fall of the Paris Commune – ironically one of the 'holiest' days in Lenin's revolutionary calendar.

Revolutionary defensism was out; whilst defeatism was to be encouraged, together with fraternization with the enemy. A revolutionary war could only be conducted under a government controlled by workers and peasants and never for the purpose of conquest. The revolution was passing through a transitory *bourgeois* phase. Bolsheviks must take advantage of their new-found freedom to expose the bankruptcy of the Provisional Government. As they were still a minority in the Soviets, party members should persistently engage in propaganda and criticism in order to give them direction. The ultimate aim was a republican Soviet of Workers' and Peasant Deputies 'throughout the land from top to bottom'. In turn this would enable them to transform the existing socio-political structure. A people in arms would replace the professional regulars. The hated police force and bureaucracy were to be abolished. Landed property would be confiscated and agricultural communes set up. A National Bank would absorb all others, so that monopolistic control of finance would be invested in the hands of the central Soviet. The latter would also be responsible for the overall production and distribution of commodities. Finally the party was to sever itself from its social chauvinistic connections, that is the reformist Social Democrats, and rename itself the Communist Party. It would then provide the fountainhead of a new revolutionary International.

His party was as appalled as the Mensheviks, whom Lenin had confronted separately, and scornfully derided in a speech later the same day. An old comrade of the Bolshevik hierarchy, Goldenberg, replied indignantly that Lenin's theses were, 'the rejection of Social Democratic doctrine and scientific Marxism. What we have listened to is a clear and unequivocal declaration of anarchism.' Almost immediately the man who had returned as a saviour was rejected as a pariah. His motives were now questioned. There were murmurings, which grew in volume, that he was in the pay of Germany or a police spy. It needed all the courage and determination that he could muster to overcome this universal onslaught – when even his closest comrades appeared to have denied him. His iron will prevailed. He was also, if anything, a realist. An objective appreciation of the situation revealed that time was on his side. The Provisional Government was talking itself out of existence. Its foreign minister, Milyukov, seemed blindly unaware of the growing intensity of anti-war feeling. He was still parroting the old pledge to continue the war to a nation which had rejected it. In these circumstances, Kerensky, a brilliant orator with a sense of drama, worked a miracle in stiffening the ranks of the front-line troops and mobilizing sufficient forces for a renewed offensive in Galicia. It proved a damp squib. Thousands of deserters made their way back from the front leaving a trail of looting, rapine and murder in their wake. The nation now faced a complete breakdown as old institutions collapsed or were swept away in an orgy of destruction. It brought frustration and despair to all leaders – except Lenin. In the developing crisis of anarchy would come his salvation.

Events moved relentlessly to his advantage. The Bolsheviks stepped up their ceaseless sapping and mining. Lenin's watchwords – Peace, Bread, the Land – crystallized the aspirations of *les malheureux*, offering them the panacea, as no others could. The armed workers of Petrograd formed a popular militia, the Soviets the real centres of power. The Bolsheviks were rapidly dominating both. At the first all-Russian Congress of Soviets on June 18th, Tseretelli, Menshevik minister of Posts and Telegraphs, addressed the delegates. He strongly questioned the feasibility of single party government replacing the present coalition. Lenin immediately stepped to the rostrum and accepted the challenge: 'Yes, there is. . . . We are prepared at any moment to take over complete power!' The delegates laughed but the spectators cheered.[1] On the 22nd June the government revealed that Lenin was preparing a *coup* under the guise of a peaceful demonstration in which soldiers and Red Guards would participate. Lenin was prevailed upon to call it off. Tseretelli had got the message. 'This is nothing but a

---

[1] The Bolsheviks received 105 votes against 500 from the coalition delegates. The new Central Executive Committee elected by Congress consisted of 35 Bolsheviks against 221 others.

conspiracy . . . they will try again tomorrow and the next day. . . . We must disarm the Bolsheviks!' It was wishful thinking. A weak government recognized its own impotence and did nothing.

Tension mounted during the days of July. The Galician offensive had petered out; the Cadet members had quit the government over what they felt was a precipitate granting of autonomy to the Central Ukrainian Soviet; local garrison and naval units were being stirred up by Bolshevik agitators. On July 16th a second, spontaneous uprising took place in the capital. Lenin was absent and a hesitant leadership missed its opportunity. Soldiers, sailors and Red Guards roamed the capital shouting anti-government slogans and threatening its destruction. But there was no leadership to give them direction. Lenin returned the next day but seemed unable to make up his mind. He addressed a huge crowd of demonstrators from the balcony of his headquarters. There was no call to attack, at a moment when, as the chronicler Sukhanov recorded, 'ten or twelve men could have arrested the government'. The aimless rioting quickly subsided as the mob dispersed. It was a serious defeat for the Bolsheviks. A panic statement by the Minister of Justice accused Lenin and his associates of being paid hirelings of the Germans. Their assignment was to subvert the war effort. The accusation paid off. At that moment the thwarted rioters felt betrayed and would believe anything. Papers found at the deserted Bolshevik headquarters, together with some forged documents, purported to show that Lenin was in fact receiving money from a German source. It sparked off a chain reaction against him and his party. On July 19th Lenin, heavily disguised, left Petrograd. He went into temporary exile, first hiding in a barn at Ragliv, inside Russia, then living under the pseudonym of Konstantyn Ivanov, a writer at Yalkala in Finland. He was kept well informed of the situation in Petrograd by a system of underground couriers operating from party headquarters within the capital.

The Bolshevik retreat was only temporary. Lenin, standing just outside the centre of events, could assess objectively the

o*

possibilities of a Bolshevik *coup*. His intelligence reports suggested that the government was fast losing control. The appointment of the reactionary general Kornilov (July 31st) rebounded to its disadvantage. Kornilov, on the grounds of restoring law and order, insisted on assuming control of all troops in the Petrograd area and on despatching a cavalry corps to the capital. For Kerensky this meant the choice of calling on the armed workers or armed reactionaries to help prop up a government which was already crumbling under the onslaught of both. He would lose either way. He chose the workers and gave Lenin his ultimate opportunity. Kornilov was ordered to surrender his command. He refused and prepared to march on the capital. The government distributed additional weapons to the Soviets, which, in turn, passed into the hands of the Bolsheviks, who were rapidly assuming control of the Petrograd Soviet. Kerensky had, therefore, armed the Red Guard. By the beginning of October the Bolsheviks had captured control of both Petrograd and Moscow Soviets. Kornilov's attempt had failed before it began. The railwaymen refused to man the trains which would transport his troops, and his soldiers' morale was already undermined by revolutionary propaganda. Lenin knew that the moment to strike was imminent.

On September 30th he moved to Viborg near the Russian frontier. He was in a state of suspense since he saw too clearly that the Bolshevik leaders were vacillating in the hour of decision. A Democratic Conference of all parties had agreed on the formation of a pre-parliament to discuss the means of invoking a Constituent Assembly. The Bolsheviks were torn between supporting this or following Lenin's insistence on an immediate uprising. His nerves at high pitch, he fulminated against them: they were traitors, their sterile inactivity was a betrayal in favour of the *bourgeoisie* and landlords. On October 12th he sent in his resignation from the Central Committee of the party with the threat to continue his activities among the lower ranks of the party. As before, he would stand alone, even if his party was torn to pieces, to make his Revolution. By October 14th he was urging, in Tkachevist terms, 'Delay is a crime', with the prophecy that 'Victory is assured, and the chances are nine out of ten that it will be bloodless'. The hunted man re-entered Petrograd (October 20th) and stayed under cover at the flat of a publisher's assistant Margarita Fofanova in the Bolshoi Sampsonievsky. The commander was now in a position to confront his party comrades face to face; he was determined to cajole, threaten, and finally push the vanguard into the act of insurrection. On October 21st, under terrible strain, he wrote a military directive to his party leaders, *Advice from an outsider*, as a manual of tactics to be employed which would ensure ultimate victory. Here one detects the influence of Marx. But he is also in accord with Blanqui's belated recognition[1] that the insurrection could never succeed without the most detailed pre-planning and organization of the armed vanguard; the maintenance of the aggressive spirit (defensism being 'the death of an armed uprising'); the concentration of *superior* forces at the right time and place; and the proposition that the side whose morale is intact at the end will be the victor. On October 23rd he called a meeting of party leaders at Sukhanov's flat on the Karpovka. Amongst those present were the backbone of the future old guard: Trotsky, Stalin, Sverdlov, Kamenev, Zinoviev and Dzerzhinsky. The mood was dramatic, the scene tragicomic. The small shabby man wearing overlarge spectacles, a false wig, and minus his usual beard, leaped up to confront them just as the chairman had finished his report. He was like an irate headmaster chiding his pupils for prevarication, which he could only assume was derived from lack of purpose or downright cowardice. At that very moment when the masses were calling for decision, they were found dithering. All night long he harangued them until an open vote was forced. Only two out of the twelve present voted against an immediate seizure of power. They were Kamenev and Zinoviev. The dissenters put the question: 'Is the sentiment among the workers and soldiers of the capital really such that they see salvation only in street fighting . . . ? No, there is no such

[1] Blanqui, *Instructions pour une prise d'armes* (1869), Archiv für die Gesichte Arbeiterbewegung, XV (1930), pp. 270–300.

sentiment,' and they concluded, 'it would be self-deception to build any plans on it.' To prevent, in their view, a premature *coup*, which could only be abortive and therefore damaging to the future of both the party and the Revolution, on October 31st they released a written statement to Gorky's *Novaya Zhizn*. They revealed publicly their conflict of views with Lenin. Lenin, appalled at this betrayal of party confidences, demanded their expulsion. Meanwhile events were overtaking both antagonists. Trotsky, as President of the Bolshevik Military Revolutionary Committee, had already gone ahead with his plans to seize the centres of power.

In the Smolny Convent, exclusive school for the daughters of the aristocracy for over a century, Trotsky and his arch-conspirators were meticulously organizing the *coup*, of which Blanqui would have been proud. A government, which had already ceased to govern, was talking out its last few days. Its replacement by any powerful group, which had any chance of producing order out of a negative anarchy, was a mere formality. Kerensky decided on the gambler's last throw. He knew that a *coup* was imminent, but he would attack first. A few loyal troops of the Petrograd garrison were despatched to the *Rabochee Put* – the Bolshevik newspaper's office. The presses were dismantled, the current issue destroyed and the doors sealed. Telephone wires from the Smolny were cut. The cruiser *Aurora* was ordered to sea, but it was already under the Revolutionary Committee's control. Kerensky had made a fatal error. He had accorded the pending Bolshevik act the excuse for defensive action, and therefore made it from that moment morally reprehensible. This was during the night of November 5th and 6th. Trotsky could then issue the decree to the local military next morning that 'the enemy of the people took the offensive. . . . The Military Revolutionary Committee is leading the resistance to the assault of the conspirators.' It was a shrewd piece of opportunism. The Bolsheviks could reasonably identify themselves as the sole defenders of the Revolution.

On November 6th, whilst Kerensky talked, Trotsky sent in his preliminary forces to take their first objectives. The *Rabochee*

Put offices were retaken by the Lithuanian Regiment and the presses reassembled. The Bolshevik Central Committee met and Trotsky allocated posts for the 'new' government. From the Smolny, orders were sent out to local party leaders entrenched in regiments, factories and ships to proclaim the uprising. The key points were the bridges, which if raised, as ordered by Kerensky, would isolate the inner city from the incoming insurgents. But the most important of these had already been taken over quietly, without bloodshed. But what of Lenin? Still straining at the leash in hiding he persisted in his message to the party leaders. They must seize power immediately. With extraordinary precision he anticipated the final outcome. His last exhortation was written at the very moment when the uprising was taking place. In a famous letter, written on the eve of 'October'[1] he made his final plea. In many ways it marked the culminating point of the conspiratorial élitist experience in the revolutionary tradition common to Russia and Western Europe:

Comrades

I am writing these lines on the evening of the 24th at a time when the situation is critical to the utmost degree. It is clear as can be that it is death to delay the uprising now.

With all my strength I want to persuade the comrades that everything now hangs by a thread, that on the order of the day are questions which are not solved by conferences, by congresses (even by congresses of Soviets), but only and exclusively by the people, by the masses, by the struggle of the armed masses.

We must not wait! We may lose everything!

Who should take power?

This is not important at the moment. Let the Military Revolutionary Committee take it, 'or some other body' which declares that it will relinquish the power only to the true representatives of the interests of the people, the interests of the Army (immediate offer of peace), the interests of the peasants (immediate

---

[1] That is November 6th of the New Style Calendar.

seizure of the land, private property abolished), the interests of the hungry.

History will not forgive revolutionaries for delays, when they could be victorious today (and will certainly be victorious today), while they risk losing much tomorrow, while they risk losing everything.

Seizure of power is the basis of the uprising; its political purposes will be made clear after the seizure.

The government is tottering. It must be given the *final push* at all costs!
Delay in starting is death.

Lenin, having despatched his letter in advance, made his way through the hostile streets to the Smolny. It was, for him, the end of the long journey to the promised land. He arrived in disguise at the centre of Bolshevik operations at the very moment when Trotsky was issuing final directives for the seizure of the strategic power centres. His leadership was accepted without hesitation. After an exhaustive examination of Trotsky's plans he 'gave his sanction to the course that events had already taken'. During the long night of November 6th and 7th the Bolshevik Red Guards moved silently and relentlessly towards their objectives. They occupied the State Bank, the power stations, the main telephone and telegraph exchanges, the main Post Office and railway stations. It was a bloodless *coup*. By early morning all that was left was the Winter Palace, which housed a government of make-believe administrators debating in a vacuum. Twelve hours later a whiff of blank shot from the *Aurora* signalled the assault which, within the hour, would end in the capture of the few ineffectual figures in their debating salon. Almost simultaneously, Trotsky, called to the Second Congress of the Soviets in the Smolny, had contemptuously dismissed the Mensheviks. With the conceit of the victor he relegated them to the dust heap of history. At that moment the

Bolsheviks had, under their own hegemony, reconciled the opposing poles of Soviet and central Government. The insurrectionists had finally and irrevocably seized power.

The next day a small, shabby, almost insignificant figure stood up to address a cheering mass of workers and soldiers at the Smolny. He grasped the sides of a bare reading-stand, his small eyes roved over the vast audience. The noise ceased abruptly as the small man prepared to speak. In his quiet, unassuming manner Lenin began

'We shall now proceed to build Socialism . . .'

The legacy of Babeuf, transmitted through the great insurrectionists, was now fulfilled.

Index